Sustainable Management for Managers and Engineers

Sustainable Management for Managers and Engineers

Edited by

Carolina Feliciana Machado
J. Paulo Davim

iSTE

WILEY

First published 2020 in Great Britain and the United States by ISTE Ltd and John Wiley & Sons, Inc.

ISTE Ltd
27-37 St George's Road
London SW19 4EU
UK

www.iste.co.uk

John Wiley & Sons, Inc.
111 River Street
Hoboken, NJ 07030
USA

www.wiley.com

Library of Congress Control Number: 2020944442

British Library Cataloguing-in-Publication Data
A CIP record for this book is available from the British Library
ISBN 978-1-78630-439-1

Contents

Preface

Based on two main concepts – sustainability and management – Sustainable Management is understood as the application of sustainable practices in different areas, namely business, the environment, society as a whole, as well as in daily life, and managing them in order to benefit both current and future generations. With the possibility of being applied to all aspects of our lives, sustainable management is critical as it is seen as the ability to successfully maintain the quality of life on our planet.

In a competitive and complex world where requirements from the different fields are ever increasing, organizations need to be responsible for their actions in the markets in which they operate. However, this responsibility cannot be seen as a one-time action but as a continuous process, under which organizations ought to use the different resources effectively, that will answer to the present and future requirements of the different stakeholders. Indeed, if from one side the organization influences the market, from the other side, the market – understood in its different perspectives, economic, social, environmental, political – also influences the organization. As a result of the interaction between the organization and the market, in order to be effective, the organization needs to think and act in a sustainable way. Occupying critical positions within the organizational structure, with a significant influence on their collaborators' performances, the role developed by managers and engineers is highly relevant in the sustainable success of the organization.

Taking into account these concerns, and giving particular attention to the needs of managers and engineers as they look to develop sustainable management – able to answer to the present and future needs of the organization – this book covers the issues related to sustainable management in a context where organizations are, increasingly, facing deep challenges such as the need to introduce recycling and repurposing practices, waste reduction, lower cost and more timely production, add value, as well as develop sustainable behaviors. Nowadays organizational activities should be managed under strategic and sustainable policies.

Conscious of this reality, this book contributes to the exchange of experiences and perspectives about the state of the research related to sustainable management, with a particular focus in the role that needs to be developed by managers and engineers, as well as the future direction of this field of research. The content provides support to academics and researchers, as well as to those operating in the management field who need to deal with policies and strategies related to sustainable management issues.

Organized in nine chapters, this book covers the following: Chapter 1 focuses on "Choice Architecture: Nudging for Sustainable Behavior"; Chapter 2 covers "Embedding Corporate Sustainability in Human Resource Management Practice"; Chapter 3 centers on "Competency Cultivation of Mechanical Engineers in the Process of Social Sustainable Development"; Chapter 4 addresses the "Essentials of Sustainability: A Roadmap for Businesses"; Chapter 5 looks at "Styles of Leadership and Perceptions of Corporate Social Responsibility"; Chapter 6 focuses on "Corporate Social Responsibility Reporting: Background, Evolution and Sustainability Promoter"; Chapter 7 covers "Integrated Management Systems Under the Sign of Sustainable Development: Risks and Opportunities"; Chapter 8 analyzes "Mentoring… Really? And Why Not?"; and finally, Chapter 9 draws a distinction, "Stop Camouflaging it in Green: Do Not Confuse Corporate Social Responsibility with Sustainable Management".

The mission of this book is to provide a channel of communication to disseminate knowledge of how to manage in an environment where concerns around sustainable management present a challenge, among academics/researchers, managers and engineers.

In other words, in order to be used by academics, researchers, human resources managers, managers, engineers, and other professionals in related matters, this book looks to:

– share knowledge about sustainable management through debate and information exchange;

– find out how organizations around the world are defining and implementing their sustainable management strategies;

– keep at the forefront of innovative theories and the latest research activity related to sustainable management;

– participate in an international, interdisciplinary exchange of information, ideas and opinions about the new challenges and changes in the sustainable management field.

The editors acknowledge their gratitude to ISTE-Wiley for this opportunity and for their professional support. Finally, we would like to thank all the chapter authors for their interest and availability to work on this project.

Carolina Feliciana MACHADO
Braga, Portugal
J. Paulo DAVIM
Aveiro, Portugal
September 2020

1

Choice Architecture: Nudging for Sustainable Behavior

Sustainable management demands an in-depth understanding of current global economic, social and environmental pressures. This chapter deals with the use of choice architecture and its potential to influence decision-making. It focuses primarily on the discussion of how nudges influence choice, their applications to design interventions to promote behavioral change, and the challenges and ethical concerns to individuals' freedom of choice.

1.1. Choice architecture and nudging

1.1.1. *Choice architecture*

People are becoming more concerned about the impact of their choices and are increasingly motivated to engage in sustainable behavior. Being environmentally sensitive in consumption, making healthy choices, and changing troublesome habits are critical to individual and societal well-being.

Choice architecture refers to the context or environment in which people make choices. Behavioral science has come to realize that the way in which options are presented can have a significant impact on the option that is chosen, and that small changes in the decision environment may influence the decision-making process.

People make countless choices in daily life, including decisions on how to use money, time, effort and attention. As individuals face a wide range of possible choices, have limited cognitive resources, and need quick decisions, they use

---

Chapter written by Cristiana Cerqueira LEAL and Benilde OLIVEIRA.

heuristics to facilitate routine choices. Heuristics are shortcuts or rules of thumb that simplify and facilitate decisions. They are not bad *per se* but do not always produce the best outcomes. Frequently, they produce systematic biases in thinking and judgment that generate expected mistakes and postponement of complex decisions. For instance, in terms of formal logic, having more options should always be better than having fewer options. Nevertheless, due to limitations of time, attention and self-control, individuals often feel overloaded when given too many options. They may perceive having more options as worse than having fewer options, when, rationally, adding more options should always be better. Indeed, people do not have time, motivation, or attention to carefully and consciously think about every decision. For instance, research has shown that we make more than 200 daily food-related decisions [WAN 07]. In general, habits and impulses govern our decisions without awareness. Nudging overcomes this problem by recognizing that choice architecture has a huge impact on the decision-making process and that small changes in that process may generate better outcomes. Small changes, such as organizing the way the food is displayed in cafeterias, where healthy food is made more visible, contribute to healthier choices.

1.1.2. *Nudging: using choice architecture for good*

Nudges are changes in the choice architecture or in the design of the choice environment that facilitate better decision-making without affecting the freedom of choice. Coined by Thaler and Sunstein [THA 08], the term gained immediate worldwide notability when Thaler was awarded the 2017 Nobel Prize in Economics.

Nudges are nearly imperceptible premeditated changes in the choice environment that influence the chosen option. A nudge does not regulate, sanction, or ban certain choices. Rather, it simply emphasizes particular options and moves individuals' choices onto a more sustainable track. A nudge is a slight change in the way options are presented, enhancing the best option without removing the other set of options to promote the best interest of the individual. Techniques that can be used to encourage or discourage certain behaviors range from a cue to boost individual self-interest to an incentive to avoid self-defeating behavior. Most people want to make better choices but routinely persist in making poor choices, by default, or because they are seemingly easier. By defaulting or facilitating better choices without restricting individuals' freedom of choice, it is possible to promote sustainable behavior and improve individual and social welfare.

One example of a breakthrough use of nudging is organ donation policy design. Organ donation saves lives, but donations are scarce around the world when compared with waiting lists. For instance, in the US, according to the Health

Resources and Services Administration (HRSA)[1], approximately 20 people die each day waiting for an organ transplant, and more than 112,000 people needed an organ donation in March 2020. In general, research has shown that more people support organ donation than are actually registered to donate [JOH 03]. Based on this knowledge, in recent decades, many countries have changed their human organ transplant systems from explicit-consent to presumed-consent systems. Instead of an explicit opt-in organ donation system that requires the individual to express their consent to become a potential donor, many countries have moved to an explicit opt-out system where consent is presumed unless the individual explicitly refuses to become a potential donor. Countries such as Austria, Belgium, the Czech Republic, Finland, France, Greece, Hungary, Israel, Italy, Luxembourg, Norway, Poland, Portugal, Slovenia, Spain, Sweden and Turkey have significantly increased their organ donation rates by changing the default status from explicit to presumed consent [JOH 03, UGU 15].

Neutrality is a key feature of nudging incentives, which means that all options should remain easily available at no relevant cost or effort to the participant. Nudges are neutral because the entire set of options is still available (individuals can still choose whether or not they want to be a donor), and individuals can opt-out of the nudge "incentive" without difficulty or relevant cost. However, in practice, nudging may strongly influence the decision-making process and, consequently, the final outcome.

Singapore, Israel and Chile went even further in organ donation policies by establishing an allocation priority clause for donors [ZÚÑ 15]. This clause states that if a person opts out of the donation system, he or she will lose priority if they need an organ donation in the future. While priority for donors is part of policy design, it is not classified as nudging because it is not neutral, and therefore, there is a clear advantage for those who are donors and a sanction against those who are not. To be classified as a nudge, the intervention cannot change incentives significantly.

Moreover, all organizations that use nudging should be transparent about why they aim to influence choices. For example, when organ donation default is altered from explicit consent to presumed consent, the purpose of the change is clearly to increase organ donation. This begs the question of whether transparent nudges are effective. If people understand that they are being nudged, they might deliberately choose to deviate from the suggested choice. However, evidence has shown that nudges can be transparent yet effective [BRU 18, SUN 16]. Transparency is key to making nudging policies ethically acceptable. For example, being aware that

1 Figures collected from the US Government Information on Organ Donation and Transplantation. Available at: https://www.organdonor.gov/statistics-stories/statistics.html, accessed June 2020.

organ donation policies have been designed to increase donations does not discourage people from donating. It has been an effective policy and has saved lives.

Nudges are neutral and transparent interventions that specifically aim to steer people's behavior, ethically using behavioral insights to do good. However, the dark side is the emergence of the symmetric term: sludge. Sludging techniques use the same behavioral insights to favor others' interests, at the expense of self-interest. The main difference between nudging and sludging is the intention: if the purpose is to increase individual welfare, then it is classified as nudging; if the purpose is to deliberately harm individual interest, however, then it is classified as sludging. The main goal of nudging is to promote effective and ethical ways to improve behavior which conventional policies have failed to reach.

1.2. Theoretical roots and applications around the word

Improving decisions while preserving freedom of choice is clearly ideal. These theoretical principles are not new and have been developed by behavioral sciences for the last four decades. The major contribution of nudge theory was to aggregate and bring the concepts to the public debate and encourage its application by governments and policymakers in large-scale public policy.

1.2.1. *Heuristics and systematic errors*

Behavioral economics has developed over the last few decades in opposition to rational economics, which assumes that people rationally maximize self-interest. Humans are not *homo economicus*, who consistently use rational judgment, as defined by John Stuart Mill in the 19th Century in his *Principles of Political Economy* [MIL 48]. Rather, humans behave in surprising and irrational ways. Due to cognitive limitations, people use heuristics or rules of thumb to speed up the process of finding a satisfactory outcome and to ease the cognitive load of making a decision. These mental shortcuts are quick, effortless and work efficiently in routine decision-making, however, mental shortcuts do not work well all the time. Frequently, people are affected by cognitive bias as they process information and, consequently, act against their own self-interest [TVE 74]. And, they do so in ways that are systematic and predictable.

Daniel Kahneman, an influential psychologist – who was awarded the 2002 Nobel Prize in Economics for bridging economics and psychology – has distinguished two types of thinking that govern the decision-making process – System 1 (S1) and System 2 (S2). S1 is a fast, unconscious, effortless, automatic and error-prone system used in everyday decision-making (based on heuristics and rules of thumb). S2 is a slow, conscious, effortful, reliable system used for complex decision-making. S1 works quite well in routine decisions – most of the time. While S2 produces better decision-making, it makes heavy demands on our cognitive resources, and would therefore require an effort beyond what is humanly possible; humans cannot constantly be in S2 mode. Humans fluctuate between S1 and S2, and most often, rely on S1 [KAH 11]. Nudging can be very effective when used with the S1 way of thinking because nudging does not compete with this way of processing information. It respects S1 thinking and uses clues to influence a person's choice. Nudges often seek either trigger or avoid the use of certain heuristics of S1.

1.2.2. *Libertarian paternalism*

Nudging is sometimes considered libertarian paternalism. A paternalist state, also denominated a nanny state, interferes with individuals excessively, in an effort to protect them by controlling several aspects of their behavior. The mandatory use of helmets, high taxes on junk food and road markings can be considered state paternalism. Although welcome in many cases, paternalism is frequently criticized in many others because it assumes that the state knows better than the individual and has the duty to protect people from themselves. Libertarian paternalism is a soft form of paternalism that rearranges the structure of choice so that it emphasizes and facilitates the so-called "best choice", without mandatory regulation or reducing personal freedom of choice [SUN 03, THA 03]. Ethical limits to the use of nudging, and whether or not paternalistic libertarian interventions influence freedom of choice, are under examination, and in some cases, generate strong opposition to nudges. The discussion is rooted in the concept of liberty, as discussed by John Stuart Mill. In his essay "On Liberty" [MIL 59], he defines liberty – from a civil and social point of view – as the limits of the power that can be legitimately exercised by society on individuals. Governments must respect individuality and diversity of choice, and nudges generate choices that threaten that diversity.

1.2.3. *Pro-self and pro-society nudges*

In this respect, pro-self nudges addressing individual self-interest and private welfare generate better acceptance than pro-social nudges addressing social welfare. Thaler and Sunstein [THA 08] stress that the goal of a conscientious choice architect is to help people make better decisions "as judged by themselves". Nudges addressing overall social welfare are more likely to be disapproved of by individualistic societies that may interpret the nudge as contrary to freedom of choice. Even if the intervention aims to benefit society, using nudges may depart from individual interest, and is the sum of those individual interests that produces desirable social welfare.

1.2.4. *Nudging around the world*

Nudging initiatives are increasingly widespread. They are used in varying ways and at different levels throughout the world. International governmental and non-governmental organizations are leading the dissemination of the design and implementing of a wide range of public policies, based on the understanding of individuals' behavior biases and rationality boundaries. According to Whitehead *et al.* [WHI 14], a total of 51 states worldwide have developed policy initiatives using behavioral science insights. These are centrally orchestrated policies that are applied uniformly to the entire population of a state in a large range of areas such as health promotion, pension planning enrolment, tax payment initiatives, and opt-out organ donation policies. However, the way in which some nudging units work may produce loose and scattered interventions with very specific aims, instead of a systematic definition of politics.

The following are some breakthrough initiatives of nudging around the world.

1.2.4.1. *The United States*

In 2009, the Obama Administration appointed Cass Sunstein (President Obama's friend and former colleague from the University of Chicago Law School) as the head of the Office of Information and Regulatory Affairs (OIRA). OIRA was established in 1980 and is, among other roles, responsible for reviewing the writing of regulations as well as developing and overseeing their implementation. Sunstein used his knowledge of behavioral and social sciences – particularly of nudging – to improve the effectiveness of policies. Sunstein worked with several national agencies to write rules that are clear and generate a consensus based on facts and evidence. The book *Simpler* [SUN 13] describes his experience during the four years he served in the Obama Administration and his vision of regulation based on a realistic, informed view (rather than a fanciful conception) on how people behave, to reduce complexity and increase effectiveness. Recognizing the benefits of this process, in 2015 President Obama established the White House Social and Behavioral Sciences Team and signed an executive order to make federal government agencies apply behavioral science insights to improve the effectiveness of their policies and to benefit the people.

1.2.4.2. *The United Kingdom*

In 2010, David Cameron established the Behavioural Insights Team (unofficially known as the Nudge Unit) led by David Halpern, which has been promoting initiatives related to public health, energy, financial fraud, and charitable contributions. "Since its formation, it has successfully designed several interventions" and, in 2012, it was estimated that the Nudge Unit would save over GBP 300 million in the next five years [BEH 11]. The Behavioural Insights Team is now independent of the UK government and works in partnership with local authorities, businesses, charities and governments in 31 countries. Areas of intervention cover a broad range, including education, equality, health, wellbeing, energy, environmentalism and sustainability [BEH 18].

1.2.4.3. *The European Union*

The European Union has also used behavioral insights in policy initiatives. The European Commission first used such insights to inform policymaking back in 2009 when it acknowledged the impact of default options. It approved a Directive on Consumer Rights that included a clause to limit the use of default options in consumer contracts. Thereafter, behavioral insights have been explored in several policy fields and, in 2014, the European Commission created the Foresight and Behavioural Insights Unit within its Joint Research Centre [LOU 16]. Several countries in the European Union, such as the Netherlands and Germany, have also developed and implemented national policy initiatives based on behavioral insights.

1.2.4.4. *The Organization for Economic Co-operation and Development*

The Organization for Economic Co-operation and Development (OECD) also highlights how behavioral economics can be applied to regulatory policy across the world. In 2014, the OECD classified this understanding as critical for businesses and governments, presented the description of several successful behaviorally-informed policies, and urged their broader dissemination [PET 14].

1.2.4.5. *The World Bank*

In 2015, the World Bank addressed the need to understand human behavior and apply that understanding to economic development, early childhood development, household finance, productivity, health and climate change [WOR 15]. The World Bank pursues better solutions in policymaking to achieve development, particularly for those who are in regions of extreme poverty. Understanding the context of the regions is considered critical for successful interventions for behavioral change.

1.2.4.6. *The United Arab Emirates*

In 2016, the United Arab Emirates (UAE) appointed a Minister of State for Happiness and Wellbeing who supervised plans, programs and policies to achieve a happier society. The responsibility of this office is to align and drive government policy to create social good and satisfaction[2]. The program consists of five pillars: the science of happiness and positivity, mindfulness, leading a happy team, happiness and policies in government work, and measuring happiness. The minister's goal is to make the country among the top five happiest in the world by

2 https://u.ae/en/about-the-uae/the-uae-government/government-of-future/happiness.

2021 by harmonizing all government plans, programs and policies. In 2019, as per the United Nations World Happiness Report, the UAE ranked 21st among 157 countries. Interestingly, one factor that influences the classification is the freedom to make life choices, in which the UAE was ranked fourth.

1.2.4.7. *Other initiatives worldwide*

Nudging has also gained increased relevance among companies and micro-initiatives that, based on individual insight, generate behavioral change toward healthier, wealthier, or more sustainable choices. Companies and governments are widely taking advantage of behavioral science. Those designing nudging interventions can draw on apparently trivial clues and characteristics of the environment, which people are often not aware of. By adjusting the social context, emotions, mental shortcuts and automatic responses jointly with small stimuli, nudges can keep people on a better path. Protecting individuals from themselves and others, while maintaining freedom of choice, is a puzzle that introduces new challenges and ethical concerns.

1.3. Nudging for sustainability

1.3.1. *Nudging tools for sustainable behavior*

Nudging is often described as the application of behavioral economics. However, the systematic application of nudging to macroeconomics and management is still rare. Using behavioral change to promote sustainability involves approaches that can be applied in several areas, such as consuming, saving, investing and productivity.

Nudging uses different sets of behavioral insights and we distinguish between two kinds of nudges: heuristics-based nudging and information-based nudging.

1.3.1.1. *Heuristics-based nudging*

Heuristics-based nudging acts mainly in automatic S1 for fast, everyday decisions where people rely on rules of thumb. Interventions to promote behavioral change can be designed to trigger or cease specific heuristics. It optimizes fast thinking and unconscious behavior.

1.3.1.2. *Information-based nudging*

Information-based nudging acts throughout conscious S2, creating awareness and encouraging reflexive thinking for better choices and behavior. It promotes information, learning and rational thinking in the decision-making process, to form true preferences.

Behavioral change and nudging initiatives can use both types of behavioral insights, despite their different nature.

1.3.2. *Behavioral insights*

The application of nudging has been increasingly generalized in recent years and some of the most common insights used as nudging tools range from simplification, framing and defaults to inform campaigns.

The following are some of the most disseminated insights in policy design.

1.3.2.1. *Simplification*

Simplification is always the first step in the decision-making process. If you want to make someone do something, make it simple and easy. The message or action should be short and focused on improving efficiency.

Simplification heuristics are generally used due to constraints of cognitive resources, attention, processing capacity, and memory [HIR 01]. Individuals often ignore information and create intentional selective barriers to focus only on some relevant features of the decision process [GOL 99].

Nudging initiatives based on simplification must be easy but reliable. For instance, Newell and Siikamäki [NEW 14] demonstrate that simple information, such as on energy efficiency labels, is the most important element pointing to cost-efficient energy investments. Even when there are several relevant elements, individuals tend to use an aggregator indicator to make their decisions. For example, energy companies often provide indicators of energy consumption to encourage better usage. To be effective, information should be simple and the recommended action should also be easy to follow.

1.3.2.2. *Environment or context*

Slight changes in the environment may have a significant impact on the final choice. Tversky and Kahneman [TVE 74] claim that availability is an important heuristic for determining choice. People do not have access to the same information to the same degree and the more accessible the information, the more frequently it is considered. Collecting information occurs mostly at the unconscious level. However, decisions on how to use information with different levels of accessibility are made at the conscious level [GOL 99]. Depending on how important a decision is and how much a person wants to avoid bias and error, an individual will decide whether to access layers of information stored at less accessible levels. In this way, the term cognitive availability arises to refer to the information that is potentially accessible to the individual, but not currently available [TVE 73].

The information available currently defines the decision environment. Small changes in the disclosed information may encourage better behavior. This knowledge can be used in several areas to highlight features in order to improve consumer behavior, such as environmentally sensitive production practices, non-animal testing, or sustainability consciousness.

1.3.2.3. *Framing and salience*

When deciding on options, the choice architecture frames the features an individual should pay attention to, or make salient, and those an individual should disregard. This is another form of simplification that was identified by Kahneman and Tversky [KAH 79] as the isolation effect. According to this, in order to simplify alternatives, people often ignore the characteristics that the alternatives share and decide by comparing the components that differentiate them. This form of choice can produce inconsistent preferences because a pair of possibilities can be decomposed into common or different characteristics in many ways, and different decompositions may lead to different preferences; therefore, framing is critical in driving preference.

Tversky and Kahneman [TVE 86] present a paradigmatic example of how framing and salience may influence decision-making. In an experiment[3], patients with lung cancer were presented with two different frames of the same treatment options. In one group, patients received a "survival frame" and were told that through surgical treatment, of 100 people, 90 individuals who had the surgery lived through the post-operative period, 68 were alive at the end of the first year, and 34 were alive at the end of five years; alternatively, through radiation therapy, of 100 people, 77 were alive at the end of one year and 22 were alive at the end of five years. Patients in the second group received the same figures in a "mortality frame" and were told that through surgical treatment, of 100 people, 10 died (instead of saying that 90 were alive) during surgery or within the post-operative period, 32 died by the end of the first year and 66 died by the end of five years; however, through radiation therapy, of 100 people, none died during treatment, 23 died by the end of one year, and 78 died by the end of five years. The seemingly inconsequential difference in the presentation of the procedures produced a marked effect. The preference for radiation therapy was 18% in the survival frame and 44% in the mortality frame. The same effect was also identified with physicians and business students. The terminology is critical: while the survival frame is centered in hope, the mortality frame is centered in fear. People in both cases receive the same information and should logically show the same preferences, despite the wording.

3 The experiment is originally from McNeil *et al.* [MCN 82].

This violates the principle of invariance because different representations of the same choice problem produced different preferences and it can easily be used in nudging interventions by simply choosing the wording carefully.

1.3.2.4. *Defaults: automatic enrolment and presumed consent policies*

People are frequently passive and tend to maintain the status quo, particularly when a decision is difficult and produces permanent or lasting results. The psychological phenomenon known as conservatism or status quo was identified by Edwards [EDW 68]. Conservatism or the status quo is observed in many decision problems in which individuals demonstrate a predisposition to what has already been established. The status quo can result from a decision, delaying a decision, or simply the inability to decide – also referred to as decision paralysis. The theory of choice under conflict by Tversky and Shafir [TVE 92] argues that the decision to postpone action or to take no action becomes more frequent when several attractive options exist. An individual is more likely to delay a decision or search for new alternatives when the conflict between alternatives is high because the alternatives are difficult to contrast (for instance, one alternative may have simultaneously more advantages but also more disadvantages when compared to the alternative options). The more alternatives there are to consider, the more difficult it will be to rank choice preferences, and the longer a decision is delayed, the more likely a person is to continue to hesitate, therefore maintaining the status quo.

Defaults work well for passive individuals who struggle to make a decision. Using defaults as the status quo makes people adhere simply because they do not need to take any action. Automatic enrolment works well for retirement planning, automatic saving planning, immediate bill charging or credit card payment. By the same order of ideas, presumed consent removes the burden of the decision. Organ donation is one example of presumed consent that does not require any action and also yields substantial results.

Despite the benefits of defaults, many people defend the importance of active decision-making because it ensures that they will be responsible for their choices. For instance, the banning of pre-ticked boxes on websites tends to become the rule. In 2009, the European Union Directive on Consumer Rights prohibited pre-ticking for charging extra payments. Additionally, in 2019, the Court of Justice of the European Union determined that active consent is required for a website to store cookies on user devices. A pre-ticked box, that users can actively deselect to opt-out, is not considered a valid form of consent; instead, affirmative (opt-in) consent is required. However, in general, active consent is often obtained in a routine and distracted way by ticking a box on a form. It is a slightly different way to drive the same result, where there is tenuous involvement of the individual. Personal data protection policies require active consent, and although ticking a box on a form is considered active consent, it does not genuinely engage the individual. It assumes awareness but is mainly based on presumed trust and routine clicking (namely, the unread rules of data protection).

1.3.2.5. *Reminders and deadlines*

Reminders, gentle reminders and deadlines create urgency for action. Digital nudging often uses these strategies and helps people accomplish their tasks and obligations on time.

Government institutions and corporations actively use reminders and deadlines to nudge people. Taxpayers receive recurrent reminders about tax payment deadlines and information on simple steps to complete their taxes, such as pre-completed tax declarations, bank transfer codes and automatic debit (or credit) payments from their bank account. Likewise, Gmail users are nudged in several ways. By default, Gmail accounts have a nudge option activated to remind users to reply to important emails (as classified by the Gmail account) and follow up on emails sent for which no response was received (again, Gmail classifies emails to which a response would be desirable). It uses artificial intelligence to scan and identify which emails should come to the top of the inbox. Being nudged can be helpful but also annoying if it occurs too frequently. If users prefer, they can manage their nudges by turning off the nudge feature and using the snooze feature to create a custom reminder; alternatively, both options can be used. Additional productivity tools offered by Gmail include "Smart Reply" and "Smart Compose". When reading an email, Gmail suggests an answer that is just one click away (this is not offered with every email as Gmail needs some context to generate a reply). Such features drive people's actions and sometimes cause users to feel guilty if they do not act in accordance. And, guilt avoidance is a strong incentive for action.

1.3.2.6. *Social norms*

Emphasizing what most people do is a strong cue to make others engage in the same desirable behavior. Highlighting positive behavior, recognizing accepted social norms and cultural dynamics may influence people's actions accordingly. Educators know that reinforcing good behavior is far more effective than calling attention to and correcting bad behavior. Policymakers use this insight frequently and are often criticized for creating a nanny state. Nevertheless, the results may justify the intervention.

The Behavioural Insights Team in the UK proved to be very efficient when it informed taxpayers that 9 out of 10 people in their area had already paid their taxes. The more personal and focused on their residential area the message, the more effective the nudge proved to be. Moreover, positively reinforcing taxpayers' good behavior could eventually also be used as a cue. It has not been tested, but one could argue that if the government added a sentence stating that a taxpayer was one of the 9 out of 10 who paid their taxes on time, their motivation to continue to comply would increase.

Banks use this kind of message to help improve payment time, and companies use this idea with bill recurrent payments. For instance, when sending a bill letter, a company could reinforce that other customers pay on time or that the customer always paid on time. It can also be very effective to reinforce good behavior in areas such as recycling, energy-saving, and reducing plastic use. Demonstrating that others have sustainable behaviors encourages individuals to develop these same behaviors.

1.3.2.7. *Information: generate awareness and empower people for better decision-making*

Generating awareness to help people make informed decisions is much more powerful than using soft persuasion by turning on or off some heuristics. People who make active decisions and commit to sustainable behavior generate real and lasting behavior changes.

Educational campaigns can be very effective. Financial literacy campaigns and programs have been used to promote financial knowledge and help people improve their financial decisions. They facilitate responsible and sustainable financial behavior and give people confidence in making financial choices, engaging in long-term financial planning and saving and investing. It is always better for individuals to feel in control of their choices instead of feeling that a policy designed their choices for them.

Individuals may avoid judgment bias and consequent decision errors as they learn from their own mistakes. Learning by experience enhances decision-making if individuals receive disclosure, proper information and feedback. In the long run, educated people taking control of their own decisions eliminate ethical concerns about excessive intervention in policy design. Behavioral change based on information and disclosure generates conscious, diverse behavior based on participation and true active choice.

1.3.2.8. *Self-nudging and self-regulation*

People often realize that they are biased or make poor decisions and seek mechanisms to overcome these shortcomings. In general, people want to save more, be more conscious of their consumption and be more productive at work.

Individuals can use self-nudging to regulate their behavior when they recognize systematic self-control failures. Examining the larger picture, enhancing education and data-driven decisions, planning for the long run, and defining rules *a priori* increases individual autonomy to create an environment architecture that encourages better choices. Individual self-nudging may be self-motivated or promoted by policymakers through education, information disclosure and programs.

To save more and invest better, individuals can set up automatic savings plans by defining an amount to save monthly or saving with a pension scheme. Planning *a priori* for the long-term, and considering tax efficiency, is a key feature for success in saving and investing. Individuals can also nudge themselves to control consumption by paying off credit cards in full each month (avoiding high penalty interest rates of 20–30%) and can avoid overconsumption by reducing credit card debt. For more sustainable consumption choices, it is possible to subscribe and receive local, seasonal and organic fresh food boxes (for example, weekly boxes catered to household size) or to subscribe for recurrent supply needs. Individuals stay on track to make better choices when they are in control of defining simpler choices or suitable defaults.

Individuals can likewise define *a priori* rules to reduce temptation. For instance, to develop self-discipline in deep work, people can use apps that reduce distraction, such as access to social media or recreational websites. Many free apps set rules of productivity *a priori*, such as blocking certain websites completely or at specific dates and times (e.g. from Monday to Friday, from 9 a.m. to 5 p.m., no more than 30 minutes per day). Once set, some apps require the user to wait up to 24 hours before changing the settings. Obviously, it is possible to get around these limits, but the goal of self-nudging is not to block access but to filter negative impulses, improve self-regulation and facilitate self-determination.

1.3.2.9. *Reducing sludge*

Nudging can also come in the form of reducing sludging, that is, eliminating the barriers that make otherwise good decisions difficult. Nudging and sludging are the good and evil sides, respectively, to the architecture of choice and use the same behavioral insights.

Legislation has been issued to reduce the risk of misleading information and enhance the consistency and comparability of the information provided. However, the same behavioral insights that are used in nudging can also be used to make judgments based on disadvantage. In March 2020, during the coronavirus disease (COVID-19) pandemic, some UK patients with life-limiting conditions (such as heart disease, cystic fibrosis, terminal cancer and neurological conditions) received letters from their local doctors requesting them to complete "do not resuscitate" forms in case they contracted COVID-19 and their health deteriorated. They were also advised not to call emergency services if they had symptoms or contracted COVID-19 and were urged to leave scarce health resources such as ventilators and hospital services to care for younger and fitter patients who are more likely to survive. The National Health Service apologized after a viral reaction on social media called the letter cruel and criticized the idea that some lives are not worth saving. This is just one example of how sludging uses the same insights as nudging. In this case, local doctors facilitated certain behaviors in an attempt to establish a social norm that favored others' interests over the individual's self-interest. While nudging can be pro-society, it must primarily be pro-individual.

1.4. Challenges and final remarks

Nudging connects antagonistic principles such as freedom of choice and the improvement of decision-making by routing preferences and choices. Under the principle of "maintaining the freedom of choice", nudging utilizes the power of influencing choices like never before.

Freedom has defined ethical limits. The nudging model departs from these limits – so-called "proper" behavior – and uses knowledge from social sciences to encourage ideal behavior. Even in the presence of transparent nudging, where people are aware that they are being nudged, nudging increases uniform behavior. In a nudged world, opposing the nudges requires assuming "irrelevant" costs and exerting constant effort. In an environment designed to influence subconscious decisions, a person must be continuously attentive to escape the framing design. It requires continued attention to escape default decisions, collect complete information while avoiding salience, frame and simplify the options set and develop critical thinking. Simply put, it would require that people stay permanently in the S2 way of thinking, which, by definition, is impossible.

Nudging also depends on whether people trust a system – governments, institutions and corporations – enough to accept their interventions. Intervention designers need to recognize that people care, are committed to, and need to be involved in accepting interventions. Nudging will require greater ethical examination as people become more aware of being nudged, and as digital nudges become increasingly complex, personalized and developed by artificial intelligence systems using personal information. People can oppose the widespread use of nudging if they believe it interferes with true choice and preference, or even harms an individual's self-interest. Public scrutiny of the nature of nudging policies will be critical for acceptance and should increase as nudging interventions spread.

Analyzing how effective nudging interventions are over time requires a longer period of data collection to determine how permanent the effects of nudging are. Meanwhile, nudging will continue to develop rapidly as different sets of behavioral insights appear alongside new applications.

1.5. References

[BEH 11] BEHAVIOURAL INSIGHTS TEAM, Behavioural Insights Team annual update 2010–11, report, 2011.

[BEH 18] BEHAVIOURAL INSIGHTS TEAM, Behavioural Insights Team annual update 2017–18, report, 2018.

[BRU 18] BRUNS H., KANTOROWICZ-REZNICHENKO E., KLEMENT K. *et al.*, "Can nudges be transparent and yet effective?", *Journal of Economic Psychology*, vol. 65, pp. 41–59, 2018.

[EDW 68] EDWARDS W., "Conservatism in human information processing", in KLEINMUNTZ B. (ed.), *Formal Representation of Human Judgment*, John Wiley & Sons, New York, 1968.

[GOL 99] GOLDBERG J., VONNITZSCH R., *Behavioral Finance*, John Wiley & Sons, Chichester, 1999.

[HIR 01] HIRSHLEIFER D., "Investor psychology and asset pricing", *Journal of Finance*, vol. 56, no. 4, pp. 1533–1578, 2001.

[JOH 03] JOHNSON E., GOLDSTEIN D., "Do defaults save lives?", *Science*, vol. 302, no. 5649, pp. 1338–1339, 2003.

[KAH 79] KAHNEMAN D., TVERSKY A., "Prospect theory: An analysis of decision under risk", *Econometrica*, vol. 47, no. 2, pp. 263–292, 1979.

[KAH 11] KAHNEMAN D., *Thinking, Fast and Slow*, Macmillan, London, 2011.

[LOU 16] LOURENÇO J., CIRIOLO E., ALMEIDA S. *et al.*, Behavioural insights applied to policy, report, European Union, Brussels, 2016.

[MCN 82] MCNEIL B., PAUKER S., SOX H. *et al.*, "On the elicitation of preferences for alternative therapies", *New England Journal of Medicine*, vol. 306, no. 21, pp. 1259–1262, 1982.

[MIL 48] MILL J., *Principles of Political Economy*, John W. Parker, London, 1848.

[MIL 59] MILL J., *On Liberty*, John W. Parker, London, 1859.

[NEW 14] NEWELL R., SIIKAMÄKI J., "Nudging energy efficiency behavior: The role of information labels", *Journal of the Association of Environmental and Resource Economists*, vol. 1, no. 4, pp. 555–598, 2014.

[PET 14] PETE L., Regulatory policy and behavioural economics, OECD publishing report, OECD, 2014.

[SUN 03] SUNSTEIN C., THALER R., "Libertarian paternalism is not an oxymoron", *The University of Chicago Law Review*, vol. 70, no. 4, pp. 1159–1202, 2003.

[SUN 13] SUNSTEIN C., *Simpler: The Future of Government*, Simon and Schuster, New York, 2013.

[SUN 16] SUNSTEIN C., "Do people like nudges?", *Administrative Law Review*, vol. 68, no. 2, pp. 177–232, 2016.

[THA 03] THALER R., SUNSTEIN C., "Libertarian paternalism", *American Economic Review*, vol. 93, no. 2, pp. 175–179, 2003.

[THA 08] THALER R., SUNSTEIN C., "Nudge: Improving decisions about health, wealth, and happiness", *The Social Science Journal*, vol. 45, no. 4, pp. 700–701, 2008.

[TVE 73] TVERSKY A., KAHNEMAN D., "Availability: A heuristic for judgment frequency and probability", *Cognitive Psychology*, vol. 5, no. 2, pp. 207–232, 1973.

[TVE 74] TVERSKY A., KAHNEMAN D., "Judgment under uncertainty: Heuristics and biases", *Science*, vol. 185, no. 4157, pp. 1124–1131, 1974.

[TVE 86] TVERSKY A., KAHNEMAN D., "Rational choice and the framing of decisions", *Journal of Business*, vol. 59, no. 4, pp. 251–278, 1986.

[TVE 92] TVERSKY A., SHAFIR E., "Choice under conflict: The dynamics of deferred decision", *Psychological Science*, vol. 3, no. 6, pp. 358–361, 1992.

[UGU 15] UGUR Z., "Does presumed consent save lives? Evidence from Europe", *Health Economics*, vol. 24, no. 12, pp. 1560–1572, 2015.

[WAN 07] WANSINK B., SOBAL J., "Mindless eating: The 200 daily food decisions we overlook", *Environment and Behavior*, vol. 39, no. 1, pp. 106–123, 2007.

[WHI 14] WHITEHEAD M., JONES R., HOWELL R. *et al.*, Assessing the global impact of the behavioural sciences on public policy: Nudging all over the world, report, Economic and Social Research Council, 2014.

[WOR 15] WORLD BANK, World development report 2015: Mind, society, and behavior, World Bank Report, 2015.

[ZÚÑ 15] ZÚÑIGA-FAJURI A., "Increasing organ donation by presumed consent and allocation priority: Chile", *Bulletin of the World Health Organization*, vol. 93, no. 3, pp. 199–202, 2015.

2

Embedding Corporate Sustainability in Human Resource Management Practice

There is a growing trend for corporations to act in ways that are socially responsible and that acknowledge the interests and concerns of the society in which they are positioned and within which they operate. In the organization, the human resource management function has the potential to develop procedures, policies and practices that encourage and support the organization's attempts to embrace social responsibility and corporate sustainability. This chapter explores three significant areas of current academic and professional literature: the meaning, scope and implications of corporate responsibility and corporate sustainability; the nature and function of human resource management; and the nexus of corporate social responsibility possibilities and human resource management engagement. The chapter reviews these areas of interest in order to suggest a means by which the end goals of corporate social responsibility can be reached, or at least become more attainable, through thoughtful and socially responsive human resource management practice.

2.1. Introduction

As the title suggests, this chapter explores the ways in which the functionality of human resource management (HRM) – that is what the HRM department does through its policies, procedures and practices – can shape and reinforce the organization's position on, and commitment to, corporate social responsibility (CSR) and corporate sustainability (CS). A central theme of this chapter is the *exploration* of concepts and possibilities. Sizeable bodies of literature and research already exist which focus separately on the roles of HRM and the aspirations of CSR and CS. A smaller but growing body of literature has also developed around the

---

Chapter written by David STARR-GLASS.

nexus of HRM practice and CSR goals. This chapter does not attempt to deliver a succinct synopsis of this material – such an attempt would undoubtedly fail to capture the richness of the literature or include its diversity. Rather, the chapter explores themes that seem to be of greatest interest and significance to the practitioner when HRM and CS are brought together.

However, the exploration is not simply a pragmatic solution for an abundance of richness in the field – it is undertaken for a specific purpose. Identifying CSR and CS principles and embedding them in HRM practice is an ongoing challenge for all organizations. The field is dynamic and changing, the social and environmental context is shifting and evolving, and the task of clarifying CSR demanding. There is also a constant challenge for HR practitioners to appreciate the role of CSR and CS in their organization and to align their practice and outcomes with corporate goals. It is hoped that this chapter – as an informed exploration of possibility, rather than an ideological prescription – might be useful for managers and HR practitioners faced with aligning and coordinating efforts to make HRM reflect and support CSR visions.

At the outset, it might be prudent to appreciate that "corporate social responsibility", "sustainability" and "human resource management" all have multiple and contested meanings. Each is understood differently within individual organizational contexts. Each is approached and defined differently within the scholarly literature that discusses it. In particular, the notion of corporate sustainability – and of the related and overarching construct CSR – has evolved in a fragmented manner. It has been described in a multitude of significantly different ways and defined in just as many variant forms [CAR 99, DAH 08]. After decades of consideration, these constructs still remain tantalizingly ambiguous. Currently, what *can* be agreed upon with certainty is that there is no single or all-encompassing definition that is generally accepted and which precisely pinpoints the nature, scope, and anticipated outcomes of CSR or sustainability [AGU 12, CAR 99, DAH 08].

Arguably, the conceptual trajectory of HRM has been smoother and less erratic; nevertheless, the meanings, intents and organizational practices associated with HRM have shifted considerably over the last 40 years and continue to evolve [KAU 14, KEE 90]. Faced with such a diversity of meaning, any attempt to link sustainability with HRM – or even to suggest that such a linkage is possible – hinges upon the specific and contextual ways in which we choose to define and understand these constructs. This chapter presents the multiple meanings that have been attributed to HRM, CSR and sustainability and suggests definitions that may be useful in understanding how they might be linked and interdependent.

The chapter is structured as follows. The first section reviews the various meanings and definitions that have emerged regarding CSR and CS, in order to understand their scope and implications for contemporary corporations and the society within which they operate. The section following this similarly explores the shifting and evolving meanings, roles and functions that are ascribed to HRM. In turn, this is followed by a section that considers the coming together, or nexus, of HRM and CSR, in an attempt to understand how HRM presence and practice can complement, support and further organizational efforts in moving towards a goal of sustainability. The penultimate section considers how selected HRM functions and practices can advance a pervasive and coordinated ethos of sustainability within the organization and its workforce. The final section briefly reviews some of the main issues, concerns and strategies that have been presented in the chapter.

2.2. Corporate social responsibility and corporate sustainability

Traditionally, corporate social responsibility (CSR) and corporate sustainability (CS) have often been linked and, to a degree at least, subsumed in one another. For example, Garriga and Melé [GAR 04], in mapping the territory of CSR theory, see CS as a subordinate and included construct that provides a specific avenue along which an organization can move towards the realization of corporate responsibility. From this perspective, CS is represented as a particular demonstration and concrete example of a more tenuous CSR agenda. This perspective is straightforward and appealing. However, before considering the ways in which CS and CSR are related and complementary, it might be useful to first look at each of these constructs separately and to examine their differences.

2.2.1. *Corporate social responsibility*

In 1962, neoliberal economist and future Nobel Prize laureate Milton Friedman [FRI 62] famously declared what many took to be a self-evident truth: "there is one and only one social responsibility of business – to use its resources and engage in activities designed to increase its profits" (p. 133). He captured a sentiment that was widespread in both economic thinking and business practice and which was neither controversial nor contentious. Interestingly, he added a caveat that is less well remembered and less frequently quoted: "… so long as it [business] stays in the rules of the game, which is to say, engages in open and free competition, without deception or fraud" (p. 133).

Friedman's [FRI 62] perspective was rooted in a particular understanding of the purpose of economic activity, the sovereignty of the marketplace, and a minimalist role for government and other regulatory institutions that might wish to curb or restrain market enthusiasm. His central ideas focused on a narrow definition of agency and a strict interpretation of the corporation's fiduciary duty towards its shareholders. His position resonated strongly with many involved in the marketplace and corporate world. The quoted passage originally appeared in *Capitalism and Freedom*, published in 1962, and it was a reiteration of normative neoliberal ideology, not a defense of that ideology or a reaction to a competing approach.

However, several years later, when the same article was reprinted in *The New York Times Magazine*, the climate had changed significantly [FRI 70]. There was now a clear sense that Friedman's words were a challenge to – indeed, more a rebuttal of – nascent ideas that were beginning to surface about the firm's broader obligations towards society, ideas that were pejoratively characterized as an "ideology of social responsibility". In the event, Friedman's admonition did little to stop the growing re-evaluation of the corporate role in civil society. It failed to check the increasing scrutiny of corporate agendas and practices. It certainly did not prevent an ongoing and more expansive reassessment of the relationship, responsibilities, and obligations that corporate players had to the wider society – a society through which those corporations were created and in which they were sanctioned to operate.

Through the 1970s, there was an increasing volume of articles in the academic literature that advanced CSR agendas, even although the construct remained fuzzy and was presented in different ways and from different perspectives [ADI 73, ELB 70, KEI 78]. In his extensive analysis of the academic literature, Montiel [MON 08, p. 257] noted that this early wave of interest in CSR focused almost exclusively on social issues – as opposed to environmental and ecological ones – and that this social perspective dominated the literature well into the 1990s, when it was overtaken by an increasing interest and concern for newer constructs such as corporate social performance, corporate sustainability and environmental management. It was during the 1970s, however, that Carroll [CAR 79] proposed what has become the most cited definition of CSR: "the social responsibility of business encompasses the economic, legal, ethical, and discretionary expectations that society has of organizations at a given point in time" (p. 500).

This definition provides a number of functions and clarifies a number of issues:

– it identifies responsibility along four significant but separate domains: economic, legal, ethical and discretionary. The latter domain (discretionary) refers to acts of sharing and beneficence initiated by the business for the benefit of those who reside beyond the firm and who are not directly impacted by its actions – acts such as philanthropy and community enrichment;

– it implicitly recognizes that corporate responsibility is a reaction, a *reciprocated response*, to legitimate expectations that arise in society and beyond the corporation. That is, corporate responsibility is an obligation demanded by others and not an option that originates within the corporation or which is defined by it;

– it anticipates that the exact nature and specific extent of corporate responsibility are contextual – the existence of the corporation's responsibility is enduring but how that responsibility will manifest itself, what it will include, and what it will not include, will shift over time and change under altered circumstances.

Corporate responses to social expectations and demands for responsibility are contextually shaped. Likewise, the precise manner and extent to which corporations will engage with their stakeholders (shareholders, employees and community members) will differ under different circumstances. Different socially embedded systems of understandings and practice will produce different expressions of CSR. For example, the expression of CSR is impacted by national culture, normative economic models, corporate governance assumptions and political institutions and norms. This has produced wide variations in how CSR is conceptualized and in how it is expressed – variations that have led to its distinct but inevitable fuzziness [AGU 06, GJØ 09, GUP 17, PRE 16]. This conceptual and operational fuzziness exists in the corporate world but it is perhaps even more pronounced in the academic world, leading Sandra Waddock [WAD 04] to observe of CSR that "parallel and sometimes confusing universes exist within the scholarly domain, not to mention between scholarship and the world of practice" (p. 5).

Further, local understandings mediate not only how CSR is conceptualized but the manner in which corporations identify their perceived stakeholders, respond to CSR challenges, and engage with these stakeholders. For example, in the U.S. many observers identify an *explicit* conceptualization of CSR in which corporate efforts tend to be clearly identified, specifically defined and forcefully articulated. However, there is a more *implicit* approach to CSR in Europe and Japan, where corporate responsibility tends to be more nuanced, embedded within the corporation itself and tacitly assumed in the efforts of corporations and recognized in the actions of their governance bodies [FIL 14, KUM 19, MAT 08].

Voegtlin and Greenwood [VOE 16], in their systematic review and conceptual analysis of CSR and HRM, acknowledged the slippery and tenuous nature of all definitions. They also sought to underscore the contextual malleability that confronts those trying to understand CSR, noting that "although we resist the temptation to provide a conclusive definition of CSR, we would be remiss to not make explicit our understanding of CSR … a shifting political contest between business, government and civil society actors over governance of the corporation" (p. 182).

This "inconclusive" definition is useful but limited. It identifies business, government and civil society as the main actors in the CSR enterprise. It recognizes CSR as essentially a political contest and, in doing so, tacitly understands business as a direct political contributor [RAS 14]. It further envisages CSR as a dynamically unfolding process rather than a stable or static equilibrium. However, it does little if anything to identify the salient issues and anticipated outcomes. Perhaps more focused – and making the conceptual bridge between CSR and corporate sustainability – is the definition offered by Aguinis [AGU 11]: "context-specific organizational actions and policies that take into account stakeholders' expectations and the triple bottom line of economic, social, and environmental performance" (p. 855).

2.2.2. *Corporate sustainability*

Compared with CSR, the conceptualizations and considerations of corporate sustainability (CS) developed somewhat later. Ideas and concerns about sustainability – from an environmental and ecological perspective at least – had slowly gained a place in American public awareness and social commentary during the early 1960s, following the publication of Rachel Carson's *Silent Spring* [CAR 62]. The book had a profound impact, focusing widespread attention on the environmental damage caused by pesticides (particularly DDT) and ultimately leading to these agents being restricted or banned [BOU 13, PAR 17].

The notion of global sustainability was also vividly brought to public attention in 1972 by the release of a photograph of the earth taken from the *Apollo 17* space mission. The photograph – which was the first time those on earth were able to see their planet from space – showed a small, beautiful and fragile globe that was undivided by national or geopolitical boundaries. This was the iconic Blue Marble image [WUE 12]. Perhaps more than the growing environmental rhetoric, ecological concerns and Cold War belligerency, this single image captured minds and galvanized interest about our shared global future [STE 17]. Despite these early beginnings, however, sustainability concerns and responses only gained significant traction within business and corporate communities towards the close of the 1980s.

Many commentators see CS as coming to the fore in 1987 with the publication of the report from the World Commission on Economic Development: *Our Common Future* [WOR 87]. This document – often referred to simply as the Brundtland Report in honor of the commission's chairman Gro Harlem Brundtland – sought to raise awareness of global sustainability. It also proposed tentative long-term environmental strategies for achieving sustainable development by the beginning of the new millennium. The Brundtland Report argued that corporate or development activities could only be deemed sustainable if their present levels of needs and consumption could be met "without compromising the ability of future generations to meet their own needs" (p. 43).

In the years that followed, Montiel [MON 08] observes that CS has taken two separate pathways. In one, it became increasingly and perhaps exclusively focused on ecological concerns, which many observers identified as providing the primary future resources that were in danger of being compromised [SHR 95, STA 95]. There was, however, a second pathway through which sustainability was deemed possible. This pathway, more in line with the Brundtland Report, was broader and embraced multiple dimensions: economic, social, and ecological [BAN 05, GLA 95]. It was reflected in the work of Elkington [ELK 97], who is credited with coining the term "triple bottom line", an idea that was subsequently expanded and elaborated on in his 1997 book, *Cannibals with Forks: The Triple Bottom Line of 21st Century Business*. This perspective sought to measure and evaluate CS performance against a framework of the 3Ps – people, profit and planet – reflecting a triple concern for social, economic, and environmental issues.

Commenting on the subsequent trajectory and impact of the triple bottom line project, Elkington [ELK 04] conceded that progress had been slow but that this was only a beginning and that "developing this comprehensive approach to sustainable development and environmental protection will be a central governance challenge – and, even more critically, a market challenge – in the 21st Century" (p. 16). Whether – or to what degree – that challenge is met by corporate governance, or by significantly altered market forces, remains an open question with many researchers and corporations reporting that there is no unequivocal relationship between levels of corporate profits and sustainability initiatives [KAP 10, PAN 14, MAR 09].

It should be appreciated that CS is inherently an ambiguous term that can be viewed from two different, but arguably connected, perspectives [IOA 19, LO 07]. From the first – what might be considered a *macro-level perspective* – sustainability is framed against the larger (global-centered) aims and outcomes associated with CSR. Here, the central issues are how the corporate community perceives and responds to common sustainability challenges in ethical, economic and political terms. At a macro level, corporate responsibility and corporate obligations are directed to a broad base of legitimate societal *stakeholders*. This seems to be the present dominant understanding of CS. As such, according to many scholars and commentators, it has merged with CSR to the extent that its present similarities and commonalities outweigh its prior historical difference and separation [ASH 18].

But there is also a second perspective of CS – what might be thought of as a *micro-level perspective* – that relates to how individual firms secure their own continuing futures (firm-centered). Here, the considerations are likely to be predominantly economic with ongoing value-increasing and wealth-creating strategy for *shareholders* being central. It might be argued these two levels of sustainability are compatible and complementary: the results of micro-level sustainability efforts naturally aggregating into macro-level outcomes. However, this logic is problematic and there is no clear evidence that it holds. It is more than likely that there is – as with many economic models – a disconnection between micro and macro levels of activity such that the aggregation of the individual parts (micro) is not the same as the observable whole (macro) [DYL 16, LAN 18].

A firm-centered understanding of CS – rather than a macro ecologically-centered one – seems more realistic for the corporation and more probable for its leaders. It makes CS not an isolated concern but one that is compatible with, and integral to, the broader CSR enterprise. Fundamentally, as Carroll [CAR 79] has observed, "before anything else, the business institution is the basic economic unit in our society … it has a responsibility to produce goods and services that society wants to sell them at a profit" (p. 500).

2.3. Human resource management

Human resource management (HRM) has had a considerably longer evolutionary trajectory and developmental history than either CSR or CS. In the U.S., the developing story of HRM theory and practice has been unfolding for more than a century and although the story has been at times confused – and often subjected to revisionist retellings – there is growing consensus as to what HRM is and to what it is not [DEN 14, KAU 14].

2.3.1. *A short evolutionary history of HRM*

Given its history, it is hardly surprising that HRM has come to mean different things to different people. It has been considered an integral function of general management activities in the manufacturing and service sectors: "omnipresent in all employment relationships, regardless of the type of economy, size of the enterprise, title of person doing the bossing, or particular approach used to acquire, control, and coordinate the labor" [KAU 08, p. 3].

At times, HRM has been seen in a more focused way: a separate component of the organizational structure, performing a distinctive function for management – best understood as a staff, advisory, or facilitating function – that involves a series of distinct activities such as employee recruitment, selection, training and development, evaluation and performance appraisal. For example, Wright and McMahan [WRI 92] understood HRM within organizations as performing four interlocking activities: "(1) the determinants of decisions about HR practices, (2) the composition of the human capital resource pool, (3) the specification of the required human resource behaviours, and (4) the effectiveness of these decisions given various business strategies and/or competitive situations" (p. 298).

A third reconfiguration of HRM, which emerged in the 1980s, contrasted its presently understood purposes with those it was considered to have had in the early decades of the 20th Century. Then, it was argued, the management of human resources was seen in terms of the bureaucratic activities connected with "personnel management" generally, and with the negotiating and bargaining side of industrial relations. The key issues were employee control, efficiency (in terms of cost reduction and containment), and labor union interface – all rather routine, low profile and non-strategic in nature. It should be noted that this historical "low" in the profile, power and influence of the HRM function is vigorously contested. Many scholars and observers see "new" HRM – with its heightened levels of power and influence – as the result of a project to reshape image, enhance professional prestige and capitalize on prevailing managerialism [KAU 12, KAU 14, MUE 05].

In the 1980s, there was a broad and relatively successful effort to rebrand HRM as a more active, responsive and strategic corporate player. Now, it was argued, the HRM function in the firm sought to make those firms and their employees "a source of long-term competitive advantage through a strategic approach that emphasizes human capital investment, employee involvement, an integrative alignment of labor management practices, and mutual gain reward systems" [KAU 08, p. 4].

By its nature, and implicit in its name, HRM deals with *people* but it construes them not as human beings but as "human resources" or "human capital". Throughout the last 30 years – particularly with a recognition that increased organizational productivity often correlated with HRM, a prevailing resource-based view of the firm, and the growing awareness of the strategic dimension of HRM [HUS 95, MAH 92, WRI 94] – many commentators felt that the "human" dimension of HRM had been lost or at least forgotten.

Indeed, economist Gary Becker [BEC 96], in his Nobel Prize speech, noted that "human capital is so uncontroversial nowadays that it may be difficult to appreciate the hostility in the 1950s and 1960s toward the approach that went with the term [...] demeaning because it treated people as machines" (p. 10). Some years later, Wright and McMahan [WRI 11], reflecting on this and on their earlier definition of HRM that had embodied a strategical perspective, observed that although the original hostility towards the notion of human capital had faded, there was still a risk "that strategic HRM researchers may similarly treat human capital as a form of capital owned and controlled by the firm. To do so would miss the complexity of the construct and continue to ignore the 'human' in strategic HRM" (p. 102).

Some reviewers consider that the intentions of HRM over the last few decades – and its attempts to reposition itself in the corporate world – may be admirable but that its promises and enthusiasm overtake its results. Ulrich [ULR 11], celebrating the fiftieth anniversary of the founding of the journal *Human Resource Management*, noted the gap between promise and results and asked: "Should we do away with HR? [...] There is good reason for HR's beleaguered reputation. It is often ineffective, incompetent, and costly: in a phrase, it is value-sapping" (p.128).

In a similar vein, Kaufman [KAU 12], reviewing the previous 30 years, gave HRM a "failing grade" so far as its performance was concerned. Others, [DIP 07] identify more specific problems such as the failure of research findings to percolate into the HRM world, with Cascio and Aguinis [CAS 08] noting the "serious disconnect between the knowledge academics are producing and the knowledge that practitioners are consuming" (p. 1,062). Commenting on this pervasive gap that exists between academic and practitioner understandings, Vosburg [VOS 17] tells the joke of the academic and practitioner who walk into a bar: "this is a very short joke since it turns out they sit at different ends of the bar and never speak. It's also not very funny; more of a sad allegory..." (p. 1).

These criticisms are helpful in moving beyond what are often overly optimistic claims and rhetorical exuberance to better consider how HRM practice can actually contribute value to organizations and their employees. Whatever its perceived shortcomings, HRM provides powerful mechanisms through which organizational cultures, climates, and attitudes can be *perpetuated* and reproduced. HRM also provides a vehicle through which collective attitudes can be *reformulated* and changed.

2.4. The nexus of human resource management and corporate sustainability

In recent years, there has been a spectacular rise in the volume of academic research and literature connecting HRM and CSR [HER 20, JAN 20, MAL 20, MUÑ 20, SAN 20, VOE 16]. The research literature is rich in content and diverse in nature. As Herrera and de las Heras-Rosas [HER 20] have noted, in the current period, "the most striking thing in the CSR thematic network is the incorporation for the first time of sustainability, with a very high level of production and, performance and research-methods-analysis with a special evolution from previous periods" (p. 17).

The attention and interest in the CSR-HRM nexus is understandable. CSR could well be no more than an organizational aspiration or espoused ideology. HRM is a corporate function that deals primarily with people and it is *people* – corporate members, employees and organizational participants – who hold the corporation's aspirations and who are uniquely capable of furthering its ideologies. Aspirations and ideologies, no matter how positive and well intentioned, remain abstractions – words written in corporate memos and phrases recorded in the minutes of board of directors' meetings – unless and until they are actively brought into reality and affirmed by those who populate the corporation. The question is how to bring CSR and HRM together in ways that are coherent, mutually advantageous and which further corporate notions of sustainability.

In a recent review of research and literature, Voegtlin and Greenwood [VOE 20, p. 189] propose a typology of CSR-HRM perspectives and the varying impact that these perspectives have on research and practice. They suggest three ways in which CSR and HRM might be linked:

– *Instrumental CSR-HRM*: characterized as a blend of instrumental CSR and an equally instrumental, or "hard", version of HRM. Here, CSR and HRM are in accord, complementing one another and directed towards improving the firm's economic performance and benefiting its shareholders.

– *Social integrative CSR-HRM*: a blend of integrative CSR at the corporate level and a more socially responsive, or "soft" version, of HRM. Here, CSR and HRM also work together in a complementary fashion but they are directed to the broader goal of not only improving the firm's economic performance but also of enhancing its social outcomes in a manner that adds value to all of its recognized stakeholders.

– *Political CSR-HRM*: this is a blend of political CSR, in which the firm recognizes its role as both an economic and political actor, and a more radical and critical version of HRM. Here, as in other cases, CSR and HRM work in a coordinated way to accomplish their joint outcome. However, the firm is actively engaged in proactive strategy in order to advance its position, while HRM practice centers on assisting, facilitating, and (if necessary) on addressing and rectifying institutional deficits.

2.4.1. *Instrumental CSR-HRM*

Instrumental CSR-HRM understands that the corporate HRM function is designed to contribute to the overall operation of the organization, which is generally understood in classical neoliberal economic outcomes: maximizing profit, adding to corporate value, and increasing shareholder wealth. From this understanding, other broader social or economic outcomes – such as environmental stewardship or global sustainability – are appreciated as valid but are determined to be beyond the corporation's remit. These broader social and economic goals, it is assumed, will be addressed independently by others, by market forces and by governmental intervention. The corporation remains passive, neutral and agnostic regarding these broader social and economic outcomes; instead, it focuses on what it can do and on what it construes to be its central and legitimate fiduciary responsibility to its shareholders [JEN 02].

In this CSR-HRM alignment, the activities and priorities of the HRM function are instrumental in realizing the corporation's primary objectives. The extent to which CSR is recognized and responded to – within the corporation and within its HRM practices – revolves around its impact on the firm's performance, strategic advantage or brand image [BOE 10]. In instrumental HRM, policies, procedures and practices are created to cultivate what have been termed "the micro-foundations of CSR" at the level of individual workers and organizational members. Efforts are designed to shape employee attitudes towards, and acceptance of, the corporation's engagement with CSR. Among other things, research in this area has tried to elucidate "the underlying psychological processes (i.e. mediators), as well as contingencies (i.e. moderators) of CSR and its outcomes" [MOR 13, p. 813].

In considering the human resource practices employed in instrumental CSR-HRM, Voegtlin and Greenwood [VOE 20] are of the opinion that an appreciation and understanding of CSR enhance practice "insofar as they contribute to organizational goals and economic performance" (p. 190). Specifically, instrumental CSR-HRM is, and can be, employed "to improve recruiting practises [sic] to attract the best talent, to motivate employees and increase their commitment to organizational goals, and to train employees in CSR to avoid reputational penalties" (p. 190). These improvements and outcomes are again directed towards enhancing corporate, economic, and financial performance and less concerned with, or directed towards, the firm's social performance.

2.4.2. *Social integrative CSR-HRM*

This second CSR-HRM nexus is characterized by a quite different understanding of the nature and purpose of the *corporation* – a corporation that is created, authorized and sustained by the society within which it is embedded and within which it operates and prospers. The firm has an economic mission but that mission is moderated by – but also responsive to and responsible for – the ambient community and outer world within which the firm operates. From this perspective, "the purpose of the firm and the capitalist system within which it operates, when viewed rightly, [is] the creation of value for *all* stakeholders" [NOL 10, p. 40, emphasis added].

This is the fuller and more expansive understanding of CSR and CS that was outlined previously in this chapter. There, it was suggested that CSR and CS overlap because both focus on the creation of corporate and economic value that could be shared to provide "meaningful benefit to society and the environment, all whilst balancing and integrating social, environmental, and economic components [where] sustainability implies the notion of both internally – and externally facing responsibility and a temporal focus that encompasses both short-term and long-term views" [ASH 18, p. 676].

From these common and shared perspectives of CSR and CS, the triple bottom line is regarded as an emblematic, albeit conceptually flawed, measure of corporate performance and outcomes. CSR and CS have a normative understanding of the corporation as an enterprise that will not purposefully harm or damage its multiplicity of stakeholders. Efficient performance and profit optimization are desirable but they must be balanced against the ethical duty of care, the creation of negative externalities and the negative impact of performance on stakeholders.

From a social integrative perspective, HRM is conceptualized in a more flexible and adaptive way – integrating and advocating a broader CSR within the organization. Rather than seeing HRM practice in narrow instrumental terms, it is regarded as a vehicle through which broader CSR awareness can be stimulated and brought to bear in the firm's performance. There is often a conspicuous corporate commitment to sustainability concerns and "green" management – reflected in the utilization of green-operational-management, green-supply-chain-management, green-human-resource-management and green-human-capital [DUM 17, LON 18].

So far as employees and organizational participants are concerned, HRM is *relational* rather than transactional. The thrust of HRM activity is cultivating motivation and considering the inclusion of different stakeholder perspectives. HRM engagement is primarily focused on developing personal and work identities, contributing to the employee's sense of meaning and meaningfulness in the workplace, and providing opportunities for employees to engage with the wider social and environmental worlds that are not limited by corporate boundaries. Employees are valued and respected as *human beings* rather than regarded as *human resources* [GLA 16, LEP 17, MIR 12].

Voegtlin and Greenwood [VOE 20] note that social integrative CSR-HRM approaches have great appeal for many corporations and for many HRM practitioners. They offer a wide range of connections and provide opportunities to confront and reconcile different stakeholder problems. However, despite these positive characteristics, this approach to a CSR-HRM relationship is "based on somewhat idealistic assumptions about unitary interests between workers, employers and other stakeholder groups. An inherent danger of a strong focus on shared value creation lies in the appeal for practitioners to decouple these activities from the more unsustainable core-business practises [sic], thereby drawing the attention away from the 'real' problems by doing 'alibi CSR'" [VOE 20, p. 192].

2.4.3. *Political CSR-HRM*

The third approach capitalizes on the growing political nature of CSR, including the role of the corporation in society and issues regarding the extent, legitimacy and impact of corporate power structures on other stakeholders. Given the power differentials that exist, firms are regarded as *corporate citizens* with ethical obligations and social responsibilities [BAE 14, SCH 14]. The recognition of a multiplicity of stakeholders is challenging and even more difficult is the reconciliation of their different claims against the firm.

It seems expedient that in this context HRM might choose to adopt a *critical* perspective. Considering what *critical HRM* might look like – and how it might engage with the organization and its members – Delbridge and Keenoy [DEL 10] contrast it with what they see as the "moribund and limited nature of mainstream" HRM which has focused, with mixed results, on improving corporate efficiency and performance. These authors recommend that a more open, reflective and critically aware approach needs to be taken in order "that HRM might be better contextualized within the prevailing socio-economic order of capitalism; that managerialist assumptions and language may be denaturalized and challenged; and that voices excluded in mainstream HRM may be heard" (p. 800).

A critical HRM approach requires a fundamental reconsideration of the traditional employment relationship and needs a more open dialogue with, and the support of, other disciplinary areas – such as sociology, psychology, economic, management theory, organizational behavior and political science – in order to develop contemporarily relevant ways of managing the working relationship. Critical HRM is called upon to take a more informed, nuanced and leading role in the CSR-HRM interface.

It is also called upon to utilize it critical awareness in confronting the new challenges and opportunities presented by the changing nature of work and the changing relationship that this produces between employees and employers. These shifting relationships and expectations have characterized the last 40 years and will undoubtedly become more prominent and urgent in the years ahead – altered expectations about employee rights and benefits; limited conditions of employment; the transformation of the workplace; the erosion of many traditional jobs through automation, computerization and artificial intelligence; and the dawning of the Fourth Industrial Revolution with all of its economic, social and political implications [FRE 13].

Summarizing their political CSR-HRM approach, Voegtlin and Greenwood [VOE 20] consider it to be the most exciting and potentially fruitful direction for HRM, especially in terms of research and analysis. Certainly, political CSR-HRM is conceptually rich and makes connections and linkages with multiple areas of interest that have traditionally resided outside the HRM remit. Its richness, interconnectedness, and relentless spirit of enquiry may well be crucial in dealing with the ever-changing organizational and social worlds. Currently, however, political CSR-HRM is only a nascent force that lacks full conceptual development. It is perhaps more of an aspiration and a work in progress than a present reality. Nevertheless, it may well hold "the possibility of exploring the social and political embeddedness of HRM – relationships between stakeholders in the management of 'human resources' both internal and external to the firm; shifting institutional arrangements and balances of power between corporations, governments and civil society [...]" [VOE 20, p. 194].

2.5. Embedding corporate sustainability in HRM practices

Organizations committed to CSR and CS are challenged to make those commitments manifest within the organization – within its workforce, within its dominant ethos and within its observable culture. In doing so, the organization can utilize HRM practices to shape its workforce and reinforce anticipated behaviors. A degree of difference and diversity of opinion is desirable because this tends to produce an environment in which innovation can flourish and in which groupthink is reduced. If, however, the organization understands CSR and CS to be essential core values then it will want to ensure that these values are widely held and supported by organizational participants.

2.5.1. *Recruitment and selection practices*

There seems to be a positive correlation between the public image that a corporation projects and the kinds of applicants who seek employment with it. Corporations that project a strong and credible commitment to CSR through their public relations efforts, brand imaging, and placement and interaction with related stakeholders, tend to interest and attract potential talent who also rate CSR highly [GUL 13, REN 13, STO 16].

In a world where organizations are increasingly expending considerable efforts and resources in order to reach and attract highly talented individuals, it is critically important that the organization is visible to these potential employees – that its mission and ethos are clearly evident and well promoted in the conventional and social media that might be relevant to new recruits. Obviously, if that clear messaging and direct signaling is not encountered then the organization will remain invisible to interested talent who value social responsibility and sustainable practices. An awareness of, and a commitment to, CSR and CS is not only a distinctive property of the corporation: it is a philosophy and ethical commitment espoused by many individuals in and beyond the workforce. These are the individuals that the CSR-responsive organization probably wants to hire, because they will be able to readily reconcile personal (non-work) and professional ideals and ideologies if they are hired [VAN 04].

Research indicates that it is the prospective recruit's *perception* of the organization's CSR commitment – the "perception of goodness" – that is important in the recruitment/application phase, rather than an objectively measured and independently validated commitment [GLA 13]. Of course, once hired, these individuals will come to their own informed determination of the strength and depth of the corporate CSR commitment. HRM should ensure that the organization's public persona is carefully reviewed and audited so that its commitment to CSR is clearly portrayed and that it presents an attractive option for potential recruits. If the CSR impression is weak or has a low impact, HRM might consider working proactively with those in the organization who publicize and promote the corporate image or brand image [BRO 06, FAL 11, PUN 18].

Selection practices – which might include combinations of tests, personality inventories, work samples, group performance, assessment centers, etc. – are varied and chosen to meet the specific needs of the job and the organization. In making these choices, the HRM department has undoubtedly prepared a careful job analysis and identified the relevant knowledge, skills, and abilities that are required. The resulting cluster of selection instruments and approaches originates from the organization; however, once enacted, the selection process becomes visible to candidates who can be expected to scrutinize it with care. Candidates who experience the selection process inevitably make inferences about the organization, about what and who it values, and about how it understands those whom it includes and excludes.

The aim of HRM should be for *all* candidates – irrespective of whether they are hired or rejected – to have a positive experience. It seems obvious that a positive candidate experience benefits those who are hired. However, a positive experience is equally important for those who are not selected because it increases the chance that they will return to the labor pool with at least a favorable attitude toward the organization – an attitude that they may communicate to others within that potential hiring pool [ZHA 17].

Although it may take different forms, the personal interview is a universal feature of selection systems. The interview provides those who represent the organization with the direct face-to-face opportunity to meet candidates, holistically assess their attitudes and dispositions, and share some of the defining cultural values of the organization with them. In terms of process and dynamics, there is a great deal going on in the interview and yet they tend to be relatively short. Depending on the experience of the interviewer the hire/reject decision might be made within the first few minutes [FRI 16].

Selection interviews are moments of anticipation that can develop into acts of confirmation if the interviewer decides that the candidate might realistically "be one of us". Selection interviews provide a very deep insight – although an insight that might not be obvious to interviewer or interviewee – as to how significant decisions are *actually* made within the organization and, as such, have received considerable attention in the research literature [AND 92, BOL 13, BUC 00, DIP 97, SIL 76].

However, as with all assessment and selection processes, interviewees are not neutral: they inevitably become involved in the dynamics. They form their own understandings about what it would be like to be employed by the organization. They come to their own conclusions about the organization and its projected values, concerns, and CSR perspectives even if these conclusions are incomplete or inaccurate. Thus, it might be advantageous, for candidates and the organization, if HRM is represented at selection interviews. At one level, many of those who conduct selection interviews lack an appreciation of equal employment legislation, perceived bias, and the potential inappropriateness of the questions that they pose. HRM representatives can make sure that these issues do not arise or that they are professionally dealt with if they do. At a second level, HRM can make sure that significant matters of organizational culture and values, such as CSR, are brought to the table [DIP 05, SCH 12].

2.5.2. *Training and development practices*

The generally accepted meaning of *training* is "a planned intervention that is designed to enhance the determinants of individual job performance" [CAM 01, p. 278]. The reasons for training – as well as the training methods utilized and the anticipated outcomes of the training program – are obviously contextual and vary with the needs and interests of the organization. Training is designed to increase worker proficiency, performance and the value of the organization's human capital. Training is orchestrated by HRM but it is often not directly supervised by them. It is imperative that HRM is directly involved in training programs and works closely with trainees to ensure that the training delivered is appropriate, effective and perceived as valid and useful by those who are involved.

Schmidt [SCH 07] defined *training satisfaction* as "how people feel about aspects of the job training they receive. Job training satisfaction is the extent to which people like or dislike the set of planned activities organized to develop the knowledge, skills, and attitudes required to effectively perform a given task or job" (p. 483).

There is a growing appreciation that training satisfaction increases employee self-value and esteem, contributes positively to employee attitudes, boosts job satisfaction and reduces employee turnover [MEM 16, SCH 07, TRU 11].

It remains unclear whether such positive outcomes are the result of the training initiatives per se or whether the training programs serve as vehicles through which pre-existing organizational identification and organizational commitment are further advanced and solidified. In the latter case, it may well be that training satisfaction contributes to greater organizational commitment and organizational citizen behavior on the part of the employee through a process of social exchange and a norm of mutual reciprocity between employee and employer [BEN 17]. With training satisfaction, as with satisfaction developed though employee development programs, "in addition to the belief that one will personally benefit from development, the belief that the organization will benefit may motivate development activity" [PIE 09, paragraph 4].

Training opportunities may arise that are specifically geared towards organizational participants acquiring greater knowledge, skills, and abilities about CSR and CS. Obviously, these kinds of training opportunities provide HRM with the direct possibility of highlighting the relevance and importance of CSR to the organization. However, in most organizations it is more likely that direct exposure to CSR and CS will come through employee *development* programs rather than employee training [FEN 08, GAR 10].

The distinction between training and development can often be blurred. However, *employee development* generally focuses on the long-term growth of the individual, the gradual acquisition and consolidation of knowledge, and the development of competency sets that will prove useful – if not necessary – to deal with potential work-related situations and issues in the future. Development recognizes the need for personal growth, increasing responsibility within the organization, and career advancement. As an HRM strategy, employee development is predicated on recognizing organizational participants as long-term assets who have the capacity of appreciating in value over time. It suggests of an ongoing relationship in which the organization prepares employees to meet organizational change [STA 18].

Employee development can be viewed as an expression of "internal" CSR. Value, consideration, respect, mutual dependency and mutual obligation are all recognized by the corporation, with respect to its closest and most obvious stakeholder – the *employee*. There might be explicit CSR content in employee development programs; however, despite the specific *content* of the development program it is important for HRM to recognize that their social responsibility is encapsulated and demonstrated in the *process* of providing employee development programs.

It has been argued that the social responsibility that corporations engage in has *two* dimensions: "an *external* one in which organizations can affect stakeholders as business partners or suppliers and strive to become more involved in the community and participate in the social costs of whatever affects the community, and an *internal* dimension in which companies are responsible towards their own employees, maintaining a fair attitude towards the latter's problems, aspirations, and quality of life" [OBR 18, pp.1–2, emphasis added].

From such a perspective, HRM development initiatives are manifestations of an internally directed CSR. The HRM department might consider accentuating this by making sure that those who engage in development programs – whatever the particular focus or content of the program – appreciate that employee development is an integral part of the organization's CSR commitment. It might also be helpful for the HRM function to recognize that the perceived quality and value of these programs (including the employee satisfaction derived from them) will be used by employees as an index of the organization's appreciation of, and commitment to, CSR.

2.5.3. *Motivation, performance and appraisal*

Encouraging and directing performance is a managerial function rather than one assumed by HRM; nevertheless, HRM practitioners are often consulted on such matters and when they are, it will become evident if their input is grounded in CSR and socially responsible HRM perspectives [BAR 19, SHE 11a].

Moves to increase employee performance, productivity and output are frequent in most corporate environments; indeed, they may be perpetually present in some. Taking a broader picture, improved productivity and increased output are critical issues for most firms in the manufacturing and service sectors: their existence and long-term viability often depends on these outcomes. However, corporate drives to increase performance and output are often met with employee discontent, reluctance, or resistance.

Employee pushback is understandable and management has either to negotiate a productive way forward or, depending on context, to exercise its power and authority to resolve the issue. Tensions are inevitably created when increased productivity or performance is required. These tensions often focus on a critical understanding of the nature of the employee-employer relationship and the power imbalances embedded in it. These tensions can often be reduced when employees recognize themselves, and are recognized as *stakeholders* in the corporation with shared interest, mutual responsibilities and common benefits.

The extent to which employees regard themselves, and are regarded as stakeholders lies at the core of internal CSR. Employee confidence in the process and their subsequent performance are likely to be higher if HRM is able to communicate socially responsive and responsible solutions and policies. Indeed, as in all other areas of practice, socially responsive and responsible HRM can significantly promote organizational CSR among the workforce, increase organizational identification, strengthen organizational commitment and improve job satisfaction [BOM 19, DES 18, GUE 11, JAM 15, KUN 15, SHE 11b].

Employee appraisal can potentially be a contentious issue for employees and management. Performance appraisal has traditionally been the prerogative of the employee's supervisor; however, it is increasingly common for appraisals to be more extensive and to originate from multiple sources – managers, peers, clients, suppliers, etc. – leading to what is usually termed "360 degree" assessment. The form and substance of employee appraisals and assessments, however, are normally detailed in HRM policies and procedures. This provides HRM with the opportunity to incorporate socially responsible approaches in the appraisal process.

Appraisal is a direct engagement between employee and the organization: it is also a direct engagement between a recognized stakeholder and the corporation. Although designed to focus on the person being appraised, all appraisal systems implicitly reveal the concerns, motivations and philosophies of the appraiser. This engagement and interaction allow the organization, mediated by HRM input, to demonstrate its CSR commitment in a very direct manner. In particular, the inclusion of a direct CSR element, as part of employee appraisals, can substantially enhance the effectiveness of the appraisal and clearly communicates the value that the organization places on its own sustainability and its social responsibility [SHE 11b, SU 17].

2.5.4. *Rewards, compensation and benefits*

Perhaps the most direct internal meeting of corporate claims and organizational participant perceptions of social responsibility come through HRM policies on employee compensation and benefits. It is through those meetings that organizational participants can consider and assess the degree to which the corporation really places importance and value on those who are impacted by its activities. Employees, considered as internal and immediate stakeholders in the enterprise, will inevitably test CSR claims and deeds. They will also test the underlying principles and outcomes of the social exchange dynamics that are central to CSR.

Employee rewards for participation can be intrinsic or extrinsic. *Intrinsic rewards* are derived from engagement in the organization and might include positive corporate identification and a sense of belonging, perceptions of career advancement, a feeling of improved status, engagement in meaningful work and job satisfaction. Employees place their own personal value on these participation outcomes; however, employee perceptions of value can be influenced by the attitude of the organization, the emphasis that it places on these outcomes, and the ways in which it directs employee attention to these elements in their work situation [BRU 17, STU 13, STU 16].

Recent research indicates that employees evaluate their companies on four CSR domains: customer-orientated, environment-orientated, philanthropy-orientated and employee-orientated. However, employees only experience a positive sense of organizational pride and job satisfaction – both are intrinsic employment rewards – based on their evaluation of the corporation's employee-orientated CSR. They may well come to positive evaluations of these other CSR domains, but the corporation's "true attitude" towards social responsibility and sustainability are rated on the ways in which they (the employees) are dealt with as stakeholders [SCH 20]. In their evaluations of the corporation's multiple social responsibility responses, it seems that, as McShane and Cunningham [MCS 12] have suggested, employees use the maxim: "To thine own self be true."

The same maxim might also be considered when employees evaluate the *extrinsic rewards* – wages, salaries, bonuses and other pecuniary benefits – that they receive for their performance within the organization. The picture is far from clear, but it is not evident that employees in CSR orientated organizations receive greater compensation or rewards than those in non-CSR enterprises. This might be surprising given the general understanding that CSR is associated with better performance and higher value creation, even although the correlation between CSR and financial performance, while usually positive, is modest [MAR 09, PAN 14].

Some argue that employees do not necessarily receive an extrinsic CSR premium but that this is compensated and accepted because they do earn intrinsic benefits as discussed previously [NEW 20, JUN 16, NYB 17]. Others argue that not all stakeholders benefit equally under CSR and that there is a "disconnection between our understanding of CSR drivers and CSR impacts […] between CSR financial and social consequences" [CRI 15, p. 112].

It falls on HRM to provide an explanation if organizational CSR financial consequences fail to coincide with anticipated social consequences in terms of employee compensation. The task of HRM might be complicated by another growing trend in employee remuneration: executive compensation and CSR-related bonuses. Employees might perceive these executive contracts and bonuses as legitimate compensation for achieving CSR standards – a perception that would further sensitize employees to the value and "goodness" associated with CSR and sustainability efforts generally. However, executive rewards and bonuses might also be perceived as yet another example of the difference that exists between stakeholder, the bias with which corporations acknowledge and respond to some stakeholders and not others, and the fragmented and often incoherent ways in which the supposed benefits of CSR are distributed. Such employee perceptions might be further influenced by the ways in which financial and CSR information is frequently manipulated to ensure that executive rewards and bonuses are paid [CAI 11, FRA 17, IKR 19, LI 19].

2.6. Conclusion

This chapter began as an exploration of CSR and of HRM. Both constructs are complex and nuanced. Both offer a multitude of different perspectives and approaches. The key issue is for the corporation – not just academics and scholarly observers – to make sense of CSR and of its HRM function and come to an appreciation of how each might be utilized effectively in the day-to-day operations of the organization and in its future strategy. The second objective, which can only come after the first, is how to align HRM and CSR in ways that are complementary, reinforcing and mutually beneficial.

HRM practices can be instrumental in clarifying, solidifying and supporting organizational CSR values and aspirations. By aligning HRM activities with corporate actions we can consolidate and reinforce those actions and bring clarity, consistency and meaning to organizational participants. HRM has a unique position within the organization: it is the interface between corporate intent and participant perception. Indeed, HRM will inevitably come to be perceived as the corporation's *internal CSR* – corporate responsibility directed inwards to engage with the firm's most valued and significant stakeholders: its employees.

No matter what the outward projection or manifestation of CSR, the organization reveals the nature, scope and genuineness of its social responsibility through its conduct towards its internal stakeholders. HRM policies, procedures, and practices implicitly reveal the extent and quality of the organization's understanding of, and commitment to, social responsibility. For example, something seems to be inherently wrong when a corporation publicizes its reduced carbon footprint and promotes its green credentials and yet has no scruples about hiring its employees on zero-hour contracts and dismissing and rehiring them every three months so that they do not accrue work-related benefits. Seen in the most favorable light this conduct is incredibly irrational and short-sighted. It betrays a fundamental lack of understanding or concern for CRS – indeed, it is hard not to believe that this conduct is deliberately mocking and contemptuous of CRS.

If the organization views CSR simply as an au courant fad, a matter of brand image and expediency, or a perceived strategic advantage, then HRM will find itself in the unenviable position of offering smoke and mirrors to its constituency rather than anything of substance or of meaning. The problem is that employees can easily differentiate between smoke and mirrors and meaningful substance.

If, however, the organization is fundamentally, genuinely and resolutely committed to CRS then HRM must decide how it can act to reinforce and sustain CRS in its policies and practice. HRM must decide whether – given the nature of the organization – the focus should be on an instrumental, socially integrative, or political CSR-HRM approach. HRM practitioners need to carefully and honestly evaluate their ability to engage in these different CSR-HRM approaches. It is true that HRM has its own agency, but its agency is subordinate to that of the organization that it serves. HRM must take care in reorganizing its practices so that they are – and are perceived to be – coherent, aligned, and energized by the principles of the CSR-HRM approach that has been adopted. This places a great deal of responsibility on HRM practitioners.

In considering *practice*, Alistair MacIntyre [MAC 07] understands it as "any coherent and complex form of socially-established cooperative human activity through which the goods internal to that form of activity are realized" (p. 187). Individuals engage in these complex activities, with their given rules and standards, to experience and enjoy the intrinsic benefits ("internal goods") derived from these practices. They may also gain extrinsic benefits as well ("external goods") in the form of money, status, or social approval. However, those who engage in practice – whether it is architecture, farming, playing chess, or HRM – often venture beyond the normal standards of accomplishment and requirements of excellence in order to acquire a higher level of internal good. MacIntyre calls this end goal *virtue* and argues that practitioners strive towards virtue in and through their practice.

David Vogel [VOG 05], in *The Market for Virtue*, concedes that CSR is ambiguous and sometimes arrived at without plan or intent. He considers the virtuous company and observes that "activities associated with corporate virtue typically represent firms' efforts to do more to address a wide variety of social problems than they would have done in the course of their normal pursuit of profits" (p. 4).

Corporations are recognizing that society is changing and that the relationship between them and society is also undergoing a gradual shift. In a world where there are many more stakeholders than corporate shareholders, corporate actions and responsibilities are being questioned. Virtuous corporations are no longer the exception. Increasingly, they are the kinds of companies that society demands. They are also the kinds of companies that consumers prefer, that attract valuable talent, and that markets reward. In this shifting world, as corporations negotiate moves toward virtuous behavior, it is hardly surprising that there is a necessity for more thoughtful, socially responsible and virtuous HRM practice.

2.7. References

[ADI 73] ADIZES I., WESTON J.F., "Comparative models of social responsibility", *Academy of Management Journal*, vol. 16, no. 1, pp. 112–127, 1973.

[AGU 06] AGUILERA R.V., WILLIAMS C.A., CONLEY J.M. *et al.*, "Corporate governance and social responsibility: A comparative analysis of the UK and the US", *Corporate Governance: An International Review*, vol. 14, no. 3, pp. 147–158, 2006.

[AGU 11] AGUINIS H., "Organizational responsibility: Doing good and doing well", in ZEDECK S. (ed.), *APA Handbook of Industrial and Organizational Psychology, Vol. 3*, American Psychological Association, Washington, DC, 2011.

[AGU 12] AGUINIS H., GLAVAS A., "What we know and don't know about corporate social responsibility: A review and research agenda", *Journal of Management*, vol. 38, no. 4, pp. 932–968, 2012.

[AND 92] ANDERSON N., "Eight decades of employment interview research: A retrospective meta-review and prospective commentary", *European Work and Organizational Psychologist*, vol. 2, no. 1, pp. 1–32, 1992.

[ASH 18] ASHRAFI M., ADAMS M., WALKER T.R. *et al.*, "How corporate social responsibility can be integrated into corporate sustainability: A theoretical review of their relationships", *International Journal of Sustainable Development & World Ecology*, vol. 25, no. 8, pp. 672–682, 2018.

[BAE 14] BAEK P., KIM N., "Exploring a theoretical foundation for HRD in society: Toward a model of stakeholder-based HRD", *Human Resource Development International*, vol. 17, no. 5, pp. 1–15, 2014.

[BAN 05] BANSAL P., "Evolving sustainably: A longitudinal study of corporate sustainable development", *Strategic Management Journal*, vol. 26, no. 3, pp. 197–218, 2005.

[BAR 19] BARRENA-MARTÍNEZ J., LÓPEZ-FERNÁNDEZ M., ROMERO-FERNÁNDEZ P.M., "Towards a configuration of socially responsible human resource management policies and practices: Findings from an academic consensus", *The International Journal of Human Resource Management*, vol. 30, no. 17, pp. 2544–2580, 2019.

[BEC 96] BECKER G.S., *The Economic Way of Looking at Behavior: The Nobel Lecture, (Essays in Public Policy, No. 69)*, Hoover Institution, Stanford University, Palo Alto, 1996.

[BEN 17] BEN MANSOUR J., NAJI A., LECLERC A., "The relationship between training satisfaction and the readiness to transfer learning: The mediating role of normative commitment", *Sustainability*, vol. 9, no. 5, p. 834, 2017.

[BOE 10] BOESSO G., MICHELON G., "The effects of stakeholder prioritization on corporate financial performance: An empirical investigation", *International Journal of Management*, vol. 27, no. 3, pp. 470–496, 2010.

[BOL 13] BOLANDER P., SANDBERG J., "How employee selection decisions are made in practice", *Organization Studies*, vol. 34, no. 3, pp. 285–311, 2013.

[BOM 19] BOMBIAK E., MARCINIUK-KLUSKA A., "Socially responsible human resource management as a concept of fostering sustainable organization-building: Experiences of young polish companies", *Sustainability*, vol. 11, no. 4, p. 1044, 2019.

[BOU 13] BOUWMAN H., BORNMAN R., VAN DEN BERG H. *et al.*, "DDT : Fifty years since 'Silent Spring'", in EUROPEAN ENVIRONMENT AGENCY (ed.), *Late Lessons from Early Warnings: Science, Precaution, Innovation*, European Environment Agency, Copenhagen, 2013.

[BRO 06] BROWN T.J., DACIN P.A., PRATT M.G. *et al.*, "Identity, intended image, construed image, and reputation: An interdisciplinary framework and suggested terminology", *Journal of the Academy of Marketing Science*, vol. 34, no. 2, pp. 99–106, 2006.

[BRU 17] BRUNTON M., EWEJE G., TASKIN N., "Communicating corporate social responsibility to internal stakeholders: Walking the walk or just talking the talk?", *Business Strategy and the Environment*, vol. 26, no. 1, pp. 31–48, 2017.

[BUC 00] BUCKLEY M.R., NORRIS A.C., WIESE D.S., "A brief history of the selection interview: May the next 100 years be more fruitful", *Journal of Management History*, vol. 6, no. 3, pp. 113–126, 2000.

[CAI 11] CAI Y., JO H., PAN C., "Vice or virtue? The impact of corporate social responsibility on executive compensation", *Journal of Business Ethics*, vol. 104, no. 2, pp. 159–173, 2011.

[CAM 01] CAMPBELL J.P., KUNCEL N.R., "Individual and team training", in ANDERSON N., ONES D.S., SINANGIL H.K. *et al.*, (eds), *Handbook of Industrial, Work and Organizational Psychology*, SAGE, London, 2001.

[CAR 62] CARSON R., *Silent Spring*, Houghton Mifflin, New York, 1962.

[CAR 79] CARROLL A.B., "A three-dimensional conceptual model of corporate performance", *Academy of Management Review*, vol. 4, no. 4, pp. 497–505, 1979.

[CAR 99] CARROLL A.B., "Corporate social responsibility: Evolution of a definitional construct", *Business & Society*, vol. 38, no. 3, pp. 268–295, 1999.

[CAS 08] CASCIO W.F., AGUINIS H., "Research in industrial and organizational psychology from 1963 to 2007: Changes, choices, and trends", *Journal of Applied Psychology*, vol. 93, no. 5, pp. 1062–1084, 2008.

[CRI 15] CRIFO P., FORGET V.D., "The economics of corporate social responsibility: A firm-level perspective survey", *Journal of Economic Surveys*, vol. 29, no. 1, pp. 112–130, 2015.

[DAH 08] DAHLSRUD A., "How corporate social responsibility is defined: An analysis of 37 definitions", *Corporate Social Responsibility and Environmental Management*, vol. 13, no. 1, pp. 1–13, 2008.

[DEL 10] DELBRIDGE R., KEENOY T., "Beyond managerialism?", *International Journal of Human Resource Management*, vol. 21, no. 6, pp. 799–817, 2010.

[DEN 14] DENISI A.S., WILSON M.S., BITEMAN J., "Research and practice in HRM: A historical perspective", *Human Resource Management Review*, vol. 24, no. 3, pp. 219–231, 2014.

[DES 18] DE STEFANO F., BAGDADLI S., CAMUFFO A., "The HR role in corporate social responsibility and sustainability: A boundary-shifting literature review", *Human Resources Management*, vol. 57, no. 2, pp. 549–566, 2018.

[DIP 97] DIPBOYE R.L., "Structured selection interviews: Why do they work? Why are they underutilized?", in ANDERSON N. and HERRIOT P. (eds), *International Handbook of Selection and Assessment*, John Wiley & Sons, Chichester 1997.

[DIP 05] DIPBOYE R.L., "The selection/recruitment interview: Core processes and context", in EVERS A., ANDERSON N. and VOSKUIJL O. (eds). *The Blackwell Handbook of Personnel Selection*, Blackwell Publishing, London, 2005.

[DIP 07] DIPBOYE R.L., "Eight outrageous statements about HR science", *Human Resource Management Review*, vol. 17, no. 2, pp. 96–106, 2007.

[DUM 17] DUMONT J., SHEN J., DENG X., "Effects of green HRM practices on employee workplace green behavior: The role of psychological green climate and employee green values", *Human Resource Management*, vol. 56, no. 4, pp. 613–627, 2017.

[DYL 16] DYLLICK T., MUFF K., "Clarifying the meaning of sustainable business: Introducing a typology from business-as-usual to true business sustainability", *Organization & Environment*, vol. 29, no. 2, pp. 156–174, 2016.

[ELB 70] ELBING A.O., JR., "The value issue of business: The responsibility of the businessman", *Academy of Management Journal*, vol. 13, no. 1, pp. 79–89, 1970.

[ELK 97] ELKINGTON J., *Cannibals With Forks: The Triple Bottom Line of 21st Century Business*, Capstone, Oxford, 1997.

[ELK 04] ELKINGTON J., "Enter the triple bottom line", in HENRIQUES A. and RICHARDSON J. (eds), *The Triple Bottom Line, Does it All Add Up? – Assessing the Sustainability of Business and CSR*, Earthscan, Sterling, 2004.

[FAL 11] FALKENBERG J., BRUNSAEL P., "Corporate social responsibility: A strategic advantage or a strategic necessity?", *Journal of Business Ethics*, vol. 99, no. 1, pp. 9–16, 2011.

[FEN 08] FENWICK T., BIEREMA L., "Corporate social responsibility: Issues for human resource development professionals", *International Journal of Training and Development*, vol. 12, no. 1, pp. 24–35, 2008.

[FIL 14] FILATOTCHEV I., NAKAJIMA C., "Corporate governance, responsible managerial behavior, and CSR: Organizational efficiency versus organizational legitimacy", *Academy of Management Perspectives*, vol. 28, no. 3, pp. 289–306, 2014.

[FRA 17] FRANCOEUR C., MELIS A., GAIA S. *et al.*, "Green or greed? An alternative look at CEO compensation and corporate environmental commitment", *Journal of Business Ethics*, vol. 140, no. 3, pp. 439–453, 2017.

[FRE 13] FREY C.B., OSBORNE M.A., *The Future of Employment: How Susceptible Are Jobs to Computerization?*, Oxford Martin School, Oxford, 2013.

[FRI 62] FRIEDMAN M., *Capitalism and Freedom*, University of Chicago Press, Chicago, 1962.

[FRI 70] FRIEDMAN M., "The social responsibility of business is to increase its profits", *The New York Times Magazine*, section SM, p. 12, September 13, 1970.

[FRI 16] FRIEDER R.E., VAN IDDEKINGE C.H., RAYMARK P.H., "How quickly do interviewers reach decisions? An examination of interviewers' decision-making time across applicants", *Journal of Occupational and Organizational Psychology*, vol. 89, no. 2, pp. 223–248, 2016.

[GAR 04] GARRIGA E., MELÉ D., "Corporate social responsibility theories: Mapping the territory", *Journal of Business Ethics*, vol. 53, no. 1/2, pp. 51–71, 2004.

[GAR 10] GARAVAN T.N., MCGUIRE D., "Human resource development and society: Human resource development's role in embedding corporate social responsibility, sustainability, and ethics in organizations", *Advances in Developing Human Resources*, vol. 12, no. 4, pp. 487–507, 2010.

[GJØ 09] GJØLBERG M., "The origin of corporate social responsibility: Global forces or national legacies?", *Socio-Economic Review*, vol. 7, no. 4, pp. 605–637, 2009.

[GLA 13] GLAVAS A., GODWIN L.N., "Is the perception of goodness good enough? Exploring the relationship between perceived corporate social responsibility and employee organizational identification", *Journal of Business Ethics*, vol. 114, no. 1, pp. 15–27, 2013.

[GLA 95] GLADWIN T.N., KENNELLY J.J., "Shifting paradigms for sustainable development: Implications for management theory and research", *Academy of Management Review*, vol. 20, no. 4, pp. 874–907, 1995.

[GLA 16] GLAVAS A., "Corporate social responsibility and employee engagement: Enabling employees to employ more of their whole selves at work", *Frontiers in Psychology*, vol. 7, p. 796, 2016.

[GUE 11] GUEST D.E., "Human resource management and performance: Still searching for some answers", *Human Resource Management Journal*, vol. 21, no. 1, pp. 3–13, 2011.

[GUL 13] GULLY S.M., PHILLIPS J.M., CASTELLANO W.G. *et al.*, "A mediated moderated model of recruiting socially and environmentally responsible job applicants", *Personnel Psychology*, vol. 66, no. 4, pp. 935–973, 2013.

[GUP 17] GUPTA A., BRISCOE F., HAMBRICK D.C., "Red, blue, and purple firms: Organisational political ideology and corporate social responsibility", *Strategic Management Journal*, vol. 38, no. 5, pp. 1018–1040, 2017.

[HER 20] HERRERA J., DE LAS HERAS-ROSAS C., "Corporate social responsibility and human resource management: Towards sustainable business organizations", *Sustainability*, vol. 12, no. 3, p. 841, 2020.

[HUS 95] HUSELID M.A., "The impact of human resource management practices on turnover, productivity, and corporate financial performance", *Academy of Management Journal*, vol. 38, no. 3, pp. 635–672, 1995.

[IKR 19] IKRAM A., LI Z.F., MINOR D., "CSR-contingent executive compensation contracts", *Social Science Research Network*, available at: https://ssrn.com/abstract=3019985, 2019.

[IOA 19] IOANNIS I., SERAFEIM G., Corporate sustainability: A strategy?, working paper 19-065, Harvard School of Business, available at: https://www.hbs.edu/faculty/Publication%20Files/19-065_16deb9d6-4461-4d2f-8bbe-2c74b5beffb8.pdf, 2019.

[JAM 15] JAMALI D.R., DIRANI A.E., HARWOOD I.A., "Exploring human resource management roles in corporate social responsibility: The CSR-HRM co-creation model", *Business Ethics: A European Review*, vol. 24, no. 2, pp. 125–143, 2015.

[JAN 20] JANG S., ARDICHVILI A., "Examining the link between corporate social responsibility and human resources: Implications for HRD research and practice", *Human Resource Development Review*, 2020.

[JEN 02] JENSEN M.C., "Value maximization, stakeholder theory, and the corporate objective function", *Business Ethics Quarterly*, vol. 12, no. 2, pp. 235–256, 2002.

[JUN 16] JUNG H., KIM D., "Good neighbors but bad employers: Two faces of corporate social responsibility programs", *Journal of Business Ethics*, vol. 138, no. 2, pp. 295–310, 2016.

[KAP 10] KAPOOR S., SANDHU H.S., "Does it pay to be socially responsible? An empirical examination of impact of corporate social responsibility on financial performance", *Global Business Review*, vol. 11, no. 2, pp. 185–208, 2010.

[KAU 08] KAUFMAN B.E., *Managing the Human Factor: The Early Years of Human Resource Management in American Industry*, Cornell University Press, Ithaca, 2008.

[KAU 12] KAUFMAN B.E., "Strategic Human Resource Management research in the United States: A failing grade after 30 years?", *Academy of Management Perspectives*, vol. 26, no. 2, pp. 12–36, 2012.

[KAU 14] KAUFMAN B.E., "The historical development of American HRM broadly viewed", *Human Resource Management Review*, vol. 24, no. 3, pp. 196–218, 2014.

[KEE 90] KEENOY T., "HRM: A case of the wolf in sheep's clothing?", *Personnel Review*, vol. 19, no. 2, pp. 3–9, 1990.

[KEI 78] KEIM G.D., "Corporate social responsibility: An assessment of the enlightened self-interest model", *Academy of Management Review*, vol. 3, no. 1, pp. 32–39, 1978.

[KUM 19] KUMAR K., BOESSO G., BATRA R. *et al.*, "Explicit and implicit corporate social responsibility: Differences in the approach to stakeholder engagement activities of U.S. and Japanese companies", *Business Strategy and the Environment*, vol. 28, no. 6, pp. 1121–1130, 2019.

[KUN 15] KUNDU S.C., GAHLAWAT N., "Socially responsible HR practices and employees' intention to quit: The mediating role of job satisfaction", *Human Resource Development International*, vol. 18, no. 4, pp. 387–406, 2015.

[LAN 18] LANDRUM N.E., "Stages of corporate sustainability: Integrating the strong sustainability worldview", *Organization & Environment*, vol. 31, no. 4, pp. 287–313, 2018.

[LEP 17] LEPISTO D.A., PRATT M.G., "Meaningful work as realization and justification toward a dual conceptualization", *Organizational Psychology Review*, vol. 7, no. 2, pp. 99–121, 2017.

[LI 19] LI Z.F., THIBODEAU C., "CSR-contingent executive compensation incentive and earnings management", *Sustainability*, vol. 11, no. 12, p. 3421, 2019.

[LO 07] LO S-F., SHEU H-J., "Is corporate sustainability a value-increasing strategy for business?", *Corporate Governance: An International Review*, vol. 15, no. 2, pp. 345–358, 2007.

[LON 18] LONGONI A., LUZZINI D., GUERCI M., "Deploying environmental management across functions: The relationship between green human resource management and green supply chain management", *Journal of Business Ethics*, vol. 151, pp. 1081–1095, 2018.

[MAC 07] MACINTYRE A.C., *After Virtue: A Study in Moral Theory*, 3rd edition, Notre Dame University Press, Notre Dame, 2007.

[MAH 92] MAHONEY J.T., PANDIAN J.R., "The resource-based view within the conversation of strategic management", *Strategic Management Journal*, vol. 13, no. 5, pp. 363–380, 1992.

[MAL 20] MALIK S.Y., CAO Y., MUGHAL Y.H. *et al.*, "Pathways towards sustainability in organizations: Empirical evidence on the role of green human resource management practices and green intellectual capital", *Sustainability*, vol. 12, no. 8, p. 3228, 2020.

[MAR 09] MARGOLIS J.D., ELFENBEIN H.A., WALSH J.P., "Does it pay to be good... and does it matter? A meta-analysis of the relationship between corporate social and financial performance", *Social Science Research Network*, available at: https://ssrn.com/abstract=1866371, 2009.

[MAT 08] MATTEN D., MOON J., "Implicit and explicit CSR: A conceptual framework for a comparative understanding of corporate social responsibility", *Academy of Management Review*, vol. 33, no. 2, pp. 404–424, 2008.

[MCS 12] MCSHANE L., CUNNINGHAM P., "To thine own self be true? Employees' judgments of the authenticity of their organization's corporate social responsibility program", *Journal of Business Ethics*, vol. 108, pp. 81–100, 2012.

[MEM 16] MEMON M.A., SALLEH R., BAHAROM M.N.R., "The link between training satisfaction, work engagement and turnover intention", *European Journal of Training and Development*, vol. 40, no. 6, pp. 407–429, 2016.

[MIR 12] MIRVIS, P., "Employee engagement and CSR: Transactional, relational, and developmental approaches", *California Management Review*, vol. 54, no. 4, pp. 93–117, 2012.

[MON 08] MONTIEL I., "Corporate Social Responsibility and Corporate Sustainability: Separate pasts, common futures", *Organization & Environment*, vol. 21, no. 3, pp. 245–269, 2008.

[MOR 13] MORGESON F.P., AGUINIS H., WALDMAN D.A. *et al.*, "Extending corporate social responsibility research to the human resource management and organizational behavior domains: A look to the future", *Personnel Psychology*, vol. 66, no. 4, pp. 805–824, 2013.

[MUE 05] MUELLER F., CARTER C., "The 'HRM project' and managerialism: Or why some discourses are more equal than others", *Journal of Organizational Change Management*, vol. 18, no. 4, pp. 369–382, 2005.

[MUÑ 20] MUÑOZ-PASCUAL L., GALENDE J., CURADO C., "Human resource management contributions to knowledge sharing for a sustainability-oriented performance: A mixed methods approach", *Sustainability*, vol. 12, no. 1, p. 161, 2020.

[NEW 20] NEWMAN C., RAND J., TARP F. *et al.*, "Corporate social responsibility in a competitive business environment", *The Journal of Development Studies*, 2020.

[NOL 10] NOLAND J., PHILLIPS R., "Stakeholder engagement, discourse ethics and strategic management", *International Journal of Management Reviews*, vol. 12, no. 1, pp. 39–49, 2010.

[NYB 17] NYBORG K., ZHANG T., "Is corporate social responsibility associated with lower wages?", *Environmental and Resource Economics*, vol. 55, no. 1, pp. 107–117, 2017.

[OBR 18] OBRAD C., GHERHEŞ V., "A human resources perspective on responsible corporate behavior. Case study: The multinational companies in Western Romania", *Sustainability*, vol. 10, no. 3, p. 726, 2018.

[PAN 14] PAN X., SHA J., ZHANG H. *et al.*, "Relationship between corporate social responsibility and financial performance in the mineral industry: Evidence from Chinese mineral firms", *Sustainability*, vol. 6, no. 7, pp. 4077–4101, 2014.

[PAR 17] PARKS P., "Silent Spring, loud legacy: How elite media helped establish an environmentalist icon", *Journalism & Mass Communication Quarterly*, vol. 94, no. 4, pp. 1215–1238, 2017.

[PIE 09] PIERCE H.R., MAURER T.J., "Linking employee development activity, social exchange and organizational citizenship behavior", *International Journal of Training and Development*, vol. 13, no. 3, pp. 139–147, 2009.

[PRE 16] PREUSS L., BARKEMEYER R., GLAVAS A., "Corporate social responsibility in developing country multinationals: Identifying company and country-level influences", *Business Ethics Quarterly*, vol. 26, no. 3, pp. 347–378, 2016.

[PUN 18] PUNCHEVA-MICHELOTTI P., HUDSON S., JIN G., "Employer branding and CSR communication in online recruitment advertising", *Business Horizons*, vol. 61, no. 4, pp. 643–651, 2018.

[RAS 14] RASCHE A., "The corporation as a political actor: European and North American perspectives", *European Management Journal*, vol. 33, no. 4, pp. 1–8, 2014.

[REN 13] RENWICK D.W., REDMAN T., MAGUIRE S., "Green human resource management: A review and research agenda", *International Journal of Management Reviews*, vol. 15, no. 1, pp. 1–14, 2013.

[SAN 20] SANTANA M., MORALES-SÁNCHEZ R., PASAMAR S., "Mapping the link between corporate social responsibility (CSR) and human resource management (HRM): How is this relationship measured?", *Sustainability*, vol. 12, no. 4, p. 1678, 2020.

[SCH 07] SCHMIDT S.W., "The relationship between satisfaction with workplace training and overall job satisfaction", *Human Resource Development Quarterly*, vol. 18, no. 4, pp. 481–498, 2007.

[SCH 12] SCHMITT N., DIPBOYE R.L., MACAN T. *et al.*, *The Selection Interview from the Interviewer and Applicant Perspectives: Can't Have One without the Other*, Oxford University Press, Oxford, 2012.

[SCH 14] SCHERER A.G., PALAZZO G., MATTEN D., "The business firm as a political actor: A new theory of the firm for a globalized world", *Business & Society*, vol. 53, no. 2, pp. 143–156, 2014.

[SCH 20] SCHAEFER S.D., TERLUTTER R., DIEHL S., "Talking about CSR matters: Employees' perception of and reaction to their company's CSR communication in four different CSR domains", *International Journal of Advertising*, vol. 39, no. 2, pp. 191–212, 2020.

[SHE 11a] SHEN J., "Developing the concept of socially responsible international human resource management", *The International Journal of Human Resource Management*, vol. 22, no. 6, pp. 1351–1363, 2011.

[SHE 11b] SHEN J., ZHU C.J., "Effects of socially responsible human resource management on employee organizational commitment", *The International Journal of Human Resource Management*, vol. 22, no. 15, pp. 3020–3035, 2011.

[SHR 95] SHRIVASTAVA P., "Environmental technologies and competitive advantage", *Strategic Management Journal*, vol. 16 no. S1, pp. 183–200, 1995.

[SIL 76] SILVERMAN D., JONES J., *Organizational Work: The Language of Grading, the Grading of Language*, Collier Macmillan, London, 1976.

[STA 95] STARIK M., RANDS G.P., "Weaving an integrated web: Multilevel and multisystem perspectives of ecologically sustainable organizations", *Academy of Management Review*, vol. 20, no. 4, pp. 908–935, 1995.

[STA 18] STANKEVIČIŪTĖ Ž., SAVANEVIČIENĖ A., "Designing sustainable HRM: The core characteristics of emerging field", *Sustainability*, vol. 10, no. 12, p. 4798, 2018.

[STE 17] STEVENSON H., "Multilateral diplomacy: Sustainable development", in STEVENSON, H. (ed.). *Global Environmental Politics: Problems, Policy, and Practice*, Cambridge University Press, Cambridge, 2017.

[STO 16] STORY J., CASTANHEIRA F., NARTIG S., "Corporate social responsibility and organizational attractiveness: Implications for talent management", *Social Responsibility Journal*, vol. 12, no. 3, pp. 484–505, 2013.

[STU 13] STUMPF S.A., TYMON W.G., FAVORITO N. *et al.*, "Employees and change initiatives: Intrinsic rewards and feeling valued", *Journal of Business Strategy*, vol. 34, no. 2, pp. 21–29, 2013.

[STU 16] STUMPF S.A., TYMON W.G., HER R.J. *et al.*, "Leading to intrinsically reward professionals for sustained engagement", *Leadership & Organizational Development Journal*, vol. 37, no. 4, pp. 467–486, 2016.

[SU 17] SU X., LIU Y., HANSON-RASMUSSEN N., "Voice behavior, supervisor attribution and employee performance appraisal", *Sustainability*, vol. 9, no. 10, p. 1829, 2017.

[TRU 11] TRUITT D.L., "The effect of training and development on employee attitude as it relates to training and work proficiency", *SAGE Open*, 2011.

[ULR 11] ULRICH D., "Celebrating 50 years: An anniversary reflection", *Human Resource Management*, vol. 50, no. 1, pp. 3–7, 2007.

[VAN 04] VAN DICK R., "My job is my castle: Identification in organizational contexts", *International Review of Industrial and Organizational Psychology*, vol. 19, pp. 171–203, 2004.

[VEL 17] VELD M., ALFES K., "HRM, climate and employee well-being: Comparing an optimistic and critical perspective", *The International Journal of Human Resource Management*, vol. 28, no. 16, pp. 2299–2318, 2017.

[VOE 16] VOEGTLIN C., GREENWOOD M., "Corporate social responsibility and human resource management: A systematic review and conceptual analysis", *Human Resource Management Review*, vol. 26, no. 3, pp. 181–197, 2016.

[VOG 05] VOGEL D., *The Market for Virtue: The Potential and Limits of Corporate Social Responsibility*, Brookings Institution Press, Washington, DC, 2005.

[VOS 17] VOSBURG R.M., "Closing the academic-practitioner gap: Research must answer the 'SO WHAT' question", *Human Resource Management Review*, 2017.

[WAD 04] WADDOCK S.A., "Parallel universes: Companies, academics, and the progress of corporate citizenship", *Business and Society Review*, vol. 109, no. 1, pp. 5–42, 2004.

[WOR 87] WORLD COMMISSION ON ECONOMIC DEVELOPMENT, *Our Common Future*, Oxford University Press, Oxford, 1987.

[WRI 92] WRIGHT P.M., MCMAHAN G.C., "Theoretical perspectives on strategic human resource management", *Journal of Management*, vol. 18, no. 2, pp. 295–320, 1992.

[WRI 94] WRIGHT P.M., MCMAHAN G.C., MCWILLIAMS A., "Human resources as a source of sustained competitive advantage: A resource-based perspective", *International Journal of Human Resource Management*, vol. 5, no. 2, pp. 301–326, 1994.

[WRI 11] WRIGHT P.M., MCMAHAN G.C., "Exploring human capital: Putting human back into strategic human resource management", *Human Resource Management Journal*, vol. 21, no. 2, pp. 93–104, 2011.

[WUE 12] WUEBBLES D., "Celebrating the 'Blue Marble'", *EOS Transactions*, vol. 93, no. 49, pp. 509–511, 2012.

[ZHA 17] ZHANG H., FEINZIG S., The far-reaching impact of candidate experience, IBM Analytics White Paper, available at: https://www.ibm.com/downloads/cas/YMOARJJG, 2017.

3

Competency Cultivation of Mechanical Engineers in the Process of Social Sustainable Development

The essence of sustainable social development is the development of human beings themselves, which relies on the development of the scientific and technological progress based on the advances of natural and social sciences. Engineers are the organizers and implementers of the formation of science and technology. Worldwide, human societies are facing increased opportunities for development, but also challenges from various fields, and their basic competencies and capacities on society and economics are being developed. The cultivation and improvement of the quality of education and training is essential for promoting the progress of science and technology, making engineering technology serve humankind, and promoting and realizing a sustainable society. Sustainable development plays a vital role. This chapter focuses on the importance and methods of developing the competence of mechanical engineers in the process of sustainable development of society, taking mechanical engineers as an example.

3.1. The importance of the basic qualities of mechanical engineers for the sustainable development of society

3.1.1. *What are the basic qualities of a mechanical engineer?*

The engineering community is involved in many industries and has had great influence on their development, with mechanical engineers being an important part of it. With the rapid development of modern science and technology and society,

---

Chapter written by Hailong FU, Yue WANG, Marius Gabriel PETRESCU and Mirela PANAIT.

the boundaries between many disciplines are becoming less obvious. The intersection of marginal disciplines and interdisciplinarity has become widespread. For a mechanical engineer, the most basic ability is to acquire more knowledge and develop a tight knowledge structure.

As mechanical engineers are involved in a wide range of fields and engaged in many jobs, their basic qualities are more comprehensive. Mechanical engineers should have a strong and solid foundation of knowledge to enhance adaptability for future work; a solid theoretical knowledge of the profession and technical practical skills to enhance professional research and development capabilities; a passion for science to enhance research and continuous innovation ability; the broad knowledge of economic management and technical management to enhance the ability to process and solve engineering problems; abundant knowledge of sociology to enhance the integration of development, science technology and social interaction [LI 00].

3.1.2. *How to achieve sustainable development of mechanical engineers*

Figure 3.1 depicts a sustainable development process of mechanical engineers. First of all, mechanical engineers need to improve their basic skills, solve basic work problems, and continue to learn on the job, accumulate knowledge and improve themselves constantly. At the same time, engineers need to communicate with each other, exchange work experiences, discuss cutting-edge technology, expand their horizons, and build a good communication environment. Finally, the development of the next generation of engineers should focus on developing the fundamental skills of the future, describing the experience of problem-solving and looking at the big picture. A cradle for training the engineers should be formed. Sustainable development is a long-term strategic goal which requires the common struggle of human generations. Therefore, mechanical engineers should think from a long-term perspective, in order that successive generations of engineers will be more advanced. Engineering technology can continue and, ultimately, serve society and benefit the people of the future.

3.1.3. *The relationship between the sustainable development of mechanical engineers and the sustainable development of society*

Society is like a ship that sails far away, and mechanical engineers are like sailors on the ship, and only if the sailors are skilled enough will the ship be able to sail safely across the ocean. In the process, sailors can also see the vastness and the beautiful scenery of the sea, thus accumulating more experience in navigation, and improving their sailing skills constantly.

As shown in Figure 3.1, if mechanical engineers continue to innovate and promote science and technology, society will progress and evolve accordingly. However, factors affecting the development of society are not single, and as it continues to evolve under the influence of other factors, it can provide a better environment for research, better material needs, and better scientific power. Mechanical engineers can accelerate their pace and make progress for society, which also promotes the development of mechanical engineers accordingly, and improving their knowledge to keep pace with the times. It can be concluded that the progress of mechanical engineers and social development mutually promote and influence each other.

This virtuous relationship between mechanical engineers and society can not only accelerate the progress of society, but also promote continuous growth of the field of mechanical engineering and the sustainable development of the mechanical engineering team, which in turn promotes the sustainable development of society.

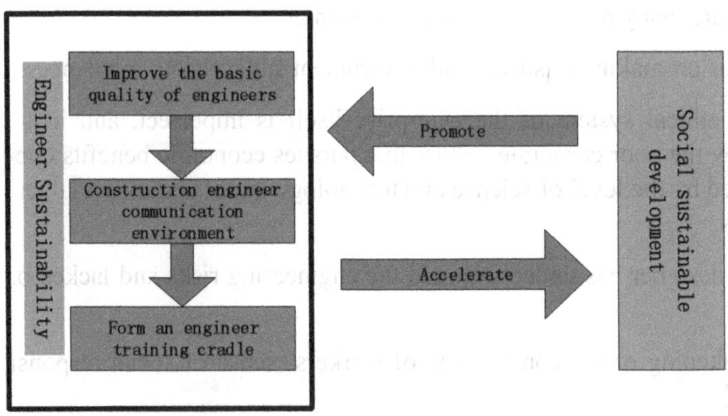

Figure 3.1. *The relationship between the sustainable development of mechanical engineers and the sustainable development of society*

3.2. Mechanical engineers must observe ethics and laws

Mechanical engineers, like other engineers, should observe ethical and legal requirements, first and foremost, in the process of implementing engineering technology.

3.2.1. *The importance of engineering ethics*

Engineering is an important production and construction process which has a profound impact on people's lives. Engineering ethics is a code of ethics that adjusts the relationship between engineering and technology, and engineering and society. It is an ethical and moral principle that must be observed in the field of engineering; a basic moral requirement for engineering and technical personnel engaged in engineering design, construction and management. People who are engaged in the profession of engineering must possess the unique ethics of the profession itself [DOU 17].

3.2.2. *Problems and causes of engineering ethics*

With the continuous development of technology, the harm of environmental pollution and the energy crisis has gradually emerged [WAN 14]. The lack of ethical care for people always occurs during the construction of the engineering project, including other ethical defects caused by the excessive pursuit of profit, etc.

There are many reasons for ethical problems:

1) decision-making mistakes and government supervision imbalances;

2) the ethical system of the enterprise itself is imperfect, and it is negatively affected by the poor corporate culture that pursues economic benefits one-sidedly. It is restricted by the level of science and technology under certain social and historical conditions;

3) the designer has underestimated the engineering risks and lacked professional ethics;

4) weakening of the construction of workers' sense of social responsibility, etc. [YAN 20].

It is obvious that engineering ethics is becoming more and more important in mechanical engineering. To achieve the sustainable development of mechanical engineering, as a mechanical engineer, observing engineering ethics should be the top priority.

3.2.3. *Legal issues in manufacturing*

As mechanical engineers, we must strictly abide by relevant laws and regulations in production and construction. If we violate local manufacturing standards or laws, it will lead to very serious consequences, such as the following:

1) observe standardization in the manufacturing field. All aspects of industrial production are closely linked. If one of the links has a size mismatch, it may cause problems within the entire production system;

2) differences in laws and regulations between countries. Many countries have different laws and regulations on industrial production. Before implementing the project, be sure to understand the regulations in the relevant regions to avoid violating the law;

3) naming and modeling a machine should avoid national and religious taboos. We must respect the human rights and religious beliefs of all people, and avoid adopting design concepts that may cause misunderstanding or discrimination.

All in all, while carrying out engineering design, mechanical engineers must be sensitive to, and respectful of relevant laws. Only under the premise of observing morality and the legal system, at the same time, can it be ensured that the project runs smoothly and achieves sustainable development.

3.3. Mechanical engineers shoulder responsibility for environmental protection

3.3.1. *Environmental pollution from industrial production is widespread*

In industrial production, particularly machine industry processes – traditional casting, forging, welding and other material forming processes, as well as traditional mechanical cutting processes such as turning, grinding, planing, milling, boring, and drilling – discharge a large amount of exhaust gas, wastewater and solid waste (directly or indirectly) and pollute the atmosphere and soil. Wastes such as metal ions, oil, acids, alkalis and organic matter, wastewater with suspended matter, chromium, mercury, lead, copper, cyanide, sulfide, dust, waste gas from organic solvents, metal shavings, slag and other solid waste. At the same time, it is accompanied by noise and vibrations during processing.

When smelting metal, corresponding smelting slag, as well as steam and dust containing heavy metals, are generated. Dust, smoke, noise, various harmful gases and various types of radiation will appear during the casting process of the material. In the plastic processing of the material, the forging hammer and punch will produce noise and vibrations during the work, heating the furnace dust, and cleaning dust will be generated during forging. High-temperature forging will also bring heat radiation. Arc welding, high-frequency electromagnetic waves, radiation, noise, etc. will be produced during the welding process of the material. As part of this process, the outer layer of the electrode and the flux decompose at high temperatures which can create a large amount of harmful dust, such as Fe_2O_3 and manganese, fluorine, etc. Ultraviolet radiation acts on oxygen and nitrogen in the ambient air to produce O_3, NO, NO_2, etc. During gas welding, a large amount of electro-slag is generated due to the production of acetylene gas from calcium carbide.

In metal heat treatment, high-temperature furnaces and high-temperature workpieces will produce heat radiation, soot and slag, and oil fumes. In addition, deoxidizers, such as titanium dioxide and silica gel, will be added to the salt bath furnace to prevent metal oxidation. Various acids, alkalis, salts, etc. and high-frequency electric field radiation are produced during chemical heat treatment. When nitriding the surface, an electric furnace is used to heat and pass ammonia gas. There is leakage of ammonia gas; when the surface is cyanided, the metal is put into the heated cyanide tank, containing sodium cyanide. Sodium cyanide is highly toxic, and will generate cyanide-containing gas and wastewater. When the surface is blackened, alkaline washing is carried out in a mixed solution of sodium hydroxide, carbonic acid and trisodium phosphate, and all waste acid liquid, waste alkaline liquid and sodium chloride gas will be discharged [LI 14].

In short, traditional metallurgy, machining and heat treatment of metal workpieces, etc. will bring unfavorable factors to people and the environment. Mechanical engineers should shoulder the important responsibility of environmental protection. The environmental protection of the human–machine environment should be considered at the early stages of the production claim.

3.3.2. *Engineers should know how to control industrial environmental pollution*

There are many methods to prevent environmental pollution, such as mechanical dust collectors, electric dust collectors, washing dust collectors and filter dust collectors, used to remove industrial exhaust gas [LI 17]. At the same time, harmful industrial gases can be purified by chemical methods such as absorption, adsorption, incineration, condensation and chemical reaction. However, from the perspective of the ability of engineers, we should master new technologies, new methods, and new material technologies for industrial pollution as soon as possible, and make them mature and perfect through production practices, and strive to achieve the sustainability of the industrial environment.

For example, the treatment method of industrial wastewater can break through the bottleneck of traditional wastewater treatment technology and specify scientific and reasonable purification process technology according to the attributes of wastewater. If it is relatively clean wastewater, such as the cooling water of the high-frequency furnace, it can be simply treated and discharged into a water channel, or treated by cooling or stabilization measures and then recycled. If it is wastewater containing toxic and harmful substances, after in-depth treatment, it can be discharged into the water channel only after meeting the national discharge standards and environmental protection requirements. For this reason, mastering wastewater treatment technology and advanced technology is essential to solve industrial water pollution.

In addition, engineers should abide by the prevention and control of industrial solid waste, and relevant standards and regulations, to mitigate industrial noise. In the process of implementing mechanical engineering technology, engineers should pay more attention to the impact of various links on the environment to ensure the rapid development of machine industry technology and avoid causing serious pollution to the environment, or have serious consequences.

3.4. Mechanical engineers must be familiar with traditions and learn to innovate

A qualified mechanical engineer should have received systematic training in mechanical theory, have good learning ability and correct learning methods, and be proficient in traditional professional knowledge and basic skills, for example:

1) familiar with the standards and representation methods of engineering drawings;

2) familiar with the performance, test methods and selection of commonly used metal materials;

3) master the basic knowledge and skills of mechanical product design, proficient in the design of parts;

4) master the basic knowledge and skills of the formulation process and be familiar with the processing technology of typical parts;

5) familiar with relevant safety regulations, ethics and legal knowledge;

6) familiar with quality management and quality assurance systems, master the basic tools and methods of process control, understand relevant quality inspection technology;

7) understand the basic concepts of computer simulation and be familiar with the characteristics and applications of commonly used computer software [ZHO 20].

The traditional engineering spirit is the unique inherent quality of the "engineering man"; it is the condensing and accumulation of long-term engineering experience, including the innovative spirit and practical spirit based on the nature of engineering, as well as the team spirit, rational freedom spirit and humanistic spirit adapted to social development. And innovation consciousness, as a generating element of innovation ability, plays an important role in enhancing innovation self-confidence, stimulating innovation motivation and maintaining innovation enthusiasm. Therefore, future mechanical engineers should not only have the traditional, professional knowledge and skills above but also have good innovation sense [ZHO 20, WAN 15].

When designing products, mechanical engineers should not only focus on meeting product demands and reducing costs but must also conduct a comprehensive analysis from a health and safety perspective, through technological innovation and invention, to solve the problems of products in order that they can meet the needs better. Besides, in a society that pays more and more attention to environmental protection and sustainable development, the role of engineers is not only seen as a technical talent but also as a thinker who is concerned with the issues from the perspective of social development. This requires engineers to have an awareness of environmental protection and energy-saving in the process of product design and manufacturing. In the stage of product development and design, new materials and technologies which are safe and environmentally friendly should be used, and the relevant methods and concepts of product lifecycle design must be learned. In the manufacturing process of products, new technologies and new processes should be used to reduce carbon and pollutant emissions. This requires mechanical engineers to comprehensively conceive from energy, environment, health and other aspects during the design of the scheme. Engineers should use innovative design as the driving force for new product development.

3.5. Mechanical engineers should pay attention to product quality management and quality assurance systems

Quality management and quality assurance systems are planning, implementation, monitoring, correction and improvement activities covering a series of processes such as procurement, research and development, production, sales and after-sales service. A process approach is most frequently adopted, combining the plan-do-check-act (PDCA) cycle and risk-based thinking [GUO 20]. At present, the most widely used is ISO 9001: 2015, which is formulated by the International Organization for Standardization Quality Management and Quality Assurance Technical Committee.

For machinery manufacturing enterprises, different quality management and quality assurance methods will produce different results. Quality management and assurance methods are composed of many factors. Therefore, enterprises are also required to choose appropriate management methods in accordance with actual conditions. Therefore, the quality of machinery manufacturing can reach the best level, and promote the development of enterprises in the direction of modernization and science.

For production processes and operations within machinery manufacturing enterprises, any link will involve a quality management and assurance system. Taking the quality capital expenditure environment as an example, if it is not controlled scientifically and reasonably, it will have an impact on the normal production and operation of the enterprise, and may even result in significant wasted funds. If an enterprise fails to properly manage and control product quality, it will lead directly to the finished product failing to meet standards, which wastes funds and is not conducive to the long-term stable development of the enterprise [PIN 20].

Therefore, in the future development of machinery manufacturing enterprises, it is necessary to establish a new quality management system. When there is a contradiction between quality and output, the enterprise must prioritize quality rather than output and, at the same time, pay attention to customer trends [HON 16], and maximize the expectations and needs of customers. Only by establishing an advanced, modern quality management system can machinery manufacturing enterprises gain a foothold within the fierce market competition, while saving capital and truly achieving the goal of sustainable development.

As a mechanical engineer, you should be able to master more modern management systems and implement them. Proficiency in various quality management techniques is needed. For the company's internal management, technical management, production activities, etc. you must have corresponding management capabilities. Only in this way can you maximize the quality of machinery manufacturing. When an enterprise encounters setbacks and difficulties, the employees should stand together with their enterprise in the same boat, devote themselves to the enterprise, and achieve growth with it synchronously.

3.6. Mechanical engineers should have a time view, a cost view and a risk view

Nowadays, with the rapid development of science and technology, stricter requirements have been put forward for the timeliness, reliability and benefits of mechanical products. As engineers, we must break the shackles of traditional design concepts and establish basic concepts such as time, cost and project risk, so as to meet the needs of economic development and mechanical product development, and to create more benefits [CHE 20, OKO 19].

3.6.1. *Establish the concept of time, follow the trend of industry development*

With the rapid development of science and technology and the emergence of new technologies, mechanical engineers urgently need to keep up with the world's new technology trends, as well as master the latest theories and technologies within their own industry. Establishing the concept of time can enable mechanical engineers to acquire the latest technical means in the shortest time, so as to create more cutting-edge mechanical products, to obtain greater benefits and serve the effect to the society.

3.6.2. *Set up the cost view, strengthen the core competition ability*

In today's market environment, especially in the changing external environment, internal competition is more and more fierce, cost pressures are increasing gradually and each enterprise can survive and develop. Cost saving has become an important measure and, as a mechanical engineer, having a cost concept is the key to making the enterprise competitive. Mechanical engineers can minimize the cost of machinery on the basis of meeting use requirements when designing products, which is the most important means to enhance the core competitiveness of enterprises [LIA 10].

3.6.3. *Establish the concept of project risk to avoid the occurrence of major losses*

Everything in the world is always evolving and changing, and risks may also extend over time and change dynamically. Mechanical engineers should establish the concept of project risk and focus on cultivating and avoiding risk awareness in the complete cycle of mechanical engineering technology implementation and all links, so as to "prevent risks". Only with a sense of project risk in mind can we avoid major losses during the project, ensure smooth progress and maximize the profits of the enterprise.

3.7. Mechanical engineers should have a global vision

3.7.1. *Establish a system concept and give play to the role of system engineering*

Today, with the rapid development of modern industry, boundaries between industrialization systems, or different countries, have become increasingly blurred.

Because the interconnections and exchanges between countries have been strengthened, the modern machine industry has been promoted; and it is the realization of common goals by machinery companies that has been the main task (improve labor productivity, reduce manufacturing costs, improve quality, product upgrading and so on). Therefore, the field of mechanical engineering is not single or multiple parts manufacturing and assembly but a large structure beyond mechanical systems. This requires mechanical engineers to observe and analyze problems with a systematic perspective when developing products. It is necessary to address the contradictions of parts and components but also to adopt a comprehensive approach from the perspective of the entire product. Engineers also need to consider the interrelationship and impact of each product and the complete set of equipment, and, ultimately, have to consider it from the highest level of the production or engineering system [HUA 15]. If a mechanical engineer does not have a systematic perspective and is not familiar with systems engineering, they would not serve all walks of life well.

3.7.2. *Strengthen international exchanges and promote common progress within the industry*

With new science and technology, the machinery industry in different countries has advantages and disadvantages. In order to develop their own technologies, they must all take advantage of their own strengths and avoid weaknesses; and must actively participate in international division of labor and cooperation in the production field, in order to save social labor and obtain better benefits. In addition, the new technological revolution is the rapid development of modern economic activities, which is followed by domestic production and sales, products and markets, and the contradiction between the supply of, and demand for resources gradually deepens. To resolve these contradictions, we must have a global perspective, achieve production configuration optimization and promote the goal of common discovery. At the same time, the development of mechanical engineers must embody a global perspective, take the world industrial system as the focus, learn from each other's strengths in technology, learn from each other in literacy, and unite and cooperate in promoting sustainable human development.

3.8. Conclusion

The social sustainable development approach is the inevitable road for human society. The harmony and coordination of human-machine-environment is the basic guarantee for the happiness of human life. The group of engineers represented by mechanical engineers is not only creator and implementer of scientific and technological progress in the advanced industrial era, it is also the promoter of human sustainable development. Under the demands of the rapid development of the global economy, engineers from various countries are urgently required to focus on global cooperation and development trends. Taking on the responsibilty of promoting the sustainable development of human society, through improving self-literacy and management capabilities, we work together to solve various problems faced by humankind in the industrial era, so that human society is truly sustainable and people's lives are happier.

3.9. Acknowledgements

The authors would like to thank the auxiliary work of postgraduate student team members: Wang Lei, Zhang Zongxu, Meng Fanchao and Zhu Honglve.

3.10. References

[CHE 20] CHEN Y., "Risk control strategy of PPP project", *Cooperative Economy and Technology*, vol. 12, pp. 60–62, 2020.

[DOU 17] DOUGHTY T.A., DILLON H., LULAY K. *et al.*, "Design and implementation of an aspirational ethics laboratory course", *ASEE Annual Conference & Exposition*, Columbus, Ohio, available at: https://peer.asee.org/28113, 2017.

[GUO 20] GUO J., "Discussion on the current status and effective countermeasures of quality management in machinery manufacturing enterprises", *Enterprise Reform and Management*, vol. 10, pp. 27–28, 2020.

[HON 16] HONG Z., HUANG X.M., ZONG W.Y., "Talents cultivation of outstanding engineering based on the plan for educating and training outstanding engineers", *Proceedings of the 2016 International Conference on Education, Training and Management Innovation (ETMI)*, 2016.

[HUA 15] HUANG H.Z., "New concepts that mechanical engineers should have", *Mechanical Engineering*, vol. 8, pp. 38–39, 2015.

[LI 00] LI L., FU G.Y., CHEN A.H., "On the quality of mechanical engineers in the new century", *Higher Education Research in Mechanical Industry*, vol. 4, pp. 67–68, 2000.

[LI 14] LI P., "Analysis of the sustainable development of chemical machinery and environment", *Chemical Engineering Management*, vol. 18, p. 131, 2014.

[LI 17] LI Y.H., "Metal environmental protection mining and mechanical automation development", *World Nonferrous Metals*, vol. 20, pp. 88–90, 2017.

[LIA 10] LIAN Y.J., "The historical mission and opportunities of Chinese engineers in the new century", *Vocational and Technical Education*, vol. 12, pp. 60–62, 2010.

[OKO 19] OKOKPUJIE I.P., FAYOMI O.S.I., OYEDEPO S.O, "The role of mechanical engineers in achieving sustainable development goals", *Procedia Manufacturing*, vol 35, pp. 782–788, 2019.

[PIN 20] PING L.Z., "On the operation of quality management systems in machinery manufacturing enterprises", *Modern Salt Chemical Industry*, vol. 3, pp. 111–112, 2020.

[WAN 14] WANG S.R., "On ethics and engineers in engineering construction", *Science and Technology Pioneer Monthly*, vol. 27, no. 10, pp. 140–141, 2014.

[WAN 15] WANG H., FU Q.C., "Teaching reform and practice of electrical engineering and electronics curriculum to strengthen engineering quality and innovative ability", *Proceedings of the 2015 International Conference on Advanced Management Science and Information Engineering (AMSIE)*, 2015.

[YAN 20] YANG S.Y., "Research on engineering ethics", *Jushe*, vol. 5, p. 188, 2020.

[ZHO 20] ZHOU Z.Q., "Research on the professional ideological education of engineers in mechanical engineering", *Mechanical Engineer*, vol. 6, pp. 17–21, 2020.

4

Essentials of Sustainability: A Roadmap for Businesses

This chapter deals with essentials of sustainability from a business management perspective. In this context, sustainability entrepreneurship, sustainable business and sustainability management tools are explained and then sustainability leadership, culture and innovation topics are addressed.

4.1. Introduction

Sustainability is a common problem for everyone in the world and unless necessary actions are taken today, there will not be a world in the future where our next generations are able to live. For this reason, all players should take the necessary responsibility for sustainable development. Businesses are also among these players and understanding sustainability from a business management perspective is important. Therefore, in the following sections, sustainability-related issues within an organization will be explained.

4.2. Definition of sustainability

Sustainability is a term which is used with different meanings in the literature. These different meanings sometimes result in confusion and misuse of the term. For this reason, it is important to clarify the concept first. Basically, the term "sustainable" means "enduring" or "continuing" and generally it is used to depict things which are "long-lasting". For example, in strategic management literature, "sustainable competitive advantage" is used to refer to the long-lasting competitiveness of the firm. Similarly, in management literature, the term "sustainable human resources" is

Chapter written by Yasemin SEN.

generally used for retaining human resources in the long run. A different meaning of sustainable is when it refers to a three-dimensional phenomenon, as in "sustainable development". These dimensions, namely, environmental, social and economic, together constitute the main factors of sustainability, and when this term is used before a word (such as sustainable business), it means applying the philosophy of sustainable development in this area (here, in business). In this chapter, sustainability will be used with this second meaning.

Sustainable development refers to the "development that meets the needs of the present generation without compromising the ability of future generations to meet their needs" [WCE 87]. Since this is a broad definition, it is possible to apply it to many fields (e.g. sustainable agriculture, sustainable architecture) and this possibility has made it a widely used definition. Based on this definition, sustainable development can be regarded as a macro level phenomenon and it is related to the development of nations within the limits of scarce resources. As stated above, it consists of three pillars (economic, social and environmental) and for sustainable development all these factors should be taken together (Figure 4.1). These pillars can be simply described as follows: the environmental dimension of sustainable development is related to preserving nature, the social dimension is related to taking care of the rights of society and the economic dimension is related to using resources efficiently for the socio-economic wellbeing of a community [JON 14].

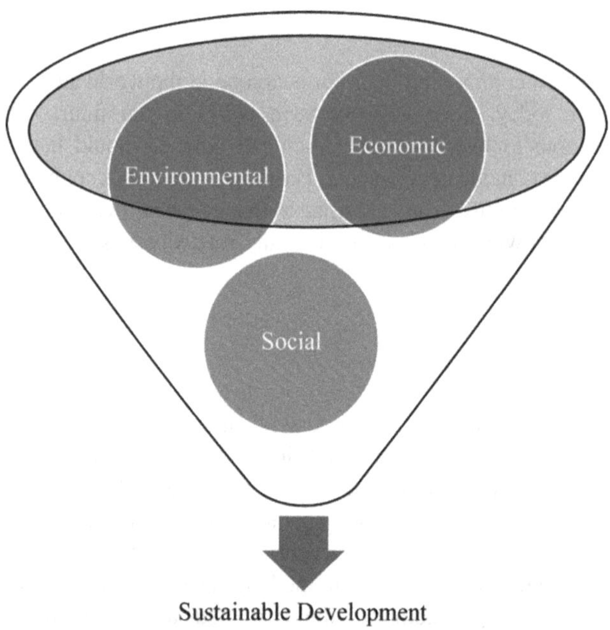

Figure 4.1. *Pillars of sustainable development*

Corporate sustainability, on the other hand, is related to applying principles of sustainable development in organizations. Based on the definition of sustainable development, corporate sustainability is defined as "meeting the needs of a firm's direct and indirect stakeholders (such as shareholders, employees, clients, pressure groups, communities etc.), without compromising its ability to meet the needs of future stakeholders as well" [DYL 02]. While achieving this goal, businesses should also take the three pillars of sustainability into account. Therefore, building on this definition, corporate sustainability can be defined as "giving importance to environmental, social and economic issues while meeting the needs of current stakeholders and, in this way, ensuring meeting the needs of future stakeholders".

4.3. History of sustainability

Sustainability has a long history. The emergence of sustainability issues can be dated back to the first industrial revolution. As a result of industrialization, nations' wealth has increased and this has triggered society's consumption. This development has been a great opportunity for the economy but more recently it has been realized that the consumption economy also created some problems. High production and consumption have brought the risk of the depletion of scarce resources. Environmental pollution and societal problems (such as negative effects on health and problems caused by bad working conditions etc.) were also problems caused by industrialization, among others. All these problems showed that action should be taken for the future of the planet, and, later on, that awareness of sustainability issues has increased.

The roots of sustainability-related awareness can be traced back to the 20th Century. In 1972, a report entitled "The Limits to Growth" was issued by the Club of Rome, an organization whose members have a common concern for the future of the planet. In this report, results of exponential growth in the world's population and economy were estimated and attention was paid to the physical limits of the planet. Again, in 1972, the United Nation's Conference on Human Environment (UNCHE) was held, in Stockholm. In this conference, which aimed to create awareness about the Earth's environment and development problems, the Stockholm Declaration was issued and thus the issue of the environment was put on the political agenda. After this conference, in 1980, an important step was taken by the International Union for the Conservation of Nature (IUCN). In this milestone, World Conservation Strategy (WCS) was formulated and launched internationally by the joint efforts of IUCN, WWFN (World Wildlife Fund for Nature) and UNEP (The United Nations Environment Program). In the report issued by IUCN, concerns about the environment and development were brought together under the umbrella of "conservation". Although the concept "sustainable development" was not yet defined, the term was used for the first time, within a chapter heading. This has been regarded as the emergence of the concept of sustainable development. In 1987, the World Commission on Environment and Development (WCED) published a report entitled "Our Common Future" (also known as the Brundtland Report) and, in this report, the definition of sustainable development was established. Since global attention towards sustainable development was created with this report, this was also an important milestone in the history of sustainable development. In 1992, the Rio Conference, which is also known as the United Nations Conference on Environment and Development (UNCED), was held, and in this conference the Rio Declaration, in which human life was mentioned as a central concern for sustainable development, was signed. Another remarkable milestone was the United Nation's Sustainable Development Summit, which was held in New York in 2015. In this global summit, in which a post-2015 agenda and sustainable development goals were determined, a universal call was made for actions needed for a better world [SEN 16].

Sustainable development is a global concern and everyone has responsibility for it. For this reason, all players in this process should take the necessary responsibilities. Businesses are among these players and for a better world it is important to manage businesses in a way that supports sustainable development (Figure 4.2).

Figure 4.2. *Players in sustainability*

4.4. Sustainability entrepreneurship

Entrepreneurship is a term used to define forming a business from scratch, and entrepreneurs are the people who take action in this process. For a start-up business, entrepreneurs bear the risk of failure and bring the factors of production together. Each enterprise has a reason for being and this reason determines its direction. Not all entrepreneurial activities are related to starting a completely new business. In order to keep up with the necessities of new market conditions, some people, namely, intrapreneurs, may execute entrepreneurial activities within an existing business, and this is called intrapreneurship. Whether it is an entrepreneurship or intrapreneurship several resources are used for serving several parties in the market and some returns (monetary or non-monetary) are gained in turn. In this process, besides other factors, the key issue is the entrepreneur themselves. An entrepreneur seeks new business opportunities and solves problems of the market. It may be hard to determine a common set of entrepreneur characteristics, but it is obvious that these kinds of people have high energy and enthusiasm with an innovative viewpoint. The focus of these innovations determines an entrepreneurship's type (e.g. social or green entrepreneurship, etc.).

The origin of the term "entrepreneur" dates back to the 17th and 18th Centuries. The French economist Jean Baptiste Say explained the term with its value-creating function. According to him, entrepreneurs take lower productivity resources and transform them into high-gain situations. Later on, in the 20th Century, Joseph Schumpeter defined the term with an innovative viewpoint. With this viewpoint, entrepreneurs are innovators and change agents of the economy. They find new ways of doing things, create new products and processes and move the economy forward. Besides these viewpoints, a widely known contemporary thinker of management, Peter Drucker, focuses on the opportunity issue. An entrepreneur may not need to be a change actor but rather it is critical to realize and take advantage of opportunities as they emerge in the market. This is also valid for not-for-profit organizations and therefore in an entrepreneurship there is no profit aim requirement [DEE 98].

Sustainable development, on the other hand, is closely related with entrepreneurship. New enterprises support economic development and, based on the main goal of an entrepreneur, an enterprise may also serve as a social and/or environmental player. Also, as explained before, sustainable development requires a collective effort of different players and businesses are among these players. As well as current businesses and their leaders playing an important role in this process, forming new businesses to support sustainability is also important. To some extent, businesses can support sustainability and strive for sector leadership in sustainability. However, forming a sustainability business from scratch and operating solely with this aim is important in creating new industries which support sustainable development. For this reason, a special type of entrepreneurship – that is, sustainability entrepreneurship – is an important issue and it needs special attention within the essentials of sustainability.

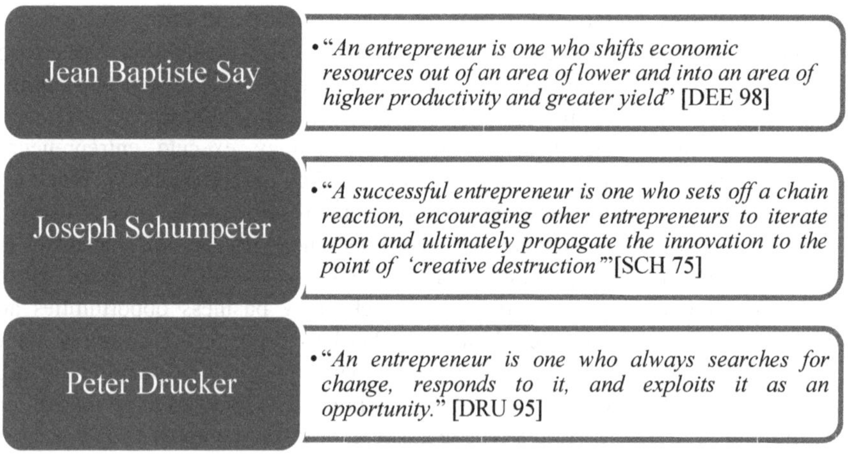

Figure 4.3. *Definitions of entrepreneurship*

In order to clarify the relationship between entrepreneurship and sustainable development, and also to explain sustainability entrepreneurship, it is important to illuminate closely related types of entrepreneurship such as ecopreneurship (green/environmental/eco-entrepreneurship) and social entrepreneurship. Although these types of entrepreneurships support sustainable development and are sometimes used interchangeably with sustainability entrepreneurship, they have distinctive specifications.

Within these types of entrepreneurships, ecopreneurship or, in other words, green entrepreneurship, is formed mainly for solving environmental problems and gaining economic value [HOC 10]. Remarkable attention about this type of entrepreneurship emerged in the 1990s and, since it is operated with an environmental driving force, this type of entrepreneurship is also known as environmental entrepreneurship [SCH 02]. Ecopreneurships basically deal with forming an innovative company providing environmental products and services [SCH 02b]. As a more specific definition, Pastakia defines ecopreneurial corporations as:

> Corporations which seek to maximize personal/organizational gains by identifying green business opportunities (eco-friendly products and processes) and transforming them into viable business ventures. [ISA 10]

In the definitions above, we can see that an environmental goal is the common characteristic of ecopreneurships. As well as environmental goals, another remarkable characteristic is innovativeness (this topic will be addressed in section 4.7 on sustainability innovation). A business idea is the most critical part of the entrepreneurial process and innovativeness is needed to determine and develop this business idea. Similarly, for an ecopreneurship, innovativeness is important for finding green business solutions and increasing business gains through the necessary innovative developments.

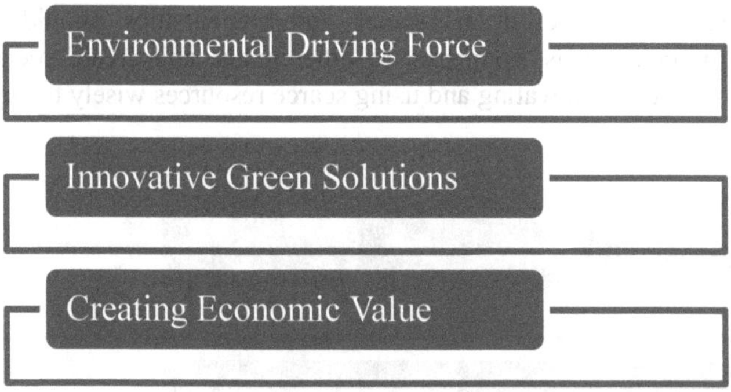

Figure 4.4. *Main characteristics of ecopreneurship*

Another sustainability-related type of entrepreneurship is social entrepreneurship. These types of entrepreneurships are new ventures which are formed by a societal driving force. According to Dees (1998), "Social entrepreneurships combine the passion of a social mission with an image of business-like discipline, innovation, and determination" [DEE 98]. Here the core issue is the social mission but, at the same time, a business discipline is important. Social entrepreneurships are generally assumed as best suited to not-for-profit organizations. Although the opposite idea is also existent in the literature, it is obvious that, for a profit-seeking organization, being highly societal is a difficult job. A profit-seeking business faced with this dilemma should decide on whether it will aim to gain more profit or rather prefer to accomplish more social aims.

On the other hand, regardless of the type of an organization (whether it is profit-seeking or a not-for-profit organization), Peredo & McLean put the importance of societal goals, among other goals, on a continuum and regard having exclusively, or in some prominent way, social goals as enough to be classed a social entrepreneurship. Based on this idea it is suggested that:

> Social entrepreneurship is exercised where some person or group (1) aim(s) at creating social value, either exclusively or at least in some prominent way; (2) show(s) a capacity to recognize and take advantage of opportunities to create that value ("envision"); (3) employ(s) innovation, ranging from outright invention to adapting

someone else's novelty, in creating and/or distributing social value; (4) is/are willing to accept an above-average degree of risk in creating and disseminating social value; and (5) is/are unusually resourceful in being relatively undaunted by scarce assets in pursuing their social venture. [PER 06]

According to this definition, social entrepreneurships should give more importance to social goals, compared to other goals, and create social value by seeking opportunities, innovating and using scarce resources wisely to support social aims.

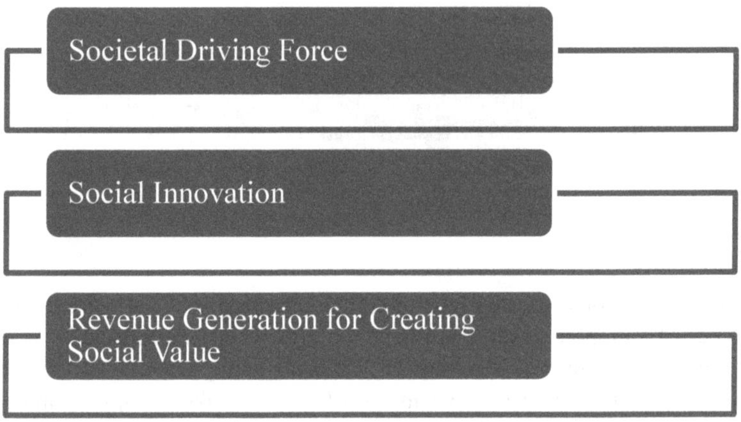

Figure 4.5. *Main characteristics of social entrepreneurships*

Different from other types of entrepreneurships, sustainability entrepreneurships are new ventures formed in order to support sustainable development. In other types of entrepreneurships, explained above, there is a dominant goal, among other goals. In some ventures, the main goal is creating environmental value (ecopreneurships – clean-technology venturing) and in other ventures the goal of creating social value is more important (social entrepreneurships e.g. health, education, community development). However, when it comes to sustainability entrepreneurships there is a balanced combination of economic, social and environmental value creation goals. These types of organizations find solutions for environmental and social problems while creating economic value to sustain the venture's operations and supporting economic development. While doing this, they monitor and realize social, environmental and economic value creation opportunities, find new ways of doing things and make innovations related to these aims, and also take a pioneering role in creating or transforming an industry to support sustainable development.

In practice, some entrepreneurships may seem to concentrate on one dimension of sustainable development-related goals (e.g. environmental) but, in fact, these different aims directly or indirectly support each other and, in the end, all of them are achieved. For example, an entrepreneurship formed to create clean energy technologies may seem to aim for an environmental goal but, at the same time, it supports social aims (such as providing health protection, increasing quality of life etc.) and economic aims (creating employment opportunities, profit generation for new investments etc.). The key point here is the entrepreneur's mindset and the enterprise's focus. Whether this entrepreneurship is formed based on a sustainability focus or not makes this issue clear. Entrepreneurships formed based on inclusive business models, for example, can also be regarded as sustainability entrepreneurships. These kinds of entrepreneurships include low income people in their value chain and create a win-win situation. Additional to social and economic goals, if they also give importance to environmental goals, then we can call them sustainability entrepreneurships.

Çöp(m)adam is a good example of a sustainability entrepreneurship and also an inclusive business model. It was formed to support women's employment and recycling/re-using in Ayvalık, in Turkey. Women who have not worked and earned money before work in this project and they produce creative products (handbags) using packaging which would be or has been thrown away as trash. These handmade products are sold and the women are paid fair wages in turn [ÇÖP 20]. This entrepreneurship has social, environmental and economic goals at the same time and, as a result, provides support for sustainable development.

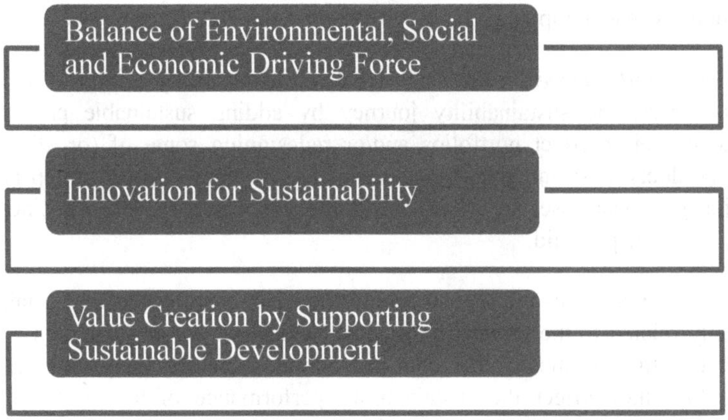

Figure 4.6. *Main characteristics of a sustainability entrepreneurship*

4.5. Sustainable business

Although it is daunting work, increasing the number of sustainability entrepreneurships is important for our future. As well as forming sustainability entrepreneurships, another way towards sustainable development goals is transforming current businesses and industries into sustainable businesses and sustainable industries. Of course, it is also not easy work to transform all industries in the short term. However, if current businesses take the necessary responsibilities, at least to some extent they can support the sustainable development goals of a country.

Based on the extent and scope of efforts towards sustainability, a business's steps in this process resemble a ladder of sustainability. In this ladder each rung represents a different progress level and as one goes up this ladder, the number of businesses that achieve this level of progress is expected to decrease. Therefore, it can also be thought of as a pyramid of sustainability. The steps in this ladder of sustainability can be listed as follows [YOU 13]:

1) products and services;

2) processes;

3) business model;

4) company focus;

5) brand identity of company;

6) supplier web and value chain;

7) industry leadership and advocacy role.

Products and services is the basic level of sustainability efforts. Most current businesses start the sustainability journey by adding sustainable products and services to their product portfolios and/or redesigning some of (or all of) their current products as sustainable. Since, compared to other steps, this step is easier, the majority of businesses are expected to fall in this category. These businesses are in the base of the pyramid.

Processes constitutes the second rung of the sustainability ladder. Sustainability is not only related to the production process, which is the transformation of inputs into outputs. In a business, other than production, there are many other processes and together they affect the sustainability performance of an organization. As Michael Porter suggested, value creation is realized through primary (inbound logistics, operations, outbound logistics, marketing and sales, service) and secondary activities (firm infrastructure, HRM, technology development, procurement) and these activities together constitute the value chain of a business. In this value chain, activities are linked to each other and total value created is affected by the interactions of these activities. For this reason, it is called a chain and, whether primary or secondary, each activity is important in the process. Similarly, for sustainability, all processes related to all activities are critical and a business which aims for sustainability may seek to make some part of or all processes sustainable. Since in this step more effort is needed than in the first step, fewer businesses (compared to first step) are expected to achieve it.

Business model is the third step in the sustainability ladder. A business model is composed of several elements which are in interrelationship, such as customer value proposition, profit formula (revenue model and cost structure), key processes and resources, and via these elements the business creates and delivers value to its customers [JOH 08]. Business models are important for all businesses (whether new or established) and based on the changing requirements of the market, the current business model may need to be reformed. In the business model step of the sustainability ladder, businesses not only make arrangements on products/services and processes, but also align their business models based on sustainability. Businesses operated with a sustainability business model create value for its customers based on the sustainability goal and for this reason it is important in the sustainability journey. EPIC Burger, a company opened in Chicago in 2008, is a good example of a sustainability business model. It was formed with a sustainability aim and the business model has been constructed accordingly. That is why its slogan is "a more mindful burger".

Company focus constitutes another important step in the sustainability ladder. The main driving force of a business affects its direction. Direction includes vision, mission statement, core values and these factors are good reflections of the way the company does business. Basically, the mission statement of a company gives information about its reason for being. The vision statement shows what the company desires to achieve in the long run and the values of a company reflect the business philosophy. A business which aims at sustainability may design sustainable products and services, make processes sustainable and change its business model based on sustainability. However, a sustainability company focus is also critical for a goal of sustainability. Since this goal needs collective action and organization-wide effort, sustainability-based orientation of management and business members affect the success of this process. Businesses at this level of the ladder have a sustainability company focus or at least they integrate sustainability goals into their current company focus.

Brand identity of company is the fifth rung of the sustainability ladder. A business with a sustainability focus can also create a strong identity which supports sustainability. Brand identity is critical for creating a brand image (customers' perception of the company) and it includes a set of elements such as a slogan, a logo or a brand name [RUK 20]. A business which is perceived as sustainable by others is closer to a sustainability goal and it becomes a role model for other businesses in the industry. In this way, transforming industries towards sustainable industries may become easier.

Supplier web and value chain is another further step towards the sustainability goal. While doing business, players on the supply chain (or within the supply network) determine the performance of a company and, therefore, businesses are linked to the players beyond the company borders. Similarly, sustainability is not an issue limited to an individual business and, in this step, businesses enlarge their sustainability efforts towards the entire supplier web. In this process the company takes control over its supply web for the sustainability goal and for this, some mechanisms, such as contracts or rules, are used.

Industry leadership and advocacy role is the final step in the sustainability ladder. If a company takes all other steps in this ladder then it becomes a role model for sustainability. This role makes it an industry leader for sustainability and it advocates this goal as a philosophy in the industry. Of course, it is not an easy job and, in reality, achieving this status is questionable. However, being at least as close as possible to this goal is important and this situation is not a barrier to a business having an advocacy role. Since this step is difficult to achieve, it is expected that the least number of businesses are at this level (Figure 4.7).

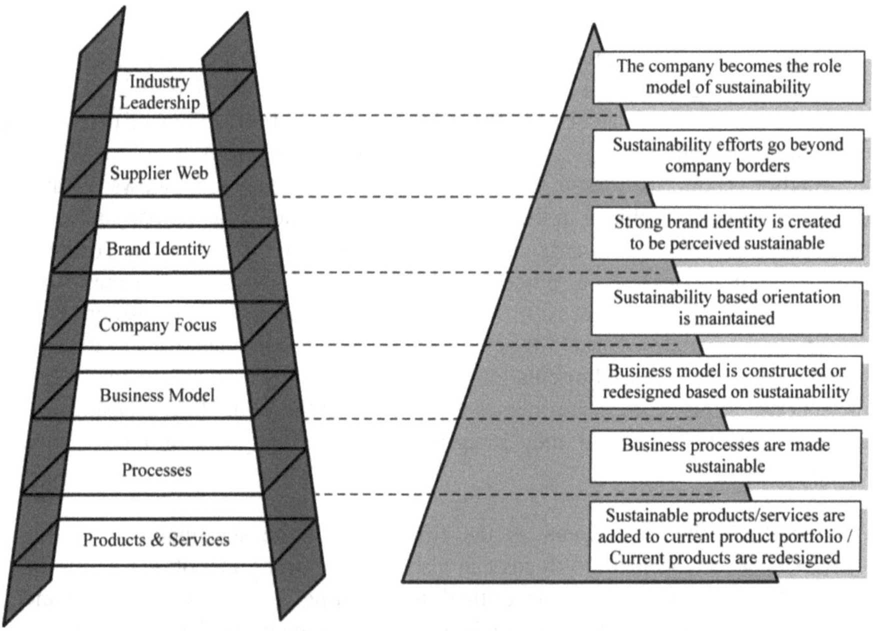

Figure 4.7. *Sustainability ladder*

Businesses need a systematic and disciplined effort to achieve the sustainability leadership level and this requires comprehensive undertakings. Therefore, organizations use sustainability management tools. Sustainability management tools which are addressed here are Environmental Management Systems (EMS), Sustainable Value Stream Mapping (Sus-VSM), Total Quality Environmental Management (TQEM) and Sustainability Balanced Scorecard (SBSC). These tools include different methodologies for applying sustainability principles and businesses may use one or more of these tools in their organizations.

Environmental Management System (EMS) is a series of systematic actions of an organization to manage and increase environmental performance. EMS is a kind of planning and execution tool and it is based on the PDCA (plan-do-check-act) cycle (Figure 4.8). Based on the preference of the business, an environmental management system can be applied formally (certified) or informally (non-certified) in the organization. If it is a certified EMS such as EMAS (Eco-Management and Audit Scheme) or ISO 14001, a scheme of subsequent steps is applied in the process. However, if it is applied informally, the process may be more flexible and management determines its own plan within the organization.

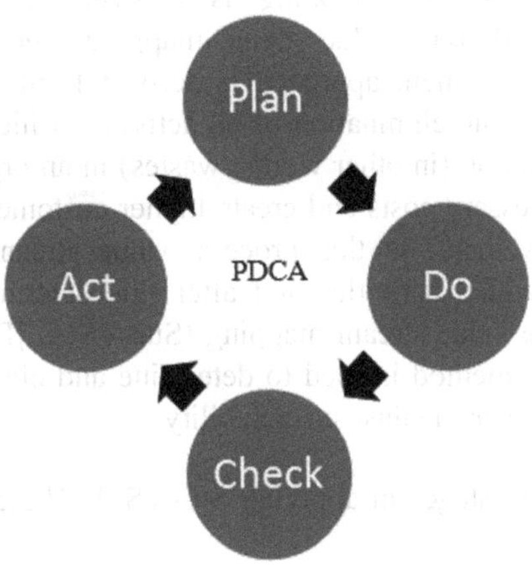

Figure 4.8. *PDCA cycle*

In a certified environmental management system, a five-stage process is followed by organizations [ISO 04]. These stages are:

1) environmental policy;

2) planning;

3) implementation and operation;

4) checking;

5) management review.

Environmental policy is related to the business's commitment to this program and it shows the philosophy of the business about environmental issues. In the planning stage, objectives are determined based on the environmental policy and after the organizational factors which affect the environment are determined, the necessary action plans are prepared accordingly. In the implementation stage, based on plans, the necessary resources are assigned for operation and the plan is implemented. When it comes to the fourth stage, the results are controlled and compared with the objectives. If there is a gap between the objectives and the results, corrective actions are taken. In the final stage, the overall system is evaluated by management and if there is something wrong with the system, the policy and objectives are revised. For a successful result, the environmental management system needs a systematic approach and organization-wide commitment. Besides, since it takes time to get results, patience and support of the top management is another important issue.

Sustainable Value Stream Mapping is a sustainability management tool developed based on traditional value stream mapping used in lean manufacturing systems. The lean management approach is derived from the Toyota Production System and is based on the elimination of all activities which are non-value added and suitable for elimination (in other words, wastes) in an organization. In this way it aims to lower unnecessary costs and create higher customer value. It is also used for continuous improvement. In this process, value stream mapping is used to determine non-value added activities and after this determination all wastes are eliminated. Sustainable value stream mapping (Sus-VSM) [FAU 12] also works in the same manner. This method is used to determine and eliminate activities which have harmful effects and are against sustainability.

There are three main stages in applying Sus-VSM. These stages are as follows [ROT 03]:

1) current state map;

2) future state map;

3) implementation plan.

In the first step, by using sustainability metrics (such as energy consumption, ergonomics or time waste), the current situation of the value stream is evaluated and mapped. After that, wastes are determined based on selected metrics. In the second step, the desired value stream map is prepared and in the third step, an action plan is prepared and applied by the organization. Sustainable value stream mapping is a comprehensive tool and can be used for one product line, product family or the whole value chain of an organization.

Total Quality Environmental Management (TQEM) is a sustainability management tool derived from Total Quality Management (TQM). Total Quality Management is a contemporary management approach which aims to ensure quality throughout the organization and seeks customer satisfaction. TQM is a management philosophy and it is based on the inclusion of everyone (from top to bottom in the organizational hierarchy) in this process.

In Total Quality Management philosophy there are four main principles. These principles are as follows [CHA 99]:

1) customer orientation;

2) continuous improvement;

3) doing the job right the first time;

4) system approach.

Total Quality Management aims at *customer satisfaction* at all times. According to TQM philosophy, the customer is not only the one who buys products and services of a company. Since output of a unit is used as input of another unit, members of the organization are also regarded as customers, namely, internal customers. Therefore, in TQM, there are two types of customers, internal and external, and satisfaction of both types of customer is important for the organization. Similarly, Total Quality Environmental Management aims for customer satisfaction. Today, quality expectations of people are evolved and support for sustainable development goals is also a criterion for quality perception. In TQEM philosophy, from top management to the employee at the lowest level, everyone is committed to this aim and organization is managed with this philosophy. Another principle of TQM is *continuous improvement*. In order to maintain quality and constant customer satisfaction, everyone searches for areas of improvement all the time and quality standards are maintained. This principle also supports innovation and, in this way, innovations do not become obsolete in time. Similarly, TQEM applies continuous improvement for the environmental performance of the organization. For this aim, an organization which applies TQEM uses similar quality improvement tools of TQM, such as the PDCA cycle. *Doing the job right the first time* is another principle of TQM. This principle is related with zero defect and the excellence aims of the organization. After happening, solving quality problems are costly and affect the customer satisfaction negatively. Therefore, preventive actions are taken at the beginning and jobs are done right at first. In TQEM, on the other hand, preventive actions are taken to increase the environmental performance of the organization. Environmental planning can be used in this process. In TQM, the *system approach* reflects a holistic viewpoint. In order to guarantee quality throughout the organization a holistic approach is needed. In this way, the origins of problems can be detected corrently and can be prevented before happening again. Similarly, for the success of TQEM, a system approach is needed. In order to improve environmental performance all interrelated parts of organization and their effects should be understood well.

TQEM is a comprehensive management tool and also has a cultural aspect. Therefore, it needs transformation and is not easy to apply. However, if applied successfully, results can be achieved permanently. Although this management tool is called "environmental management", the same principles can also be applied to the sustainable development goal. Therefore, it is regarded as a sustainability management tool.

Sustainability Balanced Scorecard (SBSC) is a sustainability management tool derived from the traditional Balanced Scorecard. Balanced Scorecard was developed by Harvard professors R. Kaplan and D. Norton as a new performance management tool, in the early 1900s [BIE 02]. While a classic organizational performance management system includes only financial performance indicators, the Balanced Scorecard method takes other indicators (such as customer satisfaction, internal processes, and innovation and learning performance indicators) which support financial results into consideration. Financial results are important for an organization's performance but, at the same time, there are many aspects which affect the success of the organization and are interrelated with each other.

Although the type and number of indicators used may differ, the widely-used indicators (perspectives) of Balanced Scorecard are as follows [KAP 92]:

1) financial perspective;

2) customer perspective;

3) internal processes perspective;

4) innovation and learning perspective.

Financial perspective is related to traditional financial performance indicators (e.g. profitability), customer perspective is related to the indicators which give information about the performance results of customer value creation (e.g. customer satisfaction), and internal processes perspective (e.g. core competencies) is related to performance indicators which give information about the success of an organization's key internal processes. Finally, innovation and learning perspective (e.g. employee growth and development) is related to performance indicators which give information about organization's capacity for development and change.

Sustainable Balanced Scorecard (SBSC) also works with the same principles. In preparation of SBSC, based on the preference of management, one of two alternatives can be selected. One alternative is preparing a SBSC by adding a fifth perspective (Sustainability Perspective) which includes sustainability performance indicators of the organization to BSC. The second alternative is embedding sustainability performance indicators to the current BSC perspectives of the organization. Sustainable Balanced Scorecard is a strong tool for management of sustainability in organizations. Any sustainability effort will be more successful if it is linked to company direction (mission and vision) and strategy. Since in SBSC the indicators are determined based on the direction and strategy of the organization, it gives a greater opportunity to organization for realizing sustainability objectives.

Businesses may choose one or more of these sustainability management tools to increase their sustainability performance. Whatever the tool(s) chosen, the important thing is applying these tools intentionally and decisively.

4.6. Sustainability leadership and culture

Leadership has a key role in the success of any businesses. Monitoring environmental changes, deciding on the right actions and applying them. While listing these behaviors, it seems easy, but in reality many organizations fail just because of the leadership style, which is not suitable for the current situation. Similarly, for a sustainable business, leadership is critical and without the right leader for sustainability it is impossible to achieve the sustainable business goals. As explained previously, it is a long journey toward becoming a sustainable business and, in this process, organizations may apply different sustainability management tools (i.e. EMS, TQEM, etc.). In all of these methodologies the success depends mainly on the support of the top management. First of all, the leader should believe in the sustainability business goal and exert effort towards it. By definition, the leader is the person who motivates others (followers) to achieve a common goal and, in leadership processes, being a role model is important. Besides, the leader should ensure any necessary conditions within the organization for a successful operation. Therefore, additional to basic leadership specifications, such as determination or being visionary etc., a sustainability leader can be defined as the person who:

1) is conscious about sustainable development;

2) believes in the goal of sustainable business;

3) has concern for the current and future needs of stakeholders;

4) acts based on sustainability values;

5) prepares the necessary conditions and takes action with others for sustainability.

As is seen from the above specifications, a sustainability leader should be conscious about sustainable development and set goals accordingly. Based on the sustainable development goal, the leader should give balanced importance to environmental, social, economic areas and ensure the longevity of the business. Of course, behaving in this way needs values (such as respect for nature, responsibility etc.) which support sustainability. Therefore, a sustainability leader should be a role model by acting based on sustainability values. Another important point in this process is preparing the necessary conditions. For a sustainable business, a system which ensures sustainability throughout the organization is important. The participation of every member (from the top to the bottom of the pyramid) in this process is necessary and this requires an organizational culture which supports sustainability. Organizational culture is related to deeply held values and the leader has a critical role in creating an organizational culture. Therefore, for a sustainable business, the leader (sustainable leader) should ensure a sustainability culture within the organization.

Although there are different viewpoints on cultural dimensions, classifications are typically based on organizational values and practices [LIN 10]. In the literature, sustainability culture is defined as "a company's recognition of the impact of the company's activities on society and communities and the need to minimize it, which translates into a philosophy and values that drive the decision-making process of the firm" [MAR 15]. In organizations which have a sustainability culture, a shared vision of and deeply held values of sustainability are critical. Based on these values, a sustainability-oriented behavioral pattern is created and maintained in a typical organization which has a sustainability culture. Basically, main characteristics of a sustainability culture can be listed as follows:

1) sustainability-oriented direction (mission, vision, values);

2) sustainability-oriented strategy and goals;

3) sustainability-oriented activities on the whole value chain;

4) providing necessary opportunities (by owners and leadership) and fostering innovation for improvement of sustainability performance;

5) commitment and involvement of everyone in the organization (from the top to the bottom of the pyramid) in the sustainability operations.

In a sustainability culture, all of the aspects of an organization reflect the sustainability orientation. This reflection mainly starts with the direction of an organization. In these kinds of organizations, sustainability is integrated with the company's mission, vision and the core values. This orientation is also reflected in the strategy and goals of the organization. Accordingly, all functions throughout the organization or, in other words, all activities on the value chain are accomplished based on this orientation. In this process, employee commitment and involvement is critical. Therefore, in order to maintain this, leaders should provide the necessary opportunities for improvement of sustainability performance. Motivating organizational members towards the shared sustainability goals and fostering sustainability innovation can be regarded among leaders' supportive activities.

As it is in every cultural arrangement, creating a sustainability culture is difficult and it needs a long time to build. Therefore, it needs passion and determination to be achieved.

4.7. Sustainability innovation

In a sustainable business, another critical point is making innovations to improve the sustainability performance of the organization. Although the variety of innovation definitions makes it difficult to pinpoint, there is a common factor of "newness" in all definitions. In one definition, innovation is defined as the "search for, and the discovery, experimentation, development, initiation, and adoption of new products, new production processes and new organizational set-ups" [DOS 88]. On the other hand, OECD defines the term as "implementation of a new or significantly improved product (good or service), or process, a new marketing method, or a new organizational method in business practices, workplace organization or external relations" [OEC 05]. When it comes to taxonomy of the term, based on different criteria, such as the object or extent of change, innovation is categorized differently. While it is categorized by OECD as product, process, marketing and organizational innovations (based on the object of change) [VAR 10], in another categorization (based on the extent of change) it is classified as incremental or radical innovation. Product (or service) innovation refers to the organization's new product or service offerings and process innovation is related to the changes in organizational operations [ROW 11]. On the other hand, marketing innovation refers to the marketing method changes in 4Ps, and organizational innovation refers to the new organizational methods in business practices, workplace organization and external relations [OEC 05]. Besides, based on the extent of innovation, radical innovation refers to significant changes whereas incremental innovation refers to minimal changes [ROW 11].

Regardless of the types explained above, another categorization can be made, as classical or sustainability innovation. Classical innovation is the innovation of any kind explained above; on the other hand, sustainability innovation is defined as "new or modified processes, techniques, practices, systems and products to reduce social and environmental harm" [KUS 19]. Although this is not a wrong definition, the economic dimension can also be added to it for businesses. Therefore, by adding this third dimension (the economic dimension) to the definition, sustainability innovation can be defined as "new or modified processes, techniques, practices, systems and products to reduce social and environmental harm *while ensuring the economic goal of business*". Although this revised definition is right, the aim of sustainability innovation is not limited to reducing harm. Finding solutions for current sustainability problems or creating new products and technologies that increase the quality of life also constitutes the aims of sustainability innovation.

Sustainable businesses should always search for sustainability innovation areas in the organization and make the necessary developments. While doing this, as well as the creativity of employees being important, the organization also needs sustainability leaders (explained above). Therefore, sustainability innovation is not an issue that can be considered alone and, for a successful sustainability innovation process, all interrelated factors should be maintained in the organization.

4.8. Conclusion

Sustainable development needs the collective efforts of each player in society and businesses are a group of these critical players. In order to support sustainable development goals, businesses either need to be formed as a sustainability entrepreneurship or transformed into sustainable businesses. Either way, businesses need systematic effort and the necessary conditions to achieve a sustainability advocacy role. In this process the leader bears a critical role. Applying appropriate sustainability management tool(s), creating the necessary conditions (i.e. sustainability culture) which support sustainability and fostering innovation for improved sustainability performance are among the responsibilities of sustainability leaders. On the other hand, each employee in the organization (from the top to the bottom of the organizational pyramid) should believe in this process and behave accordingly. As is seen from the explanations above, for a successful sustainable business, a systematic and collective effort throughout the organization is needed and this process starts with business leaders who see their organizations through a sustainability lens. Therefore, this chapter provides a roadmap for businesses towards sustainability.

4.9. References

[BIE 02] BIEKER T., "Managing corporate sustainability with the balanced scorecard: Developing a balanced scorecard for integrity management", *Oikos PhD Summer Academy*, 2002.

[CHA 99] CHANDRASHEKAR A., DOUGLESS T., AVERY G.C., "The environment is free: The quality analogy", *Journal of Quality Management*, vol. 4, no. 1, pp. 123–143, 1999.

[ÇÖP 20] ÇÖP(M)ADAM, Çöp(m)adam, available at: http://www.copmadam.com, May 7, 2020.

[DEE 01] DEES J.G., The meaning of 'Social Entrepreneurship', available at: http://www.fuqua.duke.edu/centers/case/documents/Dees_SEdef.pdf, May 30, 2001.

[DOS 88] DOSI G., "The nature of the innovative process", in DOSI G., FREEMAN C., NELSON R., *et al.* (eds), *Technical Change and Economic Theory*, pp. 221–238, Frances Pinter, London, 1988.

[DRU 95] DRUCKER P.F., *Innovation & Entrepreneurship*, Harper Business, New York, 1995.

[DYL 02] DYLLICK T., HOCKERTS K., "Beyond the business case for corporate sustainability", *Business Strategy and the Environment*, vol. 11, no. 2, pp. 130–141, 2002.

[FAU 12] FAULKNER W., TEMPLETON W., GULLETT D. *et al.*, "Visualizing sustainability performance of manufacturing systems using sustainable value stream mapping (Sus-VSM)", *Proceedings of the 2012 International Conference on Industrial Engineering and Operations Management*, Istanbul, Turkey, 2012.

[HOC 10] HOCKERTS K., WÜSTENHAGEN R., "Greening Goliaths versus emerging Davids – Theorizing about the role of incumbents and new entrants in sustainable entrepreneurship", *Journal of Business Venturing*, vol. 25, no. 5, pp. 481–492, 2010.

[ISA 10] ISAAK R., "The making of the ecopreneur", in SCHAPER M. (ed.), *Making Ecopreneurs: Developing Sustainable Entrepreneurship*, GOWER, 2010.

[ISO 04] ISO 14001:2004, Environmental management systems – Requirements with guidance for use, ISO, available at: https://www.iso.org/obp/ui/#iso:std:iso:14001:ed-2:v1:en, 2004.

[JOH 08] JOHNSON M.W., CLAYTON M.C., HENNING K., "Reinventing your business model", *Harvard Business Review*, vol. 86, no. 12, pp. 57–68, 2008.

[JON 14] JONES P., HILLIER D., COMFORT D. *et al.*, "Towards sustainable data centre operations in the UK", *Handbook of Research on Consumerism in Business and Marketing: Concepts and Practices*, IGI Global, pp. 143–154, 2014.

[KAP 92] KAPLAN R.S., NORTON D.P., "The balanced scorecard – Measures that drive performance", *Harvard Business Review*, January–February, pp. 71–79, 1992.

[KUS 19] KUSI-SARPONG S., GUPTA H., SARKIS J., "A supply chain sustainability innovation framework and evaluation methodology", *International Journal of Production Research*, vol. 57, no. 7, pp. 1990–2008, 2019.

[LIN 10] LINNENLUECKE M.K., GRIFFITHS A., "Corporate sustainability and organizational culture", *Journal of World Business*, vol. 45, no. 4, pp. 357–366, 2010.

[MAR 15] MARSHALL D., MCCARTY L., MCGRATH P. *et al.*, "Going above and beyond: How sustainability culture and entrepreneurial orientation drive social sustainability supply chain practice adoption", *Supply Chain Management: An International Journal*, vol. 20, no. 4, pp. 434–454, 2015.

[OEC 05] OECD OSLO MANUAL, The measurement of scientific and technological activities: Proposed guidelines for collecting and interpreting technological innovation data, available at: https://www.oecd.org/science/inno/2367614.pdf, 2005.

[PER 06] PEREDO A.M., MCLEAN M., "Social entrepreneurship: A critical review of the concept", *Journal of World Business*, vol. 41, no. 1, pp. 56–65, 2006.

[ROT 03] ROTHER M., JOHN S., *Learning to See: Value Stream Mapping to add Value and Eliminate Muda*, Lean Enterprise Institute, Cambridge, 2003.

[ROW 11] ROWLEY J., BAREGHEH A., SAMBROOK S., "Towards an innovation-type mapping tool", *Management Decision*, vol. 49, no. 1, pp. 73–86, 2011.

[RUK 20] RUKOSUEV D., What is brand identity and how to build it?, available at: https://www.professionalacademy.com/blogs-and-advice/what-is-brand-identity, May 7, 2020.

[SCH 75] SCHUMPETER J.A., *Capitalism, Socialism and Democracy*, Harper, New York, 1975.

[SCH 02a] SCHALTEGGER S., "A framework for ecopreneurship: Leading bioneers and environmental managers to ecopreneurship", *Greener Management International*, vol. 38, pp. 45–58, 2002.

[SCH 02b] SCHAPER M., "The essence of ecopreneurship", *Greener Management International*, vol. 38, pp. 26–30, 2002.

[SEN 16] SEN Y., "Can fast-food industry go sustainable? A company evidence from Chicago", *European Journal of Business and Management*, vol. 8, no. 12, pp. 203–208, 2016.

[VAR 10] VARIS M., LITTUNEN H., "Types of innovation, sources of information and performance in entrepreneurial SMEs", *European Journal of Innovation Management*, vol. 13, no. 2, pp. 128–154, 2010.

[WCE 87] WCED, *Report of the World Commission on Environment and Development: Our Common Future*, vol. 17, pp. 1–91, 1987.

[YOU 13] YOUNG S.T., DHANA K.K., *Sustainability: Essentials for Business*, Sage Publications, 2013.

5

Styles of Leadership and Perceptions of Corporate Social Responsibility

As there are few empirical studies analysing how styles of leadership influence perceptions of social responsibility (SR), this present research project seeks to help offset that shortcoming. This correspondingly strives to identify whether leadership styles (transformational, transactional and *laissez-faire*) influence employee perceptions as regards the SR developed by their companies. The research took place at a consultancy through the application of a questionnaire. The results demonstrate how every leadership style returns a positive result in terms of employee SR perceptions. However, transformational leadership was the style that obtained the highest overall average. This is in line with how such leaders may influence their members of staff through development of a collective vision, and inspiring others to look beyond their own respective interests in seeking to generate improvements for the organization and the community.

5.1. Introduction

Leaders perform a fundamental role not only in implementing social responsibility (SR) practices but also in the way employees perceive the organization's respective SR. These perceptions, in conjunction with building a positive image of the organization, hold relevance as they generate significant influence over the attitudes and behaviours of workers, which in turn impacts on their personal performance and that of the organization. Companies developing social responsibility policies gain higher levels of involvement from their members

---

Chapter written by Adriana Toledo PEREIRA, Maria João SANTOS and Dimas de Oliveira ESTEVAM. This work was supported by FCT, I.P., the Portuguese national funding agency for science, research and technology, under the Project UID/SOC/04521/2019.

of staff, possess more participative organizational climates and display greater capacities to attract talent, with employees frequently expressing a preference for working at such companies. Therefore, this also emphasizes the importance of discovering new means of improving SR perceptions and better understanding how employees perceive the social activities and performance standards of their organizations.

Despite growing recognition of the importance of leadership in this field, there remains a lack of research analyzing just how styles of leadership influence perceptions held by employees about the SR ongoing in their firms [DU 13]. In order to meet this shortcoming, this research project correspondingly studies the influence of leadership in this domain with the specific purpose of responding to the following question: In what way do styles of leadership influence the perspectives of employees as regards the SR practices of their company? Furthermore, the objectives include characterizing different styles of leadership (transformational, transactional and *laissez-faire*), identifying the range of perceptions on SR and studying what influence styles of leadership hold over perceptions of the prevailing SR practices, in order to identify the variables with the greatest explanatory power.

The relevance of this study also derives from returning a better understanding of the ways in which different leadership styles influence how employees perceive the company's practices in terms of sustainability. Furthermore, companies may be able to develop more assertive and concrete strategies so as to boost levels of involvement of their own staff members in SR development processes.

This chapter is structured into six parts. The first details the purpose of the research and justifies its respective relevance, before advancing with a literature review that sets out the theoretical model and the working hypotheses. The following section sets out the methodology applied and analyzes the results before the final section provides the conclusions, specifying the contribution made by this study, its limitations, alongside recommendations for possible future research.

5.2. Styles of leadership and SR perceptions

5.2.1. *Styles of leadership: transformational, transactional and* laissez-faire

The concept of leadership spans countless analytical dimensions [BOS 13], with the leadership style representing one such aspect. According to [LUS 10], leadership style reflects the combination of characteristics, abilities and behaviours that leaders apply when interacting with their subordinates. In turn, [MUL 00] defines the style of leadership as the way in which individuals undertake the functions of leadership and the way such leaders opt to behave, in relation to their employees.

Over the course of time, various different theories on leadership have emerged even while the Full Range of Leadership Model (FRLM), proposed by [AVO 91], has remained particularly prominent. This breaks down into three dimensions: transformational leadership, transactional leadership and *laissez-faire* leadership. In the transformational style, leaders inspire confidence, are admired, respected and display concern about the needs of their employees to a greater extent than their own needs. Through such means, they win over the acceptance of those they lead and develop in them the capacity to look beyond their own personal interests.

In the case of the transactional style, the leader rewards good performance standards and acts to punish for any non-compliance with the objectives set [FON 12]. The leader and the led establish a relationship that depends exclusively on the exchange of resources and rewards as a means of motivating and enabling the effective implementation of tasks [NAH 15]. This style is ideal for achieving short-term objectives and is conducive to returning swift results, despite not contributing towards those being led achieving success in any sustained fashion [NAH 15].

Finally, the characterization of the *laissez-faire* style features non-leadership or the absence of leadership. Such leaders avoid setting any clear direction and neither do they participate in developing those they lead nor do they encourage their employees [YUL 10]. On the other hand, *laissez-faire* style leaders provide their team members with the freedom to carry out their tasks and to define deadlines. They provide resources and suggestions whenever necessary but do not get involved if not needed. This autonomy may drive high levels of job satisfaction but may also be harmful whenever team members do not manage their time well or lack the knowledge, competences or self-motivation to engage in work efficiently [SOU 17]. This type of leadership may also arise when leaders lack sufficient control over their teams [OLO 13].

5.2.2. *SR perceptions*

This present study undertook analysis focused on perception, on the grounds that the behaviours of persons stem from their perceptions of what reality is and not on the actual reality prevailing. The perceived world is the world that holds importance to the behaviours engaged in [ROB 15]. These perceptions differ from individual to individual, depending on the way such information gets processed by each person [NIS 07]. If we take the particular case of SR as our reference, various studies demonstrate that when members of staff perceive the organization as socially responsible then their attitudes tend to be positively influenced, boosting their levels of involvement and performance [PET 09, TUR 09]. Such judgments shape the attitudes of workers and activate a set of behaviors [VIC 11] that return impacts in terms of performance. The perceptions around SR activities thus emerge as the extent to which employees consider that their companies foster and implement activities related to social wellbeing and environmental protection.

As stated, the perceptions of SR and building up a positive image about the company have significant influence over the performance of employees. There are diverse studies [MAR 01, ORL 01, ORL 03, WU 09, BLA 09, BAK 12] demonstrating the existence of various positive benefits resulting from SR practices. Companies developing socially responsible practices generate higher levels of involvement among their employees [LIN 10], run more participative organizational climates [RUP 06], display greater capacities to attract talent [WAD 02], with workers very often expressing their preference for working for this type of company [SMI 03].

Based on this assumption, [SAR 18] maintain that organizations should act to improve the perceptions held by their employees in terms of their SR practices while [TUR 09], furthermore, refers to the importance of grasping just what the perceptions of members of staff are about the social activities and performances of the organization. This stems from the relevance of SR in influencing their attitudes and behaviours, which impacts upon their personal performance and thus that of the respective organization [GLA 14].

5.2.3. *Relationships between styles of leadership and SR*

The implementation of SR in companies depends, to a large extent, on the actions of their leaders. There are, however, few empirical studies that analyze just how the styles of leadership (transformational, transactional and *laissez-faire*) influence the implementation of these SR policies and practices. In order to meet this shortcoming, some authors [WAL 06, GRO 11, THO 11, LUU 12, NAZ 14, GRO 14, DU 13, ROM 15] have studied the prevailing associations between leadership styles and SR practices and perceptions.

[GRO 11] identify how transformational leadership is the style that most inspires the adoption of SR practices, as this style incorporates an altruistic ethic while transactional leadership more closely interlinks with a utilitarian ethic. Hence, transactional leadership weakens the perceptions of company SR while transformational leadership is able to strengthen such perceptions. This finding aligns with those of the studies by [NAZ 14, GRO 14] that report how worker perceptions of SR are positively influenced by the transformational style of leadership, while the transactional style does not return any significant impact. Transformational leaders may influence their members of staff through developing a collective vision that inspires those being led to look beyond their own immediate interests, and/or the exclusive interests of the leaders, in the drive to obtain improvements both to the organization and the community [GRO 14]. Indeed, the characteristics of transformational leadership closely interlink with the practices of SR [DU 13] as transformational leaders deploy a broader vision of the organization and tend to display higher levels of ethical development [VER 04]. [LUU 12] and [WAL 06] affirm how transformational leaders hold a more strategic understanding, and less of a social perspective, of SR.

[DU 13] also confirms the assumption that transactional leadership weakens the perceptions of SR held by employees. This study concludes that transactional leadership does not relate to SR as this stems from utilitarian values and norms of reciprocity, unlikely to generate strong commitment towards SR from the employee perspective. Transactional leaders primarily strive to generate efficient and profitable results, deploying power, rewards and sanctions to shape the behaviours of employees. However, the research findings of [LUU 12] report how transactional leadership does correlate with legal and economic SR. Hence, transactional leaders tend to back SR practices whenever they are able to contribute towards raising the quality and security of the product and when they provide direct benefits to the organization.

In contrast with the transformational and transactional styles of leadership, leaders adopting the *laissez-faire* style wield little control over their subordinates and allow them the liberty to engage in their designated tasks without any direct supervision [WU 09]. The studies by [ROM 15, THO 11] analyzed the *laissez-faire* style and CSR before concluding that there was no such relationship.

5.2.4. *Research model and hypotheses*

Despite the sheer extent of the academic literature on both leadership and SR, there are only a handful of studies interrelating the styles of leadership with the SR activities of the organization [STR 11, DU 13]. According to [STR 11], this scarcity of research may stem, partially, from two challenges. On the one hand, this reflects how they are two particularly broad and multifaceted fields and, on the other hand, this arises due to the lack of defined, clear and consensual definitions of leadership and SR. The present study strives to understand whether the styles of leadership influence worker perceptions of the SR practices that the company develops. Studies published on the theme report that the style of leadership (transformational, transactional and *laissez-faire*) does influence SR practices, as well as the perceptions held by members of staff. Within the scope of responding to the research questions, the conceptual framework that structured the research carried out (Figure 5.1) classifies the perception of SR as a dependent variable, with the transformational, transactional and *laissez-faire* styles of leadership as the independent variables.

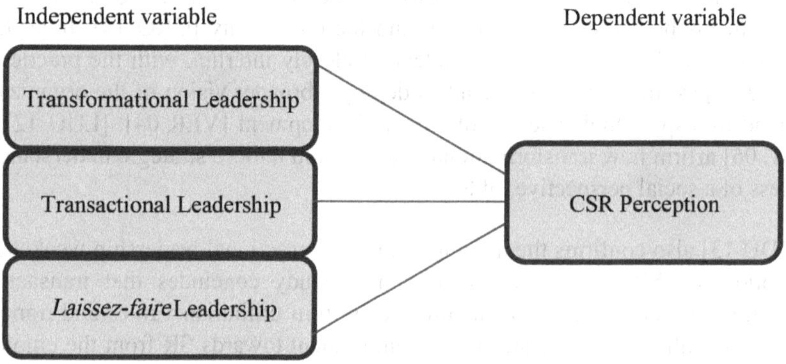

Figure 5.1. *Model of research*

This aims to report on the impact of the styles of leadership (transformational, transactional and *laissez-faire*) on the perceptions employees hold about the SR practices that their companies engage in, for a series of reasons. Firstly, based upon the existing literature [WAL 06, LUU 12, DU 13, NAZ 14, GRO 14], we expect transformational leadership to positively shape perceptions on company SR practices. Secondly, there is the further expectation that transactional leadership reports a negative relationship with the prevailing SR perceptions. Some studies (for example, [NAZ 14, DU 13]) conclude that transactional leadership weakens the SR perceptions of members of staff. This assumption is also supported by the findings of the [DU 13] study, affirming that there is no relationship between transactional leadership and SR with this style incorporating utilitarian values and norms of reciprocity that hinder the generation of strong employee belief in the respective company's SR. Thirdly, there is also the expectation for the *laissez-faire* leadership style to return a negative relationship with SR perceptions. The authors [ROM 15, THO 11] analyze the *laissez-faire* style and SR before concluding in favour of a negative association. Based on the aforementioned statements, we arrive at the following research hypotheses:

H1: transformational leadership positively relates to the SR perceptions prevailing in companies;

H2: transactional leadership negatively relates to the SR perceptions prevailing in companies;

H3: *laissez-faire* leadership negatively relates to the SR perceptions prevailing in companies.

5.3. Method

This study opted to take a quantitative approach, essentially of the correlational or explanatory type. This derives primarily because the core objective of this research is to analyze the relationship existing between leadership styles (transformational, transactional, *laissez-faire*) and the perceptions of employees about the SR of their companies. In order to achieve the objectives and research hypotheses, we used a questionnaire as our means of data collection. In turn, this questionnaire was divided up into three sections. The first section applied the SR scale put forward by [BAL 11] with its 16 classification items. This choice derived from this questionnaire having already been applied to a Portuguese sample and having returned satisfactory results, in terms of its internal consistency. The second section spans 45 affirmations designed to measure the prevailing perceptions of the styles of leadership. In this case, we made recourse to the Multifactor Leadership Questionnaire, designed by [AVO 04], which characterizes the transformational, transactional and *laissez-faire* styles of leadership by evaluating the behaviours of leaders in accordance with the perceptions of those they lead. According to its authors, [AVO 04], this questionnaire returns advantages due to its applicability across every organizational sector. Furthermore, the core model easily portrays the interrelationship between the styles of leadership and the expected results. The final section ensured the characterization of the sample both at the individual level, taking into consideration gender, nationality and academic qualifications and, at the organizational level, detailing the profession and length of service in the company.

The questionnaire was subject to pre-testing in order to verify both the relevance of its questions [FOR 00] and whether the items were easy to understand. The questionnaire was conducted at a Portuguese management software solutions firm. Unable to survey the entire population, we opted to use a stratified sample and correspondingly sent out 250 online questionnaires. Of these, we received and validated 54 completed responses that made up the final sample. Finally, we processed the data obtained through the Qualtric platform, followed by analysis using SPSS (Statistical Package for the Social Sciences).

Based on the data collected between June 11–29, 2018, we can report that of the 54 respondents, 59% are male and 41% female. In relation to their ages, we note that 46% of these employees are aged between 31 and 40, with 37% aged either 30 or younger. As regards their academic level of education, the vast majority have obtained higher education qualifications (81%), with 19% holding secondary school diplomas. In terms of their professional categories, almost a majority of respondents are senior technical staff (48%), followed by 26% classified as other, 9% are assistants, 7% are managers, 6% operational technicians and 4% directors. Finally, in terms of their respective length of service, 44% of respondents report between 5 and 10 years with the organization, 24% have been there for one year or less, with 7% having spent between 10 and 15 years at the company.

5.4. Results

5.4.1. *Analysis of scale reliability*

Analysis of the reliability involves measuring the internal consistency of the scales applied, with this measurement usually made according to Cronbach's Alpha, generally accepted as the most appropriate for studies deploying scale metrics [MAR 06].

Variables	**Cronbach's Alpha**
Styles of leadership	0.968
Transformational style of leadership	0.972
Transactional style of leadership	0.912
Laissez-faire style of leadership	0.807
Perceptions of SR	0.966

Table 5.1. *Internal consistency test*

In accordance with Table 5.1, the leadership style variable returns a total Cronbach's α value of 0.968, with perceptions of SR providing a Cronbach's α value of 0.966. In brief, all of the dimensions to styles of leadership and perceptions of SR report α values in excess of 0.80. Hence, we may state that the instrument obtains an appropriate level of reliability given that this requires an α result of over at least 0.70 [MAR 06].

5.4.2. *Mean and standard sample deviation*

After verifying the reliability of the internal consistency of each scale, we calculated the mean and the standard deviation for each scale according to the total sample.

	N	Media	Stand. Dev.
Transformational leadership	54	3.202	0.254
Transactional leadership	54	3.116	0.341
Laissez-faire leadership	54	3.249	0.454
Perceptions of SR	54	4.058	0.280

Table 5.2. *Mean and standard deviation*

According to the results above, we find that the respondents identify the presence of the three styles of leadership in fairly similar ways. As regards the SR perceptions, we may state that the respondents hold high levels of perception towards the SR of the organization for which they work. The data also demonstrates a balance between the styles of leadership and the SR perceptions even while the perception of SR returns an average value of 4.058, higher than that for the styles of leadership.

5.4.3. *Analysis of variable correlations*

In order to analyze any correlation existing among the variables, we opted to calculate the Pearson correlation coefficient. Following [MAR 11], in any correlation analysis, there is no relationship between the variables when their correlation coefficient is equal to zero ($R = 0$). The variables also vary in the same direction whenever $R>0$ and, on the contrary, head in the opposite direction whenever $R<0$. Correlations are deemed weak whenever $R<0.25$, moderate at $25 \leq R<50$, strong over the level of $50 \leq R<75$ and very strong at $R \geq 75$ or higher.

	Transformational	**Transactional**	***Laissez-faire***	**CSR Perc.**
Transformational leadership	1			
Transactional leadership	0.957*	1		
Laissez-faire leadership	0.891*	0.844*	1	
CSR perceptions	0.720*	0.699*	0.680*	1

*The correlation obtains significance at the level of 0.01 (two decimal places)

Table 5.3. *Correlation analysis*

This correlation matrix reports the existence of positive and significant correlations between the variables of transformational leadership, transactional leadership, *laissez-faire* and perceptions of SR. This conveys how every style of leadership presents a significantly positive correlation with the categories thus varying in accordance with the perceptions of SR.

5.4.4. *Multiple regression analysis*

In order to more fully understand the impacts that the different styles of leadership have on the perceptions of company SR, we made recourse to the multiple linear regression methodology, "estimated" according to the stepwise method. Table 5.4 presents the results of the models adjusted for the prevailing perceptions of SR. The SR perception dimension therefore serves as a dependent variable in the linear model. Each model thereby, in a first phase, applied the SR perception variable before advancing to the styles of leadership (transformational, transactional and *laissez-faire*), as independent variables, in a second phase.

Summary of model[b]					
Model	**R**	**R2**	**R2 adjusted**	**Standard estimate error**	**Durbin-Watson**
1	0.726[a]	0.528	0.499	0.43144	2.489
a. Predictors: (Constant), Transformational leadership, Transactional leadership and *Laissez-faire* leadership					
b. Dependent Variable: SR Perceptions					

Table 5.4. *Analysis of the regression model*

ANOVA[a]						
Model		**Sum of Squares**	**Df**	**Mean Square**	**F**	**Sig.**
1	Regression	10.395	3	3.465	18.614	0.000[b]
	Residual	9.307	50	0.186		
	Total	19.702	53			
a. Dependent Variable: SR Perceptions						
b. Predictors: (Constant), Transformational leadership, Transactional leadership and *Laissez-faire* leadership						

Table 5.5. *ANOVA regression analysis*

The tables above set out the results of the regression analysis and the ANOVA regression models. The R2 = 0.528 reflects how the styles of leadership account for 52.8% of the variation in SR perceptions. The complete model contains all of the predictors that obtain statistical significance at 5% as the p value of 0.000b is less than the 0.05 level of significance. According to [FIL 09], Durbin-Watson results of either below 1 or over 3 represent paths for consideration. Hence, the Durbin-Watson value of 2.489 indicates how there is no self-correlation in the model. The F value stands at 18.614 against a level of significance corresponding to 0.000. As the level of F statistical significance stands at below 0.050, the independent variables (transformational, transactional and *laissez-faire*) achieve a good performance in explaining variations in SR perceptions.

Coefficient[a]						
Model		**Non-standardized coefficients**		**Standardized coefficients**		
		B	**Std. Error**	**Beta**	**t**	**Sig.**
1	(Constant)	2.005	0.284		7.054	0.000
	Transformational leadership	0.359	0.339	0.419	1.060	0.294
	Transactional leadership	0.122	0.295	0.138	0.413	0.681
	Laissez-faire leadership	0.161	0.182	0.190	0.886	0.380
a. Dependent Variable: SR Perceptions						

Table 5.6. *Coefficients*

The coefficient results detailed in Table 5.6 report that the transformational style of leadership attains a beta result of 0.419, while *laissez-faire* leadership comes in with a beta reading of 0.190, and the transactional style of leadership on 0.138, with each obtaining statistical significance and strong indicators of the SR perceptions in the organization under study. The t values are also all positive which reflects how styles of leadership confidently predict the variation (positive) in SR perceptions. This correspondingly concludes that all the styles of leadership, with a particular emphasis on the transformational style, facilitate SR perceptions.

5.5. Discussion of the results

This study set out to understand how styles of leadership influence employee perceptions regarding the SR engaged in by their company. This correspondingly reports the positive and significant correlations existing between the dimensions of transformational, transactional and *laissez-faire* leadership and the perceptions of SR. Approaching each hypothesis in turn, we may therefore conclude:

Hypothesis 1: transformational leadership positively relates to SR perceptions.

This hypothesis received confirmation through analysis by the Pearson correlation, reporting a positive correlation (R = 0.891) between the transformational style and SR perceptions. These results align with the existing literature [WAL 06, LUU 12, DU 13, NAZ 14, GRO 14]. The characteristics of the transformational leadership style closely intertwine with SR practices [DU 13] as transformational leaders hold broader visions of the organization and tend to exhibit higher levels of ethical development [VER 04]. To this end, they perform important roles in facilitating engagement in SR practices. Hence, the results affirm how the transformational style of leadership helps foster high levels of SR perception.

Hypothesis 2: transactional leadership negatively relates to SR perceptions.

This hypothesis was not subject to confirmation. There was no negative relationship reported between transactional leadership and prevailing SR perceptions. The Pearson correlations confirm a positive correlation (R = 0.699) between these factors. These results thus run counter to the findings of [NAZ 14] which conclude in favor of transactional leadership weakening the perceptions of SR prevailing among employees. This assumption is also fundamental to the study by [DU 13] that affirms how transactional leadership does not interrelate with SR; and, that the transactional leadership process is based on utilitarian values and norms of reciprocity that are unlikely to generate strong beliefs in SR among members of staff.

Hypothesis 3: *laissez-faire* leadership negatively relates to SR perceptions.

This hypothesis also went unconfirmed as, according to the Pearson correlations, there is a positive link between *laissez-faire* leadership and the existing SR perceptions (R = 0.680). These results thus run counter to the research by [ROM 15] who studied the impact of the *laissez-faire* leadership style on SR perceptions and reported a negative relationship between these factors. Similarly, [THO 11] also advanced study findings attributing the *laissez-faire* style with a negative influence on SR perceptions. According to [ALM 18], this leadership style is the least efficient style of leadership, perceived more as a posture of abandoning leadership with a differing perspective resulting from these research findings.

We deployed multiple regression to obtain a model that might enable predictions of SR perceptions in accordance with the respective style of leadership (transformational, transactional and *laissez-faire*). Analysis of the regression coefficients reports that every style of leadership, with particular emphasis on the transformational style, facilitates the emergence of SR perceptions. These findings identify transformational leadership as the most effective, productive and satisfactory style for members of staff, to the extent that both parties strive for the good of the organization within the scope of shared visions and values, backed up by reciprocal trust and respect [LO 10].

Hence, we conclude that the transformational, transactional and *laissez-faire* styles of leadership generate positive impacts in terms of SR perceptions. However, in the specific case of SR, the transformational style emerges as the most productive. Therefore, business leaders should strive to adopt a transformational style of leadership and involve their team members in decision-making processes, for example, given that this confirms how this leadership style best enhances the SR perceptions of their employees.

This research seeks to report and emphasize how the styles of leadership bear an influence on the building up of employee perceptions on the SR practices of their companies. The study carried out demonstrates how leadership represents a determinant factor at this level, generating very significant impacts on SR perceptions. Within this framework, there is a need to deepen their potential, especially through further research into the relationships prevailing between styles of leadership, the perceptions of SR and the corresponding affective implications.

5.6. Conclusion

Throughout recent years there have been increasing pressures on companies to integrate SR in every area of their business within the framework of the Triple Bottom Line, which takes into account not only the financial wellbeing of the company but also positive impacts on the surrounding environment and society as a whole [ELK 04]. Building and maintaining strong and sustainable relationships with the different stakeholders is highly important to companies remaining competitive. However, SR is not only a significant factor for boosting company reputations [GRI 09] among consumers, as suggested and studied by [MOH 05, OPP 06]. This also enables the attraction and retention of better qualified human resources. Studies have reported how employees serve as active agents for SR, in line with how achieving the objectives defined in this area depends, in large part, on their commitment and collaboration [COL 07]. This furthermore conveys how they hold central importance to the implementation of any SR strategy. However, it remains no less true that the success of any strategic SR implementation also depends on the stimuli provided by the leadership and the actual perceptions held by members of staff towards the SR initiatives and practices engaged in by their companies. Within this framework, achieving high standards of performance in terms of SR greatly depends on the actions and involvement of company leadership. The profile of these leaders and their leadership styles may influence not only employee perceptions about these practices, and consequently their greater or lesser involvement in the implementation of the respective SR strategy, but also their attitudes towards their work, including their affective commitments and levels of performance.

In order to offset the scarcity of studies within this area, here we approach the association between the styles of leadership (transformational, transactional and *laissez-faire*) and the perceptions towards the SR practices ongoing in the company. The findings, as regards hypothesis 1, report a positive interlink between the transformational style of leadership and the prevailing SR perceptions. This is furthermore highlighted by the Pearson correlation result that obtains strong significance (R = 0.720). This result is in line with the existing literature, given that according to the findings of studies by [NAZ 14, GRO 14, GRO 11, DU 11, WAL 06], transformational leadership generates positive connections with SR perceptions.

As regards hypothesis 2, this was not subject to confirmation as the transactional style of leadership turned out to return a positive impact on employee perceptions towards SR, reflected in a strong correlation result of R = 0.699. Despite the conclusions of [NAZ 14, DU 13] pointing to transactional leadership weakening the perceptions of social responsibility among members of staff, research results from [LUU 12] reported the opposite, with transactional leadership correlating with legal and economic SR, thus conveying how transactional leaders tend to support SR practices whenever such are capable of raising product quality and/or security, as well as whenever these practices emphasize the key parties interested in the organization.

As regards hypothesis 3, this also failed to be confirmed. Through analysis of the Pearson correlations, we verified the existence of a positive correlation between *laissez-faire* leadership and SR perceptions (R = 0.680). This relationship also runs counter to other findings in the literature, such as the conclusions of [ROM 15, THO 11]. However, we would emphasize that leaders who adopt this style do not give up on assuming responsibility for their actions but rather attribute greater scope for manoeuvre to those under their management [GUI 91]. This style of leadership may facilitate employees gaining freedom in decision-making over the implementation of SR practices.

Leadership styles hold important relevance to the management of businesses and companies. There are added gains returned by managers and leaders adopting appropriate styles of leadership reflecting the respective situation and the values and attributes of those they manage, in order to ensure their respective motivation and commitment to the organization's goals so as to obtain better levels of performance [ZAR 15]. Ethical questions and community involvement deserve greater association with business success over the long term. Taking into account the rising interest in sustainable societies, there is a corresponding need for styles of leadership capable of nurturing the ideas and principles around SR.

This research project faced certain limitations that may have held implications for the results returned. The first limitation stems from the fact that the research focuses upon professionals from a consultancy firm located in Lisbon and, as such, hinders any generalization of results, which are correspondingly restricted to the universe studied. This is in combination with the lack of time available for the collection of data, which influenced the size of the sample, it being smaller than would otherwise be desired. In turn, the fact of having measured perceptions through recourse to a questionnaire with closed questions did not enable the collection of further knowledge about the motivations underlying those perceptions. Furthermore, the application of the Likert scale in the questionnaire may have influenced respondent answers to the extent that there is the tendency to select the central option in the scale. Finally, it is important to highlight that the questionnaires have a previously established scale and thus, without any further feedback from respondents – in a situation compounded by the potential for different interpretations of the respective questions – this further raises subjectivity, as well as the eventual occurrence of the halo effect, with the potential of introducing bias into the results.

Within the scope of achieving better results, both in organizations and in society in general, there is a fundamental need to analyze and deepen our awareness about the role that leaders assume as potential drivers or obstacles in achieving success in the relationship between SR and the affective implications. This correspondingly recommends future studies that attempt to broaden the scale of the sample, as well as extend the study into other sectors of activity, so as to enable the potential for the comparison of results among organizations with different structural characteristics and confirm the scope for establishing relationships between styles of leadership and perceptions of SR. Another suggestion involves undertaking a qualitative study on SR perceptions as a complement to a quantitative study, as this would generate deeper knowledge about the motivating factors that underpin these perceptions. Finally, we would also propose the study of different variables including, for example, gender and the number of years spent relating directly with the management. Despite the existing limitations, we consider that we obtained the objectives set and that this current research project contributes to the better understanding of the theme under study.

5.7. References

[ALM 18] AL-MALKI M., WANG J., "Leadership styles and job performance: A literature review", *Journal of International Business Research and Marketing*, vol. 3, no. 3, pp. 40–49, 2018.

[AVO 91] AVOLIO B., BASS B., *The Full Range of Leadership Development: Basic and Advanced Manuals*, Bass, Avolio & Associates, New York, 1991.

[AVO 04] AVOLIO B., BASS B., *Multifactor Leadership Questionnaire, Manual and Sampler Set.*, 3rd edition, Mind Garden, Redwood City, 2004.

[BAK 12] BAKER H., NOFSINGER J., *Socially Responsible Finance and Investing – Financial Institutions, Corporations, Investors, and Activists*, John Wiley & Sons, Hoboken, 2012.

[BAL 11] BALTAZAR P., Corporate social responsibility from an employee's perspective: Contributes for understanding job attitudes, Doctoral dissertation, ISCTE, Lisbon, 2011.

[COL 07] COLLIER J., ESTENBANN R., "Corporate social responsibility and employee commitment", *Business Ethics: A European Review*, vol. 16, no. 1, pp. 19–33, 2007.

[DU 13] DU S., SWAEN V., LINDGREEN A. *et al.*, "The roles of leadership styles in corporate social responsibility", *Journal of Business Ethics*, vol. 114, no. 1, pp. 155–169, 2013.

[ELK 04] ELKINGTON J., "Enter the triple bottom line", in HENRIQUES A., RICHARDSON J., (eds), *The Triple Bottom Line: Does It All Add Up?*, Routledge, London, 2004.

[FIE 09] FIELD P., *Discovering Statistics Using SPSS*, SAGE Publications, Thousand Oaks, 2009.

[FON 12] FONSECA A., PORTO J., BARROSO A., "O efeito de valores pessoais nas atitudes perante estilos de liderança", *Revista de Administração Mackenzie*, vol. 13, no. 3, pp. 122–149, 2012.

[FOR 00] FORTIN M., *O Processo de Investigação, da concepção à realização*, Lusociência, Loures, 2000.

[GHI 91] GHILARDI F., SPALLAROSSA C., *Guia para a organização da Escola, Edições Asa*, Rio Tinto, 1991.

[GLA 14] GLAVAS A., KELLEY K., "The effects of perceived corporate social responsibility on employee attitudes", *Business Ethics Quarterly*, vol. 24, no. 2, pp. 165–202, 2014.

[GRI 09] GRIGORE G., "Corporate social responsibility and reputation", *Metalurgia International*, vol. 14, no. 11, pp. 95–98, 2009.

[GRO 11] GROVES K., LAROCCA M.A., "An empirical study of leader ethical values, transformational and transactional leadership, and follower attitudes toward corporate social responsibility", *Journal of Business Ethics*, vol. 103, no. 4, pp. 511–528, 2011.

[GRO 14] GROVES K., "Examining leader–follower congruence of social responsibility values in transformational leadership", *Journal of Leadership and Organizational Studies*, vol. 21, no. 3, pp. 227–243, 2014.

[LEK 11] LEKO M., STIMAC H., "Internal CSR – The perceptions and attitudes of Croatian employees" *10th International Congress of the International Association on Public and Nonprofit Marketing*, Oporto, Portugal, available at: https://www.researchgate.net/publication/321875923, 2011.

[LIN 10] LIN C., "Modeling corporate citizenship, organizational trust, and work engagement based on attachment theory", *Journal of Business Ethics*, vol. 94, pp. 517–531, 2010.

[LO 10] LO M., RAMAYAH T., MIN H. *et al.*, "The relationship between leadership styles and organizational commitment in Malaysia: Role of leader–member exchange", *Asia Pacific Business Review*, vol. 16, no. 1, pp. 79–103, 2010.

[LUS 10] LUSSIER R., ACHUA C., *Leadership: Theory, Application, & Skill Development*, 4th edition, South-Western Cengage Learning, Mason, 2010.

[LUU 12] LUU T., "Corporate social responsibility, leadership, and brand equity in healthcare service", *Social Responsibility Journal*, vol. 8, pp. 347–362, 2012.

[MAR 01] MARGOLIS J.D., WALSH J.P., *People and Profits? – The Search for a Link Between a Company's Social and Financial Performance*, Lawrence Erlbaum Associates, Mahwah, New Jersey, 2001.

[MAR 06] MAROCO J., GARCIA-MARQUES T., "Qual a fiabilidade do Alfa de Cronbach? Questões Antigas ou Soluções Modernas?", *Laboratório de Psicologia*, vol. 4, no. 1, pp. 65–90, 2006.

[MAR 11] MAROCO J., *Análise Estatística com o SPSS Statistics*, 5th edition, ReportNumber, Pêro Pinheiro, 2011.

[MOH 05] MOHR L., WEBB D., "The effects of corporate social responsibility and price on consumer responses", *The Journal of Consumer Affairs*, vol. 39, no. 1, pp. 121–147, 2005.

[MU 00] MULLINS L., *Management and Organisational Behaviour*, Pitman Publishers, London, 2000.

[NAH 15] NAHAVANDI A., *The Art and Science of Leadership*, Global Edition, Pearson, New Jersey, 2015.

[NAZ 14] NAZIR A., ARSHAD M., SHAKAIB M. *et al.*, "How does managers' leadership styles influence institutional CSR activities? Employees perspective", *Journal of Basic and Applied Scientific Research*, vol. 4, no. 5, pp. 175–180, 2014.

[NIS 07] NISHII L., WRIGHT P., Variability within organizations: Implications for strategic human resource management. Centre for Advanced Human Resource Studies, available at: https://digitalcommons.ilr.cornell.edu/cgi/viewcontent.cgi?article=1468&context=cahrswp, accessed on May 10, 2018, pp. 1–33, 2007.

[OLO 13] OLOLUBE N., DUDAFA U., URIAH O. *et al.*, "Education for development: Impediments to the globalization of higher education in Nigeria", *International Journal of Educational Foundations and Management*, vol. 1, no. 2, pp. 109–130, 2013.

[OPP 06] OPPEWAL H., ALEXANDER A., SULLIVAN P., "Consumer perceptions of corporate social responsibility in town shopping centers and their influence on shopping evaluations", *Journal of Retailing and Consumer Services*, vol. 13, pp. 261–274, 2006.

[PET 04] PETERSON D., "Perceived leader integrity and ethical intentions of subordinate", *Leadership and Organization Development Journal*, vol. 25, no.1, pp. 7–23, 2004.

[ROB 15] ROBBINS S., JUDGE T., *Organizational Behavior*, Pearson Education Limited, United Kingdom, 2015.

[ROM 15] ROMÃO F., Responsabilidade Social das Organizações e Envolvimento no Trabalho: Poderá o Líder e a Satisfação no Trabalho Potenciar esta Relação? Master's degree dissertation, ISCTE, Lisbon, 2015.

[RUP 06] RUPP D., GANAPATHI J., AGUILERA R. *et al.*, "Employee reactions to corporate social responsibility: An organizational justice framework", *Journal of Organizational Behaviour*, vol. 27, pp. 537–543, 2006.

[SAR 18] SARFRAZ M., WANG Q., ABDULLAH M., "Employees perception of Corporate Social Responsibility impact on employee outcomes: Mediating role of organizational justice for small and medium enterprises (SMEs)", *Sustainability*, vol. 10, pp. 1–19, 2018.

[SMI 03] SMITH N., "Corporate Social Responsibility: Whether or how?", *California Management Review*, vol. 45, no.4, pp. 52–76, 2003.

[SOU 17] SOUGUI A., BON A., MAHAMAT M. *et al.*, "The impact of leadership on employee motivation in Malaysian telecommunication sector", *Galore International Journal of Applied Sciences and Humanities*, vol. 1, no. 1, pp. 59–68, 2017.

[STR 11] STRAND R., "Exploring the role of leadership in corporate social responsibility: A review", *Journal of Leadership, Accountability, and Ethics*, vol. 8, no. 4, pp. 84–96, 2011.

[THO 11] THOMAS S., Impact of leadership on the practice of Corporate Social Responsibility, a study in the private sector: United Arab Emirates, Dubai, Master's dissertation, British University, 2011.

[TUR 09] TURKER D., "How corporate social responsibility influences organizational commitment", *Journal of Business Ethics*, vol. 89, no. 2, pp. 189–204, 2009.

[VER 04] VERA D., CROSSAN M., "Strategic leadership and organizational learning", *Academy of Management Review*, vol. 29, pp. 222–240, 2004.

[VIC 11] VICENTE A., REBELO T., INVERNO G., "Moderadores do impacto de perceções de responsabilidade social das empresas no comprometimento organizacional", *Revista Psicologia: Organizações e Trabalho*, vol. 11, no. 2, pp. 65–83, 2011.

[WAD 02] WADDOK S., BODWELL C., GRAVES S., "Responsibility: The new Business Imperative", *Academy of Management Executive*, vol. 16, pp. 132–148, 2002.

[WAL 06] WALDMAN D., SIEGEL D., JAVIDAN M., "Components of CEO transformational leadership and corporate social responsibility", *Journal of Management Studies*, vol. 43, pp. 1703–1725, 2006.

[WU 09] WU F., SHIU C., "The relationship between leadership styles and foreign English teachers job satisfaction in adult English Cram Schools: Evidences in Taiwan", *The Journal of American Academy of Business*, Cambridge, vol. 14, no. 2, pp. 75–82, 2009.

[YUL 10] YULK G., *Leadership in Organizations*, 7th edition, Prentice Hall, New Jersey, Upper Saddle River, 2010.

[ZAR 15] ZAREEN M., RAZZAQ K., MUJTABA G., "Impact of transactional, transformational and *laissez-faire* leadership styles on motivation: A quantitative study of banking employees in Pakistan", *Public Organization Review*, vol. 15, no. 4, pp. 531–549, 2015.

6

Corporate Social Responsibility Reporting: Background, Evolution and Sustainability Promoter

Corporate social responsibility has come a long way from the first forms of unregulated, voluntary social actions of businesses to the now standardized, regulated mandatory and voluntary activity within the CSR field. As the concept became more and more complex, the need for CSR reporting became evident and standards for CSR reporting emerged. The Global Reporting Initiative (GRI) materialized as the main standard for CSR reporting. This chapter is composed of a short historical evolution of the CSR concept and associated reporting opportunities, a quantitative analysis of policy regarding CSR around the world, and a quantitative analysis of the reporting activity within five industrial sectors: energy, chemicals, metal products, mining, and automotive.

6.1. Introduction

The problem of CSR has been studied by many researchers over the last few decades. The concept has had many transformations over time and, as the world became more connected and access to information became easier, the increasing popularity of CSR forced companies to approach it more proactively, placing more and more importance on stakeholder opinion, to the detriment of shareholders.

The new paradigm of CSR activity has recently shifted from large companies, the most visible in the eyes of stakeholders, to medium and small companies, as digitalization now offers quick access to information on every aspect of a company's activity.

Chapter written by Marian Cătălin VOICA and Adrian STANCU.

Within this environment CSR became very important, not only for large companies, but also for medium and small ones, as shareholders could decide to distance themselves from companies not demonstrating good social conduct or, who appear to be socially irresponsible.

Once shareholder interest in CSR activity began to increase, companies understood its importance and the need for unified reporting standards became necessary. This necessity led to the creation of Global Reporting Initiative (GRI) standards and ISO 26000, with the role of uniformization in CSR reporting.

This chapter presents a short review of the main advances in the CSR domain and its most prestigious contributors; a short presentation of CSR standardization options and policy measures; a quantitative analyses of reporting policies around the world; and an in-depth quantitative analysis of reporting to GRI by region and by business size between 2007 and 2017 for five industrial sectors, namely energy, chemicals, metal products, mining, and automotive.

6.2. A brief history of CSR development and conceptualization

The concept of CSR has many dimensions and must be explored piece by piece, with an examination of each of the words the term comprises. According to Carroll and Brown [CAR 18] those words have the following meanings:

Corporate – corporate forms of business organizations which evolved to include all businesses: large, medium or small. The focus of today's society is on large organizations due to their visibility, but small enterprises are inside the CSR domain too.

Social – human society or the life and welfare of a community. The applicability of this notion may imply a community, a state, a nation or the world. Many times, society is considered to be a collection of stakeholders possibly influenced by a company action. We must acknowledge that today's society includes other life forms and the natural environment.

Responsibility – accountability of a business for what is subject to its power, control, or management. It involves an obligation and the possibility of being held accountable by society.

6.2.1. *Timeline of CSR development*

Over time CSR "*benefited*" from various definitions. For many, Howard Bowen is considered to be the "father of CSR", with his extraordinary book *The Social*

Responsibilities of the Businessman [BOW 53]. According to Bowen, CSR can be defined as: "the obligations of businessmen to pursue those policies, to make those decisions, or to follow those lines of action which are desirable in terms of the objectives and values of our society" [BOW 53].

Ackerman and Bauer stated that social responsibility has too much to do with motivation, rather than performance, and argued that social responsiveness is more adequate [ACK 76]. Based on this idea was the development of CSR1, as the general understanding of CSR, and CSR2, which was categorized as corporate social "responsiveness", focusing on the literal act of responding [FRE 78].

After these first advances in the field of CSR, the domain broadened further with the addition of new concepts to the basics of CSR. Starting from the performance of CSR, Carroll proposed a corporate social performance (CSP) model, composed of three dimensions [CAR 79]:

– a basic definition of CSR;

– a statement for the firm's philosophy;

– indication of social issues arenas (consumers, environment, discrimination, etc.).

This model has been further extended by Wartick and Cochran [WAR 58] who proposed that the three dimensions should be viewed as principles, processes and policies. Subsequently reformulated by Wood, who rethought the whole construction and proposed that CSP is a business organization's configuration of principles of social responsibility, processes of social responsiveness and policies, programs and other observable outcomes, as they related to the firm's societal relationships [WOO 91].

6.2.2. *Opponents and supporters of CSR*

From the start, businesses and the academic community have been divided between supporters and opponents. In the same decade as Bowen we find, as an opponent, Theodore Levitt, whose article, "The dangers of social responsibility" [LEV 58], promoted the idea that a business's goal is long-run profit maximization and that government should provide general welfare.

Milton Friedman, the renowned economist, was the toughest opponent of CSR arguing that businesses must not be concerned with social matters which should be handled by the free market. Friedman argued that management must engage in one goal: the maximization of profits for its owners or shareholders. Even though Friedman was strongly opposed, he acknowledged that a business must comply with laws and ethics, often found in CSR definitions [FRI 70].

Another aspect that attracted attention was the fact that businesses should be armed to tackle social activities. This comes from the fact that management is primarily educated in financial matters and do not have the social skills to engage in CSR [DAV 73]. Another opponent stated that CRS weakens the scope of businesses by steering them away from their aim, taking the company into uncharted waters, far beyond its defined scope [HAY 69]. Another argument is that the business already has enough power so why risk company capital to gain more, along the lines of social power [DAV 73]? Finally, engagement in CSR activities will make the business less competitive [CAR 10].

The main argument for CSR is that it is in a business's own interest to be socially responsible, in order to maintain a favorable business position in the long term. Some argued that government intervention could be reduced until standardized business policies fulfil society's expectations [CAR 10]. Davis identifies two more aspects: businesses have the resources (management, functional expertise and capital) and should be allowed to try because many have tried and failed to solve social problems [DAV 73]. Another view is that being proactive is better than being reactive, so anticipating, planning and initiating is less costly than simply reacting to social problems as they appear [CAR 09].

Another view is that the public strongly supports the CSR concept so businesses have no other option but to engage with it. Nowadays, the public steers businesses away from their inherent scope of profit maximization to a broader specter of obligations to society and stakeholders, even if making things better for them requires sacrificing some profit [BER 00].

The debate between supporters and opponents of CSR has been around since early writing on the concept. Each side presents the truth about CSR, as the concept is considered to sway between the two views. Here it can be argued that CSR is a tool for creating a better image for the business, therefore positioning it in the realm of public relations. Another could say that a business simply wants to give back to society, therefore placing it within the philanthropic arena. No matter what driver leads a company to engage in CSR, the result is a win-win for both business and society.

6.2.3. *Carroll's pyramid of corporate social responsibility*

After extensive research and debate in the field of CSR, Carroll presented a graphical view on the domain as the "pyramid of corporate social responsibility" [CAR 91] presented in Figure 6.1. As can be seen, Carroll depicted CSR as a pyramid with four categories. This form has been adopted by many researchers [WAR 85, WOO 91, SWA 95, 99, BUR 99, CLA 95, IBR 93, 95, MAL 93, ONE 89,

PIN 96, SMI 01, CIU 05, MAT 13a, PAN 15, ENE 17, AND 18, EHS 18, BRE 18, ZAM 20] therefore confirming the relevance of the framework and the four areas as the main paradigm of the CSR concept.

Carroll provided a hierarchy of corporate responsibilities composed of the economic, legal, ethical and philanthropic aspects of a business. At the base of the pyramid are economic responsibilities, the main reason for business existence being the creation of a sufficient amount of profit in order to satisfy the needs of the shareholders, to create jobs for employees and deliver goods and services to customers. Legal responsibilities are the obligation to comply with business rules and regulations to protect society from corporations' misdeeds and moral misjudgments. Ethical responsibility is the first stage of the pyramid that is not required, but it is expected. In general, businesses should care about their stakeholders and be proactive in identifying and excluding from their portfolio the activities and actions that might be detrimental to society.

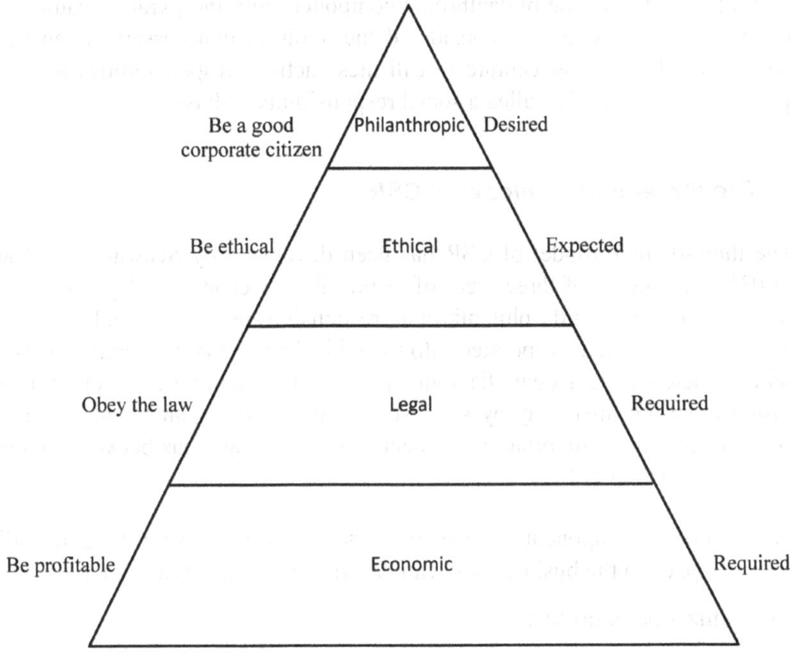

Figure 6.1. *Pyramid of corporate social responsibility (source: [CAR 91])*

Philanthropic responsibilities are one of the first forms of CSR and they take the form of donations and activities directed at improving conditions for employees and the local or global community.

Carroll's pyramid model has a few issues [SCH 03]:

– the use of a pyramid to depict the relationships between the four components of the model;

– the role of philanthropy as a separate component;

– the incomplete theoretical development of the economic, legal and ethical domains.

The pyramid framework may be confusing and inappropriate in some cases. It induces the idea of hierarchy among the CSR components and the conclusion that philanthropic activities – from the top of the pyramid – are the most important, and that the economic responsibilities – from the base – are less important. This could lead to a misunderstanding of the relationship between the CSR domains. The pyramid cannot grasp the interweaving nature of CSR components.

The introduction of the philanthropic component into the pyramid caused some confusion and some scientists considered the addition unnecessary. Even Carroll acknowledged that it is inaccurate to call these actions responsibilities [CAR 79]. So, philanthropy cannot be called a social responsibility of businesses.

6.2.4. *The three-domain model of CSR*

The three-domain model of CSR has been developed by Schwartz and Carroll [SCH 03] and consists of three areas of responsibility: economic, legal and ethical. Unlike Carroll's pyramid, philanthropic responsibilities are excluded from the model, as these can be incorporated into the ethical and economic components. The model is depicted using a Venn diagram – presented in Figure 6.2 – in order to avoid confusion regarding hierarchy by suggesting that all three components have equal importance and, more importantly, to identify overlapping areas between two or all three components of CSR.

The economic component includes those activities that have a direct or indirect economic impact on the business, and can be evaluated against two criteria:

– maximization of profits;

– maximization of share value.

The legal component of CSR consists of the response of a business to legal requirements of government and local jurisdictions. The legality can be classified as:

– compliance;

- passive,

- restrictive,

- opportunistic;

– avoidance of civil litigation;

– anticipation of the law.

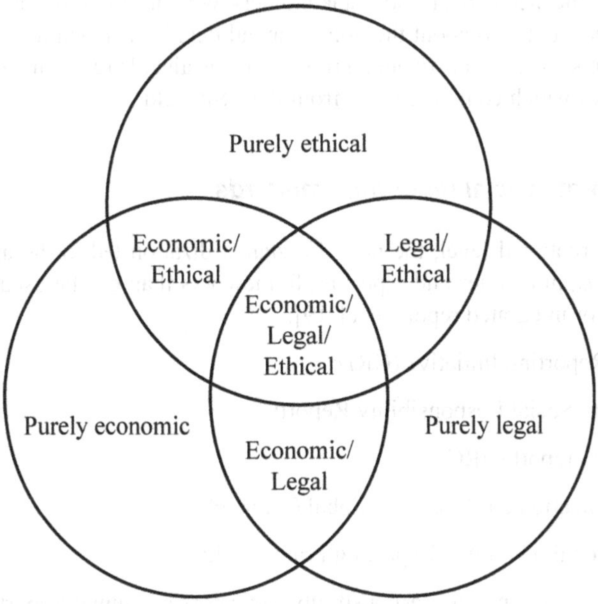

Figure 6.2. *The three-domain model of CSR (source: [SCH 03])*

The ethical component represents the ethical responsibilities of a business. The model includes only three general ethical standards that a business is expected to comply with, according to the general population and stakeholders:

– conventional;

– consequentialist;

– deontological.

An important addition of the three-domain model is the overlapping. Instead of categorizing a corporate action in one of the three components, now, it can be classified under two or all three components. A CSR activity can now be classified in one of the three components: purely economic, purely legal or purely ethical, or one of the four overlapping components: economic/ethical, economic/legal, legal/ethical and economic/legal/ethical.

6.3. Corporate social reporting – standardization and policy

Once CSR became so widely accepted, the need for CSR reporting regulations and policy grew. The shift from maximizing profits to increase long-term market value created the need to provide stakeholders with information, not only about financial aspects but also about the non-financial details. This led to the appearance of new concepts such as non-financial reporting, sustainable reporting and integrated reporting, all of which contain aspects from the CSR field.

6.3.1. *Corporate social reporting standards*

At the international level, the need for standardization led to the appearance of many standards, guidelines and reporting frameworks than can be used to prepare a non-financial or integrated report [PAT 19]:

– Global Reporting Initiative (GRI);

– Corporate Social Responsibility Report;

– Integrated report (IIRC);

– Communication on Progress (Global Compact);

– International Integrated Reporting Framework;

– Guidance on Corporate Responsibility Indicators in Annual Reports;

– KPIs for ESG;

– Model Guidance on Reporting ESG Information for Investors;

– Reporting framework in line with the UN Guiding Principles on Business and Human Rights;

– Carbon Disclosure Project;

– Greenhouse Gas Protocol Corporate Standard;

– Principles for Responsible Investment;

– OECD guidelines for multinational enterprises;

– PN-ISO 26000: 2012 regarding social responsibility;

– Account Ability 1000 Standard (AA1000);

– Eco-Management and Audit Scheme (EMAS);

– Tripartite declaration of principles for multinational enterprises and social policy (ILO) and others.

There is a strong relationship between GRI Guidelines and ISO 26000 as they provide guidelines showing the links between the two standards. This has been done in order to help companies make use of ISO 26000 to integrate social responsibility principles and to use GRI guidelines to prepare the report for businesses performance assessment. If the company decides to prepare a more advanced report, they can use the ISO 26000 guidelines.

Businesses face a big issue with CSR reporting, that is, the materiality of events on information. The potential effect of events needs complex analysis to establish how they may impact companies, in terms of opportunities and risks related to value creation. The reports are aimed at different users and might be too complex for some as they contain information pertinent to only a small group of people. This type of information could be made available as a supplement to the main report, in line with the GRI guidelines.

6.3.2. *Corporate social reporting policy*

Policies refer to national government initiatives such as market regulations, policies, and legislation, in which companies disclose or report on non-financial factors. Governments focus on CSR as businesses can help meet policy objectives voluntarily, helping governments to achieve policy goals in the field of sustainable development, environmental protection, and human development; affording it the role of redistributor of corporate resources to society. CSR policies can be used as a motive to enforce hard law regulations that are not desirable, creating new forms of state intervention. Governments try to influence development of the CSR concept by promoting softer non-binding initiatives. Further, the soft approach of CSR seems to follow a mutation of public governance from hierarchical regulations towards more network-like partnering modes of self- and co-regulation [KOO 03, PIE 00, RHO 97, STE 10, VOL 11, MAT 13b, PAN 14, AND 14, DEI 16]. The domain of CSR restructures the way management works and the relationships between businesses, governments and civil society. From the point of view of policy makers (though not only) CSR leads to shifting involvement of the public and private sectors [MOO 02]. Since CSR is far more than a management approach that could be left to the discretion of managers, governments have a vested interest in co-defining this shifting involvement of the different sectors, rather than being passive objects of change [STE 10].

The range of public policies from CSR is wide-ranging in terms of themes and instruments. The most used types of policies are [STE 10]:

– informational instruments based on knowledge resources consisting of campaigns, training and websites;

– economic instruments (carrots) based on the resources of the taxing authority and money, with the role of influencing behavior by using financial incentives and market force such as taxes, subsidies and wards;

– legal instruments (sticks) promote action by using the state's legislative, executive and judicial powers through laws, directives and regulations;

– partnering instruments (ties) build on a co-regulatory network as different actors are interested in working together towards the same objectives;

– hybrid instruments (adhesives) as many government initiatives on CSR combine two or more other instruments from above.

6.3.3. *Carrots and sticks analysis*

This analysis was conducted using data from Carrots & Sticks[1], a live tracker of all policy regarding sustainable reporting from 86 countries. This was compared with previous Carrots & Sticks reports, from 2006, 2010, 2013 and 2016. Figure 6.3 shows a world map depicting countries that have a policy, those that do not have one and those with no information.

The database currently holds 500 active policy instruments world-wide. Between 2016 and July 2020, 117 new instruments came into force meaning there was an almost 30% increase in active policy instruments. The distribution of these instruments among regions, and the most prolific countries in terms of policy instrument production, can be seen below:

– Europe with 208: Spain, 18; Italy, 16; France, 13;

– Asia Pacific with 150: Australia, 17; Japan, 16; China, 15; India, 14;

– Africa and the Middle East with 60: South Africa, 15; Israel, 7; Nigeria, 6;

– South America with 55: Brazil, Argentina and Colombia are in South America;

– North America with 27: the USA, Canada and Mexico are in North America.

1 https://www.carrotsandsticks.net (accessed on July 4, 2020).

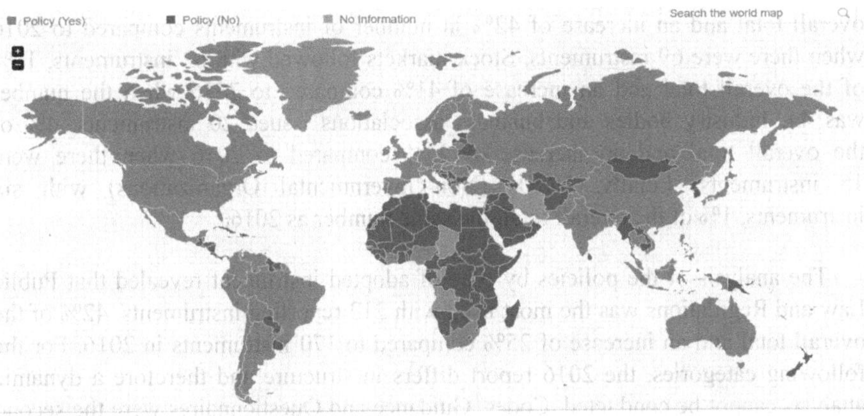

Figure 6.3. *Countries with reporting policy 2020 (source: https://database.globalreporting.org/SDG-12-6/Global-Tracker (accessed on July 4, 2020)). For a color version of this figure, see www.iste.co.uk/machado/sustainable.zip*

As previously stated, there are two forms of policy compliance: mandatory and voluntary. In Table 6.1, data regarding the evolution of two types of policy is presented:

Indicator	2006		2010		2013		2016		2020*	
Mandatory	35	58%	94	62%	130	72%	248	65%	282	56%
Voluntary	25	42%	57	38%	50	28%	135	35%	218	44%
Total	60		151		180		383		500	
Countries and Regions	19		32		44		71		86	

* data available until July 4, 2020

Table 6.1. *Voluntary and mandatory distribution of policy instruments (source: https://www.carrotsandsticks.net)*

The evolution shows an upward trend in the number of policies, of both types; however up until 2013 we observed an increasing share of mandatory policy, reaching 72%. Subsequently, more parity began to appear between the two types, with the existing gap now at 8%.

Analysis of the policy issuers revealed that governments issued the most sustainability reporting instruments, with a total of 314, 64% of the overall total and an increase of 40% in number of instruments compared to 2016 when the number was 223. Financial regulators were in second place with 98 instruments, 20% of the overall total and an increase of 42% in number of instruments compared to 2016 when there were 69 instruments. Stock markets followed with 62 instruments, 12% of the overall total and an increase of 41% compared to 2016 when the number was 44. Industry bodies and business associations issued 20 instruments, 4% of the overall total and an increase of 33% compared to 2016 when there were 15 instruments. Finally, NGOs (Non-Governmental Organizations) with six instruments, 1% of the overall total, the same number as 2016.

The analysis of the policies by type of adopted instrument revealed that Public Law and Regulations was the most used with 212 reporting instruments, 42% of the overall total and an increase of 25% compared to 170 instruments in 2016. For the following categories, the 2016 report differs in structure and therefore a dynamic analysis cannot be conducted. Codes, Guidance and Questionnaires were the second most used with 107 reporting instruments, 21% of the overall total followed by Guidelines and Standards for Non-financial Reporting with 66 reporting instruments, 13% of the total, Self-regulation with 32 reporting instruments, 6% of the total, Index Questionnaires with 5 reporting instruments, 1% of the total and Others (action plan, strategy, program, voluntary initiative) with 78 reporting instruments, 16% of the overall total.

Analysis of the policies by target organization revealed that All Companies were targeted by 209 instruments, 42% of the total and an increase of 35% compared to 155 instruments in 2016. Large Private and Listed Companies were targeted by 241 instruments, 48% of the total and an increase of 48% compared to 163 instruments in 2016. State-owned Enterprises were targeted by 18 instruments, 4% of the total and a decrease of 36% compared to 28 instruments in 2016. Small and medium-sized enterprises (SMEs) were targeted by 7 instruments, 1% of the total and a decrease of 22% compared to the 2016 number of 9 instruments.

The analysis of the policies by the Environmental, Social and Governance (ESG) coverage reveals that many of the policy instruments consist of more than one of the ESG components. Therefore, a share in the total reports by each ESG component is not a reliable method of analysis. When considering these aspects, it must be noted that each instrument may include one, two or all three ESG components. So, 303 instruments included Governance aspects, 282 instruments included Environmental aspects and 268 instruments included Social aspects.

6.4. Analysis of the GRI reporting enterprises between 2007 and 2017

This chapter focuses on large enterprises, multinational enterprises (MNEs) and small and medium-sized enterprises (SMEs) active in five sectors, across six continents and who have reported to GRI between 2007 and 2017. The five sectors under discussion are: energy, chemicals, metal products, mining, and automotive. The six continents refer to Africa, Asia, Europe, Latin America and the Caribbean, Northern America, and Oceania.

GRI has been chosen for this analysis as it is an independent organization based in Amsterdam, The Netherlands. GRI was founded in 1997 in Boston, USA under the Coalition for Environmentally Responsible Economies (CERES) and the Tellus Institute, with the support of the United Nations Environment Programme (UNEP). The first Sustainability Reporting Guidelines (SRG) went public in 1999 and the first full version in 2000. SRG are available as a free public good and are continuously improved and revised. Another important reason for selecting GRI is its Sustainability Disclosure Database (SDD) where researchers are able to see every submitted report.

6.4.1. *Analysis of the GRI reporting enterprises from the energy sector between 2007 and 2017*

Figure 6.4 shows the evolution of GRI reporting by large enterprises within the energy sector, between 2007 and 2017. Overall, throughout this period of time, the number of large enterprises from all six continents that reported to GRI has varied. The highest numbers came out of Europe, Asia, and Latin America and the Caribbean – in this order – with slight differences in four years in the case of the first two continents. More specifically, the highest numbers of large enterprises that reported to GRI were from Europe between 2007 and 2012, and in 2015. Only between 2013 and 2014 and, 2016 and 2017, respectively, were there more large enterprises from Asia who reported to GRI as compared to the companies from the other five continents.

On the contrary, the smallest numbers of large companies that reported to GRI were from Africa, Oceania, and Northern America. Although there were no large enterprises reporting to GRI from Africa between 2007 and 2009, their number started to increase in 2010 and, as a result, the same value has been reached. Furthermore, its enterprises saw a similar evolution rate to those from Oceania between 2014 and 2017.

The highest numbers of large enterprises that reported to GRI by year, for the 2007–2017 period, were: 114 companies from Asia in 2017; 118 from Asia in 2016; 97 from Europe in 2015; 101 companies from Asia in 2014; 83 from Asia in 2013; 82 companies from Europe in 2012; 64 from Europe in 2011; 46 from Europe in 2010; 33 from Europe in 2009; 32 from Europe in 2008; and 23 companies from the same continent in 2007.

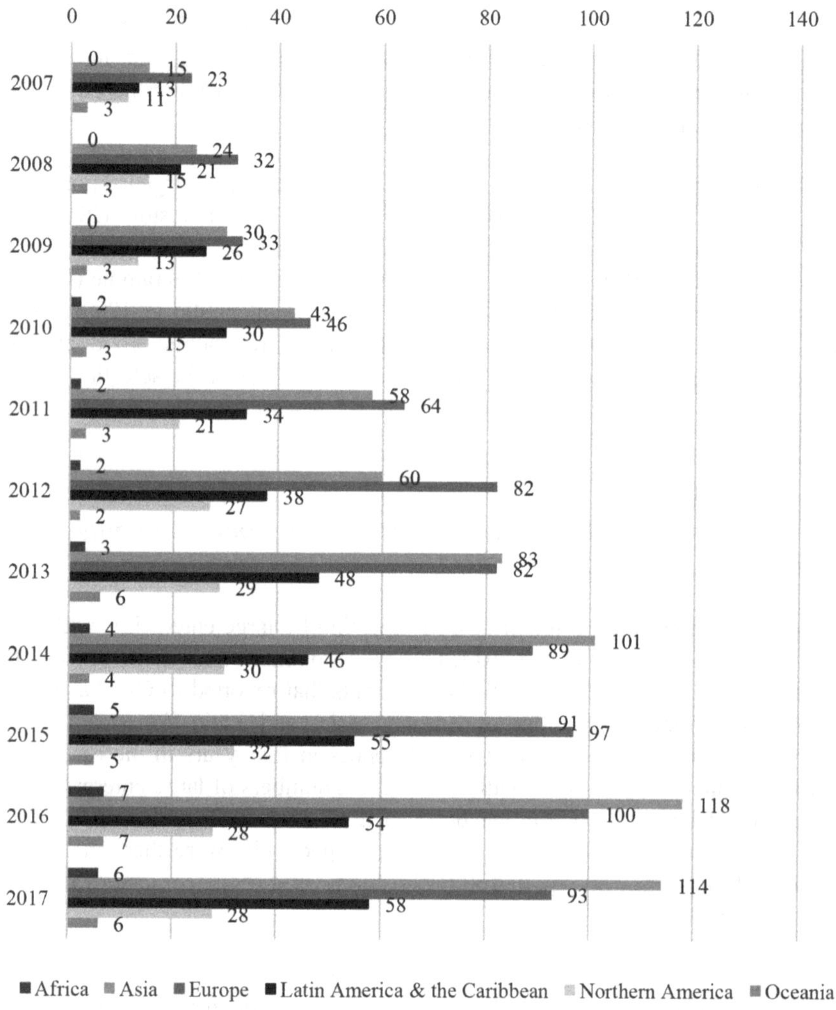

Figure 6.4. *GRI reporting evolution of large enterprises from the energy sector by region, 2007–2017 (source: compiled by the authors based on data collected from GRI SDD)*

At the opposite end, the lowest numbers of large enterprises that reported to GRI, by year, for the same period were: six companies from Africa and Oceania in 2017; seven from Africa and Oceania in 2016; five from Africa and Oceania in 2015; four from the same continents in 2014; three companies from Africa only in 2013; two from both Africa and Oceania in 2012; two companies from Africa between 2010 and 2011; and none from the same continent between 2007 and 2009.

In terms of the highest increase in the number of large GRI reporting enterprises from the same continent, there were cases such as: Oceania in 2013 as compared to 2012 (200%); followed by the companies from Africa in 2010 in contrast to 2009 (100%); those from Latin America and the Caribbean in 2008 versus 2007 (61.54%); those from Asia in 2008 as opposed to 2007 (60%); the companies from Northern America in 2011 as compared to 2010 (40%); and the companies from Europe in 2010 in contrast to 2009, and, respectively, 2011 versus 2010 (39.39%). These increases occurred in the first half of the analyzed period, with 50% of them in 2008 in contrast to 2007.

With respect to the largest decrease in the number of GRI reporting large enterprises from the same continent, the following cases can be highlighted: the companies from Oceania in 2012 against 2011, and, respectively, 2014 as compared to 2013 (-33.33%); followed by the companies from Africa in 2017 in contrast to 2016 (-14.29%); the companies from Northern America in 2009 versus 2008 (-13.33%); those from Asia in 2015 as opposed to 2014 (-9.9%); those from Europe in 2017 against 2016 (-7%); and the companies from Latin America and the Caribbean in 2014 in contrast to 2013 (-4.17%). These reductions were equally distributed throughout the 11 years and one-third of them are in 2017 versus 2016.

Figure 6.5. shows the evolution of GRI reporting by MNEs within the energy sector, by region, between 2007 and 2017. The highest numbers of MNEs that reported to GRI were from Europe, Northern America, and Asia, with Europe first out of the three across the whole period. There were more MNEs that reported to GRI from Northern America than from Asia between 2007 and 2011, and in 2013, respectively.

By contrast, the smallest numbers of MNEs that reported to GRI were from Africa, Oceania, and Latin America and the Caribbean. The number of MNEs that reported to GRI from Oceania and Latin America and the Caribbean had approximately the same evolution – with some small differences – in 2007, 2009, 2011, and, respectively, between 2013 and 2017.

The highest numbers of MNEs that reported to GRI, by year, for the 2007–2017 period, were from Europe only – that is: 30 companies in 2017, 32 in 2016, 25 in 2015, 24 in 2014, 26 in 2013, 21 companies in 2012, 20 in 2011, 13 in 2010, 9 in 2009, 7 in 2008, and 7 companies in 2007.

Conversely, the lowest numbers of MNEs that reported to GRI by year were: none from Africa in 2017; one company from Africa between 2013 and 2016; none from Africa between 2010 and 2012; none from Africa and Oceania in 2009; none from Africa in 2008, and none from Africa and Oceania in 2008.

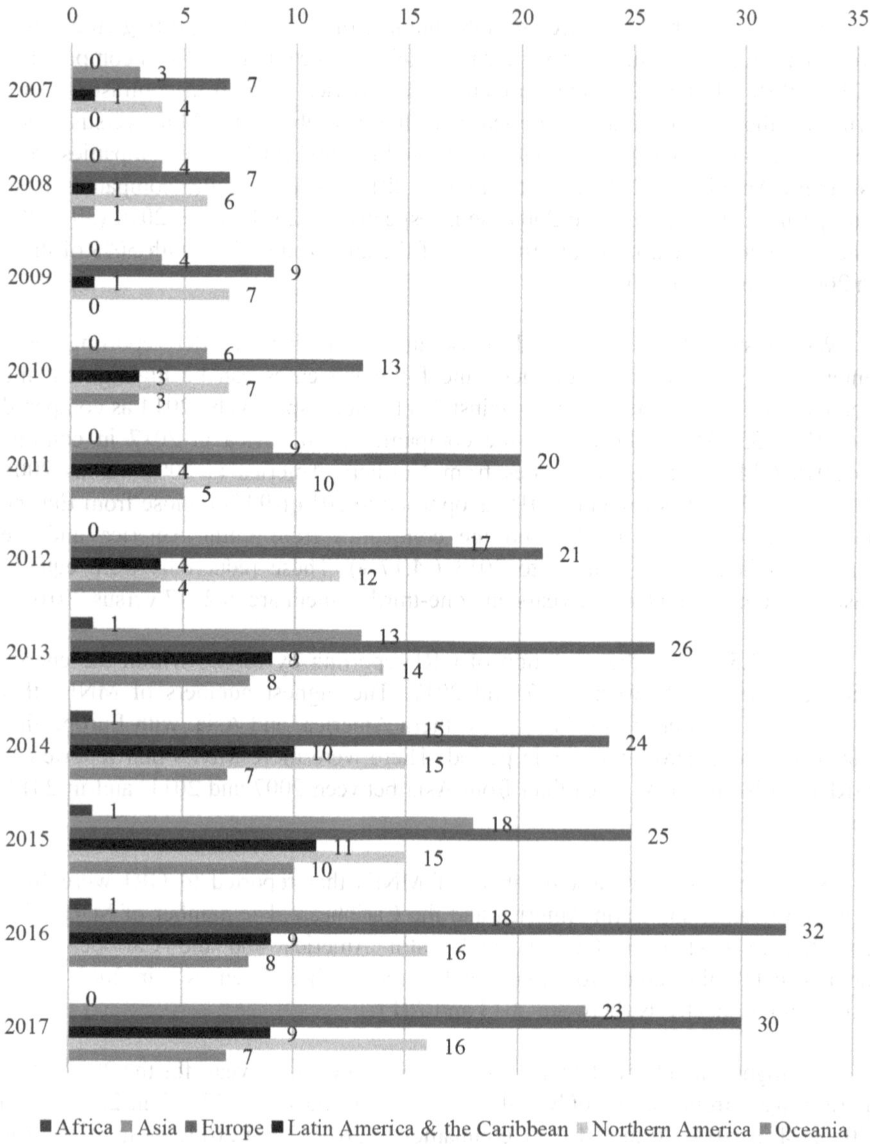

Figure 6.5. *GRI reporting evolution of MNEs from the energy sector by region, 2007–2017 (source: compiled by the authors based on data collected from GRI SDD)*

With respect to the highest increase in the number of GRI reporting MNEs from the same continent, there were cases such as: companies from Latin America and the Caribbean in 2010 against 2009 (200%); followed by those from Africa in 2013 versus 2012 (100%); companies from Oceania in 2013 as compared to 2012 (100%); those from Asia in 2012 versus 2011 (88.89%); the companies from Europe in 2011 in contrast to 2010 (53.85%); and those from Northern America in 2008 as opposed to 2007 (50%). These increases took place in the first half of the 2007–2017 period and one-third of them were in 2013 against 2012.

In terms of the largest decrease in the number of GRI reporting MNEs from the same continent, the following cases can be highlighted: the companies from Africa in 2017 versus 2016 (100%); followed by those from Asia in 2013 as compared to 2012 (-23.53%); the companies from Oceania in 2012 against 2011, and, respectively, 2016 against 2015 (-20%); those from Northern America in 2016 in contrast to 2015 (-18.18%); and the companies from Europe in 2014 as opposed to 2013 (-7.69%). It must be noted that in the case of the MNEs from Northern America, their number did not decline throughout the analyzed period of time. In 2010, 2015, and 2017, respectively, the number of MNEs from Northern America remained constant and in the years remaining their number rose. These decreases are scattered at the end of first half and throughout the second half of the analyzed period.

Figure 6.6 shows the evolution of GRI reporting by SMEs within the energy sector, by region, between 2007 and 2017. The highest numbers of SMEs that reported to GRI were from Europe, Latin America and the Caribbean, and Asia. More specifically, the highest numbers of SMEs that reported to GRI between 2009 and 2012 were from Europe, between 2013 and 2015 were from Latin America and the Caribbean, and in 2017 were from Asia.

Conversely, the smallest numbers of SMEs that reported to GRI were from Northern America, Oceania, and Africa. The number of SMEs that reported to GRI from Oceania and Africa had approximately the same evolution, with some small differences, in 2011 and 2017.

The highest numbers of SMEs that reported to GRI, by year, for the 2007–2017 period were: 17 companies from Asia in 2017; 11 from Europe and Latin America and the Caribbean in 2016; 14 from Latin America and the Caribbean in 2015; 12 from Latin America and the Caribbean in 2014; 9 companies from Latin America and the Caribbean in 2013; 9 from Europe in 2012; 8 companies from Europe in 2011; 3 from Europe in 2010; 3 from Europe in 2009; one company from Europe in 2008; and one company from Asia in 2007.

The lowest numbers of SMEs that reported to GRI, by year, were: none from Northern America between 2011 and 2017; none from Africa, Northern America, and Oceania in 2010; none from Africa, Latin America and the Caribbean, Northern America and Oceania in 2009; none from Africa, Asia, Northern America, and Oceania in 2008; and none from Africa, Asia, Europe, Northern America, and Oceania in 2007.

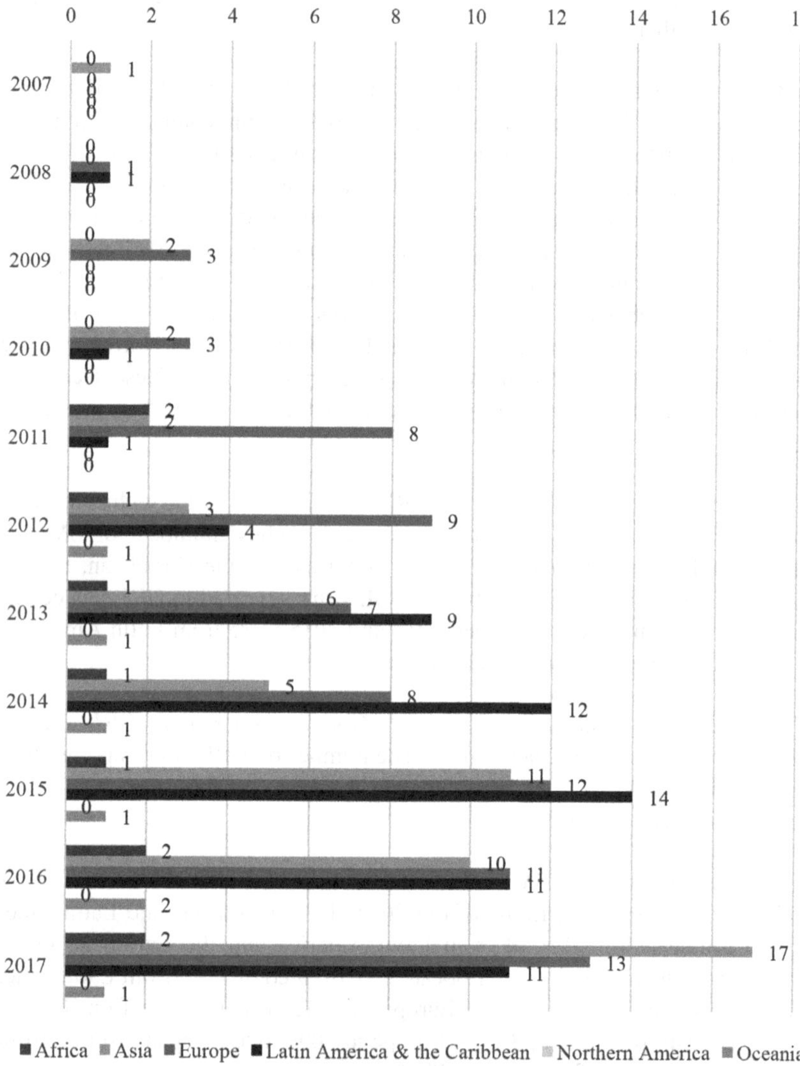

Figure 6.6. *GRI reporting evolution of SMEs from the energy sector by region, 2007–2017 (source: compiled by the authors based on data collected from GRI SDD)*

In terms of the highest increase in the number of GRI reporting SMEs from the same continent, there were cases such as: the companies from Latin America and the Caribbean in 2012 versus 2011 (300%); followed by those from Europe in 2009 in contrast to 2008 (200%); the companies from Asia in 2015 as opposed to 2014 (120%); and the companies from Africa and Oceania in 2016 against 2015 (100%). These increases were spread across all 11 years, but approximately two-thirds of them were focused in the latter half of the period analyzed.

Concerning the largest decrease in the number of GRI reporting SMEs from the same continent, the following cases can be highlighted: the companies from Africa in 2012 as compared to 2011, and, respectively, Oceania in 2017 as opposed to 2016 (-50%); those from Europe in 2013 versus 2012 (-22.22%); the companies from Latin America and the Caribbean in 2016 against 2015 (-21.43%); and the companies from Asia in 2014 in contrast to 2013 (-16.67%). There are no SMEs from Northern America that reported to GRI between 2007 and 2017. These reductions had a medium distribution range in the analyzed period, starting with 2012 and ending with 2017.

6.4.2. *Analysis of the GRI reporting enterprises from the chemicals sector between 2007 and 2017*

Figure 6.7 shows the evolution of GRI reporting by large enterprises within the chemicals sector, by region, between 2007 and 2017. The highest numbers of large companies that reported to GRI were from Asia, Europe, and Northern America, with slight differences between 2015 and 2017 for the last two continents. More specifically, the highest numbers of large enterprises that reported to GRI were from Asia between 2007 and 2008, and, respectively, between 2010 and 2017. In 2009, the number of large enterprises that reported to GRI from Asia was the same as the number from Europe.

On the contrary, the smallest numbers of large companies that reported to GRI were from Oceania, Africa, and Latin America and the Caribbean. The number of large companies that reported to GRI from Oceania was relatively constant during the 11 years.

The highest numbers of large enterprises that reported to GRI, by year, for the 2007–2017 period were: 77 companies from Asia in 2017; 72 from Asia in 2016; 56 companies from Asia in 2015; 48 from Asia in 2014; 42 from Asia in 2013; 36 companies from Asia in 2012; 31 from Asia in 2011; 20 from the same continent in 2010; 14 companies from Asia and Europe in 2009; 13 from Asia in 2008; and 7 companies from the same continent in 2007.

At the opposite end, the lowest numbers of large enterprises that reported to GRI, by year, for the same period were: one company from Oceania between 2016 and 2017; none from Oceania in 2015; one company from Oceania between 2011 and 2014; one from Africa and Oceania between 2009 and 2010; and none from Oceania between 2007 and 2008.

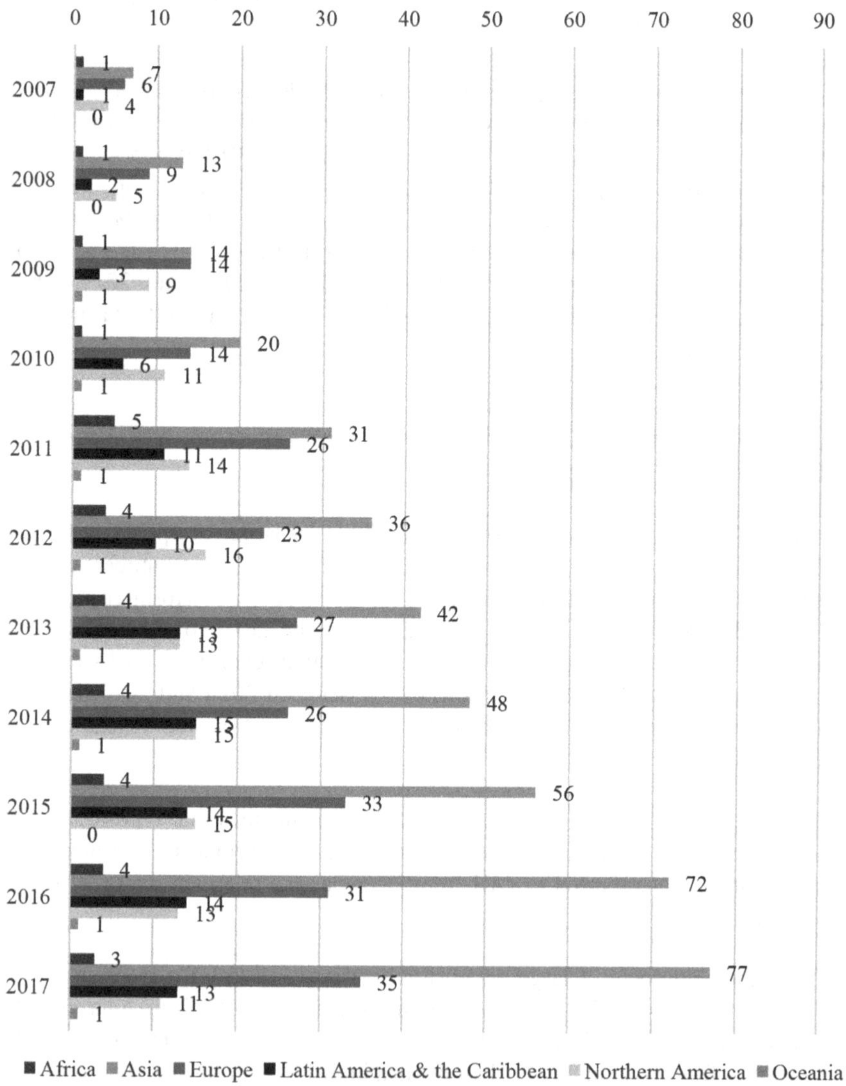

Figure 6.7. *GRI reporting evolution of large enterprises from the chemicals sector by region, 2007–2017 (source: compiled by the authors based on data collected from GRI SDD)*

With reference to the highest increase in the number of GRI reporting large enterprises from the same continent, there were cases such as: the companies from Africa in 2011 against 2010 (400%); followed by the companies from Latin America and the Caribbean in 2010 as compared to 2009 (100%); those from Asia in 2008 versus 2007 (85.71%); those from Latin America and the Caribbean in 2011 as opposed to 2010 (85.71%); and the companies from Northern America in 2009 in contrast to 2008 (80%). These increases were scattered within the first half of the analyzed period and one-third were in 2009 against 2008.

Concerning the largest decrease in the number of GRI reporting large enterprises from the same continent, the following cases can be highlighted: the companies from Oceania in 2015 versus 2014 (-100%); those from Africa in 2017 as compared to 2016 (-25%); the companies from Northern America in 2013 against 2012 (-18.75%); those from Europe in 2012 as opposed to 2011 (-11.54%); and the companies from Latin America and the Caribbean in 2012 in contrast to 2011 (-9.09%). These reductions occurred within the latter half of the 11 years with a third of them in 2012 in contrast to 2011. A particular case are the companies that reported to GRI from Asia, due to the fact that their number grew continuously in the 2007–2017 period.

Figure 6.8 shows the evolution of GRI reporting by MNEs, by region, between 2007 and 2017. The highest numbers of MNEs that reported to GRI were from Asia, Europe, and Northern America. More specifically, the highest numbers of MNEs that reported to GRI were from Asia in each of the 11 years. More MNEs from Europe reported to GRI than from Northern America, excepting the year 2011.

In contrast, the smallest numbers of MNEs that reported to GRI were from Africa, Oceania, and Latin America and the Caribbean. The number of MNEs that reported to GRI from Africa and Oceania had approximately the same evolution, with some small differences, between 2007 and 2009.

The highest numbers of MNEs that reported to GRI, by year, for the 2007–2017 period were from Europe only, that is: 75 companies in 2017; 78 in 2016; 75 in 2015; 43 companies in 2014; 36 in 2013; 30 in 2012; 25 in 2011; 19 in 2010; 15 in 2009; 15 in 2008; and 13 companies in 2007.

Conversely, the lowest numbers of MNEs that reported to GRI, by year, were: one company from Africa and Oceania between 2010 and 2017; none from Africa and Latin America and the Caribbean in 2009; none from Africa in 2008; and none from Africa and Latin America and the Caribbean in 2007.

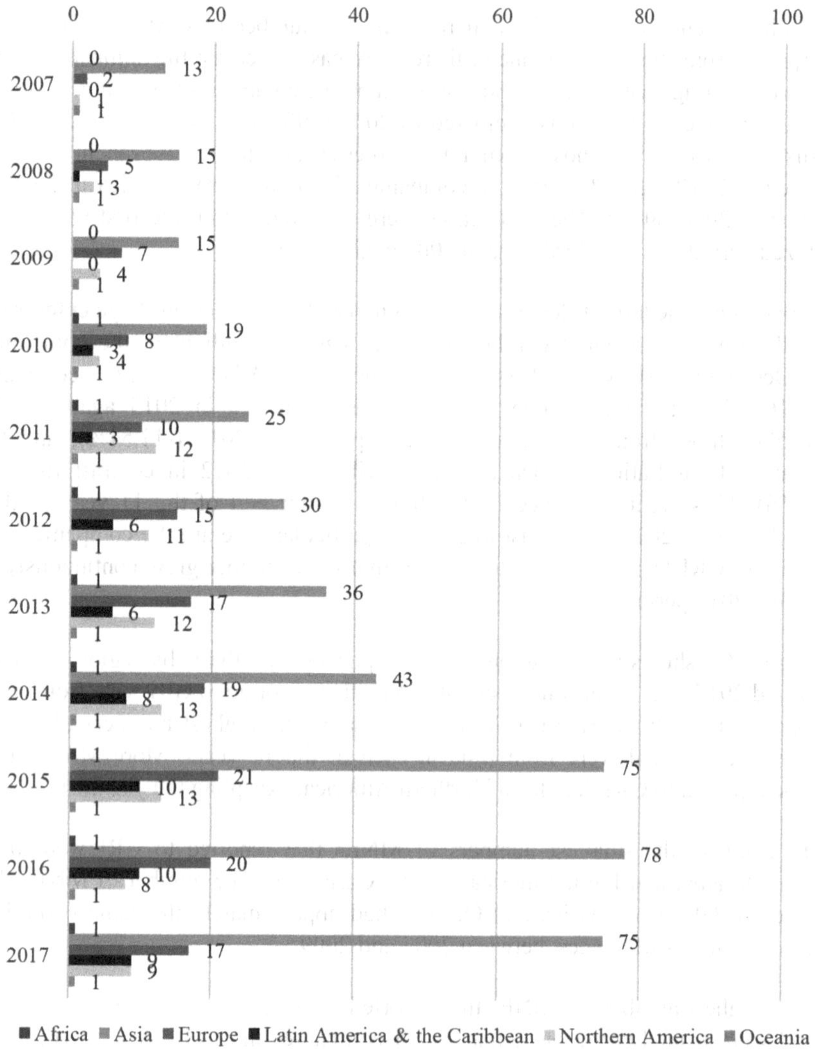

Figure 6.8. *GRI reporting evolution of MNEs from the chemicals sector by region, 2007–2017 (source: compiled by the authors based on data collected from GRI SDD)*

In terms of the highest increase in the number of GRI reporting MNEs from the same continent, there were cases such as: the companies from Northern America in 2008 as compared to 2007, and, respectively, 2011 against 2010 (200%); followed by the companies from Europe in 2008 versus 2007 (150%); those from Latin America and the Caribbean in 2012 as opposed to 2011; those from Africa in 2011 in contrast to 2010 (100%); and the companies from Asia in 2015 against 2014 (74.42%). The number of MNEs from Oceania that reported to GRI are not part of this ranking as this remained the same from 2007 until 2017. These increases had a large distribution range throughout the analyzed period, both in the first and second half. Approximately a third of them were in 2008 versus 2007.

In terms of the largest decrease in the number of GRI reporting MNEs from the same continent, the following cases can be highlighted: the companies from Latin America and the Caribbean in 2009 versus 2008 (-100%); the companies from Northern America in 2016 as compared to 2015 (-38.46); those from Europe in 2017 in contrast to 2016 (-15%); and those from Asia in 2015 against 2014 (-3.85%). The MNEs from Oceania and from Africa that reported to GRI are not in this ranking, since their number of MNEs did not decline between 2007 and 2017. These decreases were spread throughout the 11-year period and half fall in 2017 versus 2016.

Figure 6.9 shows the evolution of GRI reporting by SMEs within the chemicals sector, by region, between 2007 and 2017. The highest numbers of SMEs that reported to GRI were from Europe, Asia, and Northern America. More specifically, the highest numbers of SMEs that reported to GRI between 2008 and 2013, and, respectively, in 2015 were from Europe; in 2014 they were from Asia and Europe, and between 2016 and 2017 they were from Asia.

In contrast, the smallest numbers of SMEs that reported to GRI were from Africa, Latin America and the Caribbean, and Oceania, with the same evolution over the 11-year period.

The highest numbers of SMEs that reported to GRI, by year, for the 2007–2017 period were: eight companies from Asia in 2017; five from Asia in 2016; six from Europe in 2015; five companies from Asia and Europe in 2014; four from Europe in 2013; four from Europe in 2012; two from Europe in 2011; three from Europe in 2010; two companies from Europe in 2009; and one company from the same continent in 2008. In 2007, there were no SMEs from any of the six continents that submitted reports to GRI.

The lowest numbers of SMEs that reported to GRI, by year, for the same period were: none from Africa, Latin America and the Caribbean, and Oceania between 2013 and 2017; none from Africa and Latin America and the Caribbean between 2011 and 2012; none from Africa, Asia, Latin America and the Caribbean, and

Northern America between 2008 and 2010; and none from Africa, Asia, Europe, Latin America and the Caribbean, and Northern America in 2007.

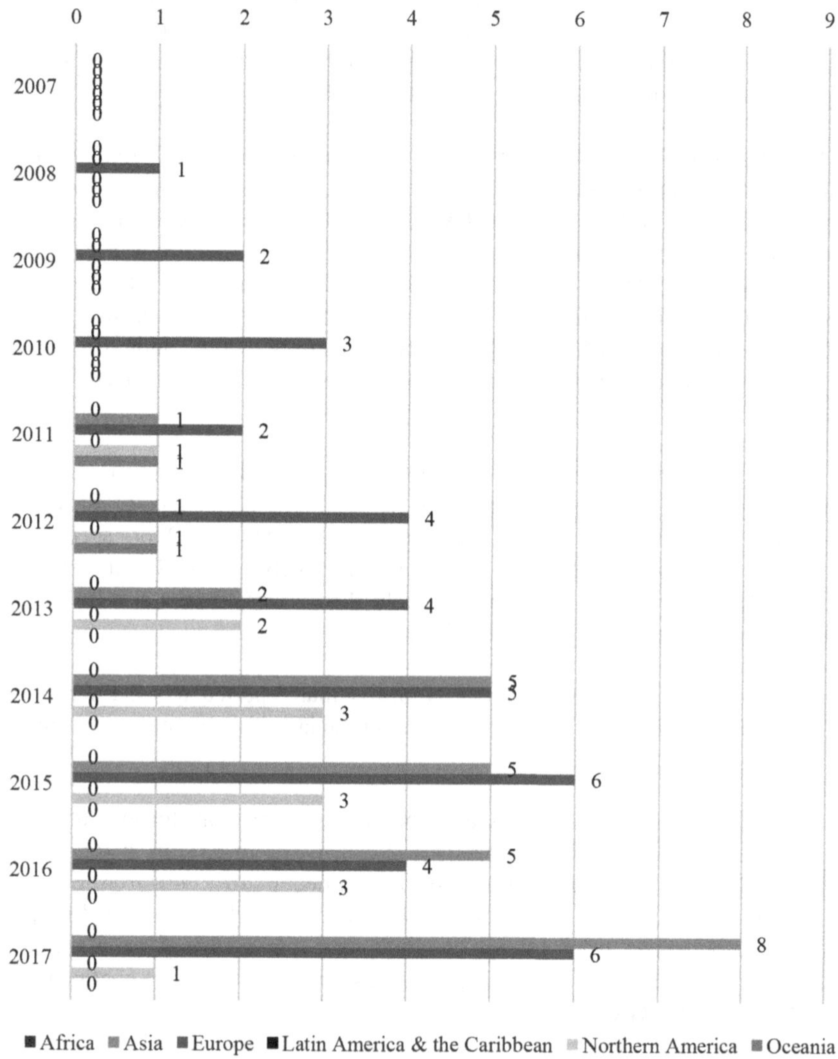

Figure 6.9. *GRI reporting evolution of SMEs from the chemicals sector by region, 2007–2017 (source: compiled by the authors based on data collected from GRI SDD)*

With reference to the highest increase in the number of GRI reporting SMEs from the same continent, there were cases such as: the companies from Asia in 2014 as compared to 2013 (150%); followed by those from Europe in 2009 versus 2008, and, respectively, 2012 against 2011 (100%); those from Northern America in 2013 as opposed to 2012 (100%); and the companies from Oceania in 2011 in contrast to 2010 (100%). These increases were not correlated and appeared in the first two-thirds of the analyzed period.

In terms of the largest decrease in the number of GRI reporting SMEs from the same continent, the following cases can be highlighted: the companies from Oceania in 2013 versus 2012 (-100%); the companies from Northern America in 2017 against 2016 (66.66%); and the companies from Europe in 2011 in contrast to 2010, and, respectively, 2016 as compared to 2015 (-33.33%). This ranking does not include the companies from Asia and Europe as the number of SMEs increased continuously during the 11 years. Furthermore, no SMEs from Africa and Latin America and the Caribbean reported to GRI between 2007 and 2017. The above-mentioned reductions occurred in the latter two-thirds of the 11 years and they are not correlated.

6.4.3. *Analysis of the GRI reporting enterprises from the metal products sector between 2007 and 2017*

Figure 6.10 shows the evolution of GRI reporting by large enterprises within the metal products sector, by region, between 2007 and 2017. The highest numbers of large companies that reported to GRI were from Asia, Europe, and Latin America and the Caribbean. More specifically, the highest numbers of large enterprises were from Europe between 2007 and 2009, and from Asia between 2010 and 2017.

On the contrary, the smallest numbers of large companies that reported to GRI were from Oceania, Africa, and Northern America. There were slight differences in the number of large companies that reported to GRI from Africa and Latin America and the Caribbean, which are in separate rankings. Although the number of reporting companies from Africa was low in the first part of the analyzed period, this increased steadily to eventually match the number of companies from Latin America and the Caribbean in 2017.

The highest numbers of large enterprises that reported to GRI, by year, for the 2007–2017 period were: 67 companies from Asia in 2017; 57 companies from Asia in 2016; 36 from Asia in 2015; 33 from Asia in 2014; 36 companies from Asia in 2013; 38 from Asia in 2012; 28 from Asia in 2011; 17 companies from the same continent in 2010; 16 from Europe in 2009; 10 from Europe in 2008; and 5 companies from the same continent in 2007.

At the opposite end, the lowest numbers of large enterprises that reported to GRI, by year, throughout the period analyzed were: one company from Oceania between 2014 and 2017; two from the same continent between 2011 and 2013; none from Oceania in 2010; and none from Africa and Oceania between 2007 and 2009.

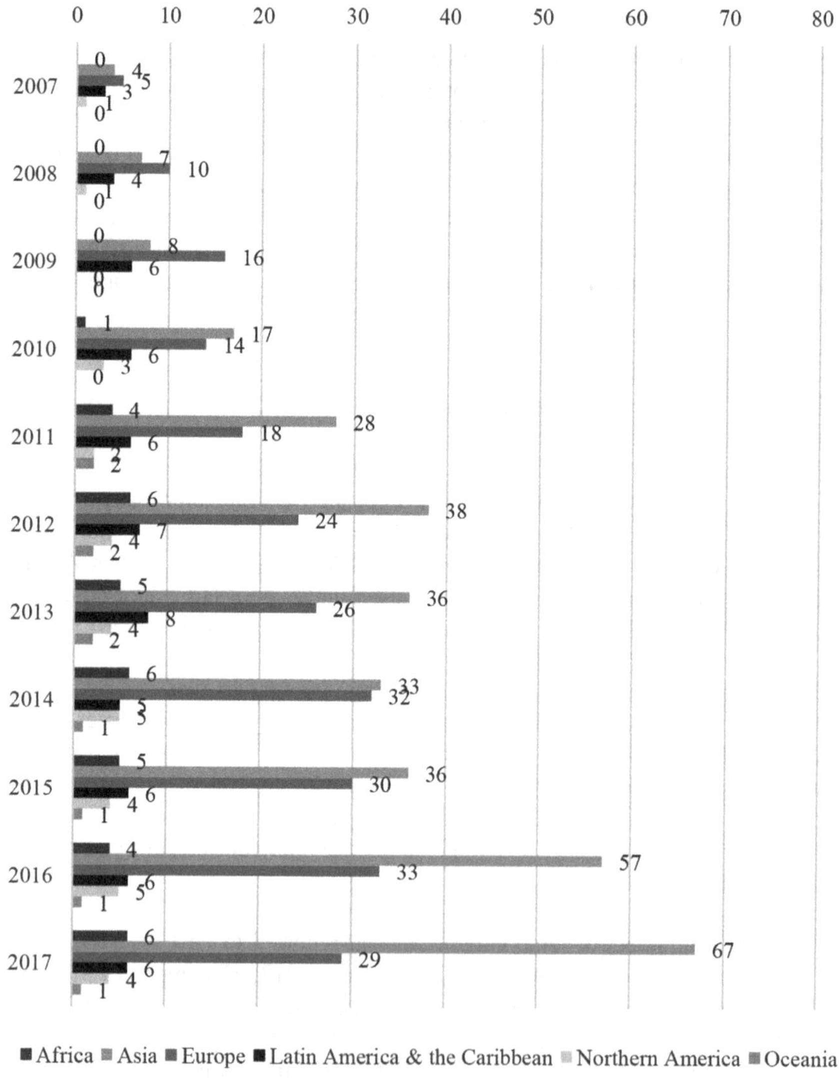

Figure 6.10. *GRI reporting evolution of large enterprises from the metal products sector by region, 2007–2017 (source: compiled by the authors based on data collected from GRI SDD)*

In terms of the highest increase in the number of GRI reporting large enterprises from the same continent, there were cases such as: the companies from Africa in 2011 as compared to 2010 (300%); followed by the companies from Oceania in 2011 versus 2010 (200%); those from Asia in 2010 as opposed to 2009 (112.5%); those from Europe in 2008 in contrast to 2007; the companies from Northern America in 2012 against 2011 (100%); and those from Latin America and the Caribbean in 2009 as compared to 2008 (50%). All of these increases were scattered in the first half of the analyzed period, and they are not linked.

Concerning the largest decrease in the number of GRI reporting large enterprises from the same continent, the following cases can be highlighted: the companies from Oceania in 2014 versus 2013 (-50%); those from Latin America and the Caribbean in 2014 as opposed to 2013 (-37.5%); the companies from Africa in 2016 in contrast to 2015 (-20%); those from Northern America in 2009 as compared to 2008 (-13.33%); those from Asia in 2010 against 2009 (-12.5%); and the companies from Asia in 2014 versus 2013 (-8.33%). These decreases had a large distribution range across the 11 years, with half in 2014 versus 2013.

Figure 6.11 shows the evolution of GRI reporting by MNEs, by region, between 2007 and 2017. The highest numbers of MNEs that reported to GRI were from Europe, Asia, Northern America, and Oceania. More specifically, the highest numbers were from Europe, leading the ranking in 8 of the 11 years analyzed against the companies from Asia. In third position are two continents instead of one, since the companies from these regions occupied this position in the ranking five times each.

In contrast, the smallest numbers of MNEs that reported to GRI were from Africa and Latin America and the Caribbean. The number of the companies from these regions had a significantly different evolution as those from Africa have not submitted reports to GRI.

The highest numbers of MNEs that reported to GRI, by year, for the 2007–2017 period were: 18 companies from Europe in 2019; 18 companies from Asia in 2016; 16 from the same continent in 2015; 19 from Europe in 2014; 15 from Europe in 2013; 15 from Europe in 2012; 11 companies from Europe in 2011; 8 from Europe in 2010; 9 from Europe in 2009; 6 from the same continent in 2008; and 3 companies from Asia in 2007.

Conversely, the lowest numbers of MNEs that reported to GRI, by year, were: none from Africa between 2011 and 2017; none from Africa and Latin America and the Caribbean in 2009 and 2010; none from Africa, Latin America and the

Caribbean, and Oceania in 2008; and none from Africa, Latin America and the Caribbean, Northern America, and Oceania in 2007.

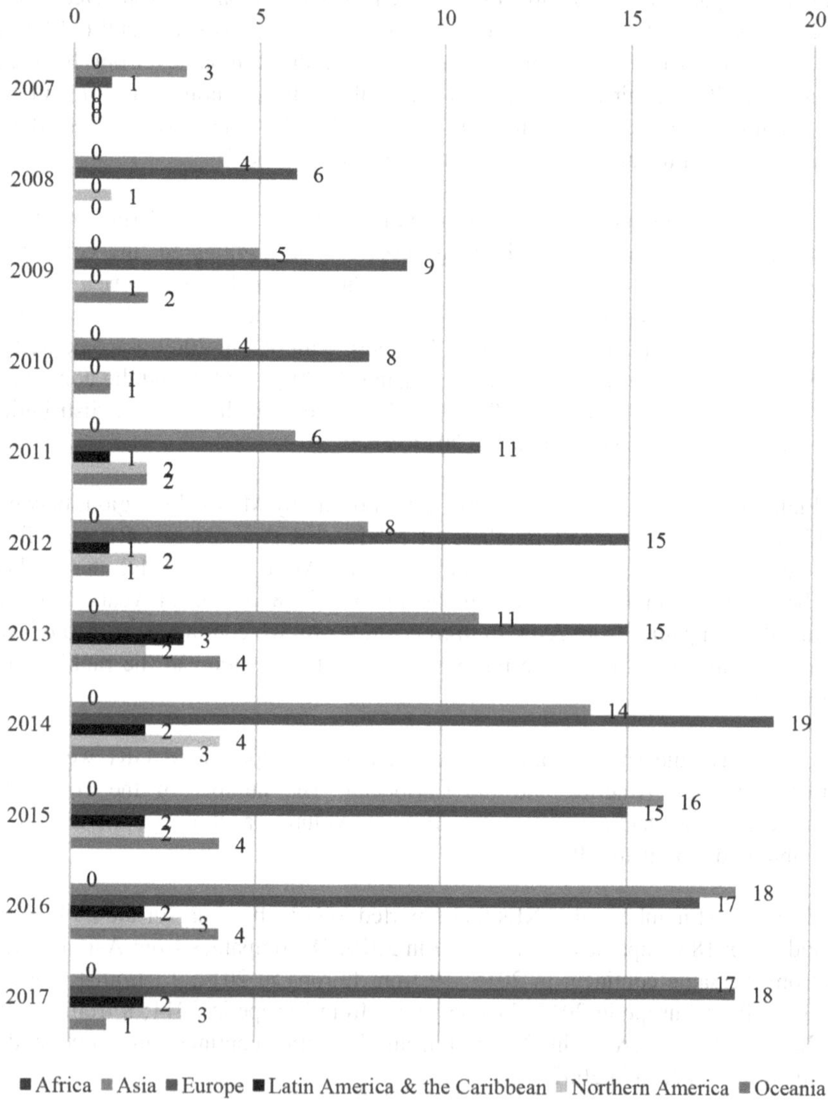

Figure 6.11. *GRI reporting evolution of MNEs from the metal products sector by region, 2007–2017 (source: compiled by the authors based on data collected from GRI SDD)*

In terms of the highest increase in the number of GRI reporting MNEs from the same continent, there were cases such as: the companies from Europe in 2008 as compared to 2007 (500%); followed by the companies from Oceania in 2013 versus 2012 (300%); Latin America and the Caribbean in 2013 as opposed to 2012 (200%); the companies from Northern America in 2014 in contrast to 2013 (100%); and the companies from Asia in 2011 against 2010 (50%). These increases appeared throughout the analyzed period but most occurred in the first half. A third of the increases were in 2008 as compared to 2007, and another third in 2012 versus 2011.

Regarding the largest decrease in the number of GRI reporting MNEs from the same continent, the following cases can be highlighted: the companies from Northern America in 2015 versus 2014 (-50%); the companies from Oceania in 2010 in contrast to 2009, and, respectively, 2012 against 2011 (-50%); those from Latin America and the Caribbean in 2014 as compared to 2013 (-33.33%); those from Europe in 2015 as opposed to 2014 (-21.05%); and the companies from Asia in 2010 against 2009 (-20%). The MNEs from Africa are not part of the two rankings since they do not appear in the statistics as having submitted reports to GRI. The above-mentioned reductions are scattered throughout the analyzed period, and they are not correlated.

Figure 6.12 shows the evolution of GRI reporting by SMEs within the energy sector, by region, between 2007 and 2017. The highest numbers of SMEs that reported to GRI were from Europe, Asia, and Latin America and the Caribbean. More specifically, the highest numbers of SMEs that reported to GRI between 2007 and 2013 were from Europe; between 2014 and 2016 they were from Asia, and in 2017 they were from both Europe and Asia.

In contrast, the smallest numbers of SMEs that reported to GRI were from Northern America, Oceania, and Africa. The number of SMEs that reported to GRI from Oceania and Africa had the same evolution throughout the 11 analyzed years.

The highest numbers of SMEs that reported to GRI, by year, for the 2007–2017 period were: three companies from Asia and Europe in 2017; four companies from Asia in 2016; five from Asia in 2015; two from the same continent in 2014; three from Europe in 2013; two companies from Europe in 2012; two from Europe in 2011; two from Europe in 2010; two from Europe in 2009; one company from Europe in 2008; and one company from the same continent in 2007.

The lowest numbers of SMEs that reported to GRI, by year, were: none from Northern America and Oceania in 2017; none from Africa, Northern America, and Oceania between 2013 and 2016; none from Latin America and the Caribbean, Northern America, and Oceania in 2012; none from Asia, Latin America and the Caribbean, Northern America, and Oceania in 2011; and none from Africa, Asia,

Latin America and the Caribbean, Northern America, and Oceania between 2007 and 2010.

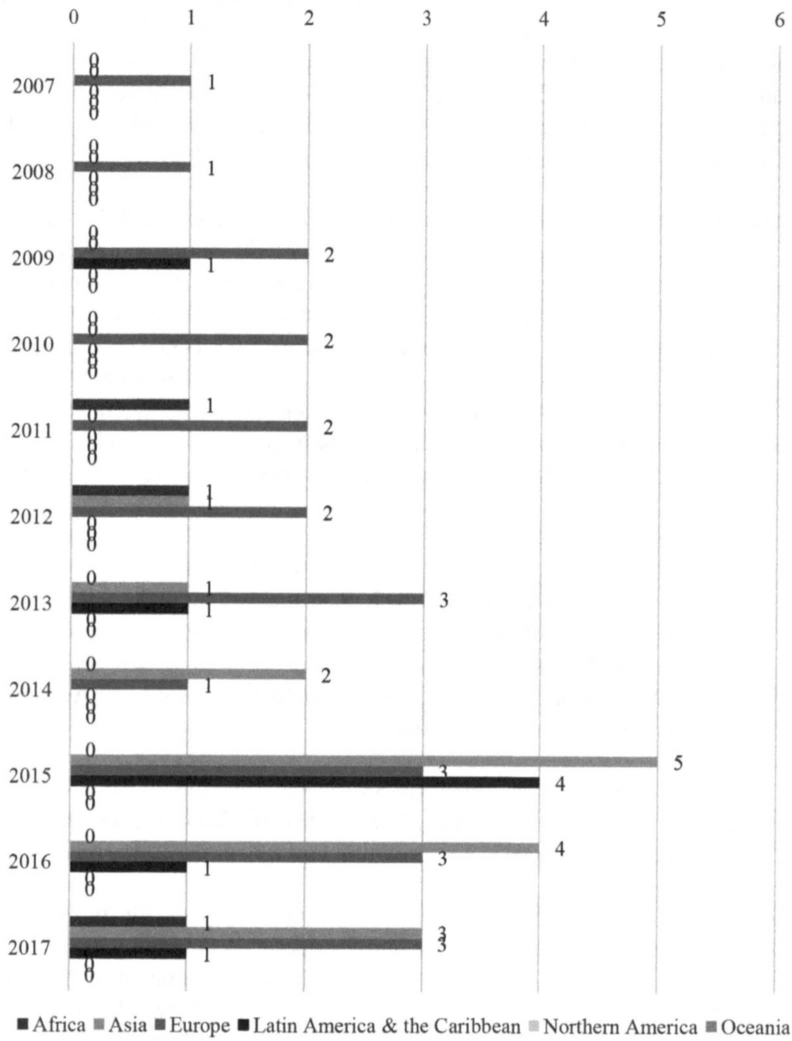

Figure 6.12. *GRI reporting evolution of SMEs from the metal products sector by region, 2007–2017 (source: compiled by the authors based on data collected from GRI SDD)*

In terms of the highest increase in the number of GRI reporting SMEs from the same continent, there were cases such as: the companies from Latin America and the Caribbean in 2015 versus 2014 (300%); followed by the companies from Europe in

2015 in contrast to 2014 (200%); those from Asia in 2015 as opposed to 2014 (150%); and the companies from Africa in 2011 against 2010, and 2017 versus 2016 (100%), respectively. These increases appeared in the latter half of the 11 years and there is no correlation between them.

Concerning the largest decrease in the number of GRI reporting SMEs from the same continent, the following cases can be highlighted: the companies from Africa in 2013 as compared to 2012 (-100%); the companies from Latin America and the Caribbean in 2010 as opposed to 2009, and, respectively, 2014 versus 2013 (-100%); those from Europe in 2014 against 2013 (-66.67%); and the companies from Asia in 2017 in contrast to 2016 (-25%). The companies from Northern America and Oceania did not submit reports and, as a result, they are not part of this ranking. All of these decreases occurred in the second half of the analyzed period, and 50% of them were in 2014 versus 2013.

6.4.4. *Analysis of the GRI reporting enterprises from the mining sector between 2007 and 2017*

Figure 6.13 shows the evolution of GRI reporting by large enterprises within the mining sector, by region, between 2007 and 2017. It must be noted that the companies from all six continents reported to GRI each year, making this one of the most reported sectors.

The highest numbers of large companies that reported to GRI were from Africa, Latin America and the Caribbean, and Asia. More specifically, the highest numbers of large enterprises that reported to GRI were from Asia in 2016 and 2017, Africa between 2010 and 2015, and Latin America and the Caribbean between 2007 and 2009.

On the contrary, the smallest numbers of large companies that reported to GRI were from Oceania, Northern America, and Europe. The number of large enterprises from Northern America and Europe had approximately the same evolution between 2007 and 2013. Starting in the year 2014, the number of companies from Europe began to grow and the number of companies from Northern America declined.

The highest numbers of large enterprises that reported to GRI, by year, for the 2007–2017 period were: 49 companies from Asia in 2017; 50 companies from the same continent in 2016; 32 from Africa in 2015; 34 from Africa in 2014; 37 from Africa in 2013; 38 companies from Africa in 2012; 38 from Africa in 2011; 20 companies from the same continent in 2010; 18 from Latin America and the Caribbean in 2009; 15 from Latin America and the Caribbean in 2008; and 11 companies from the same continent in 2007.

At the opposite end, the lowest numbers of large enterprises that reported to GRI, by year, for the same period were: six companies from Oceania in 2017; seven from Northern America in 2016; nine from Northern America and Oceania in 2015; six from Oceania in 2014; four companies from Oceania in 2013; eight from Oceania in 2012; eight from Oceania in 2011; seven from Oceania in 2010; four companies from the same continent in 2009; four from Northern America in 2008; and two companies from Oceania in 2009.

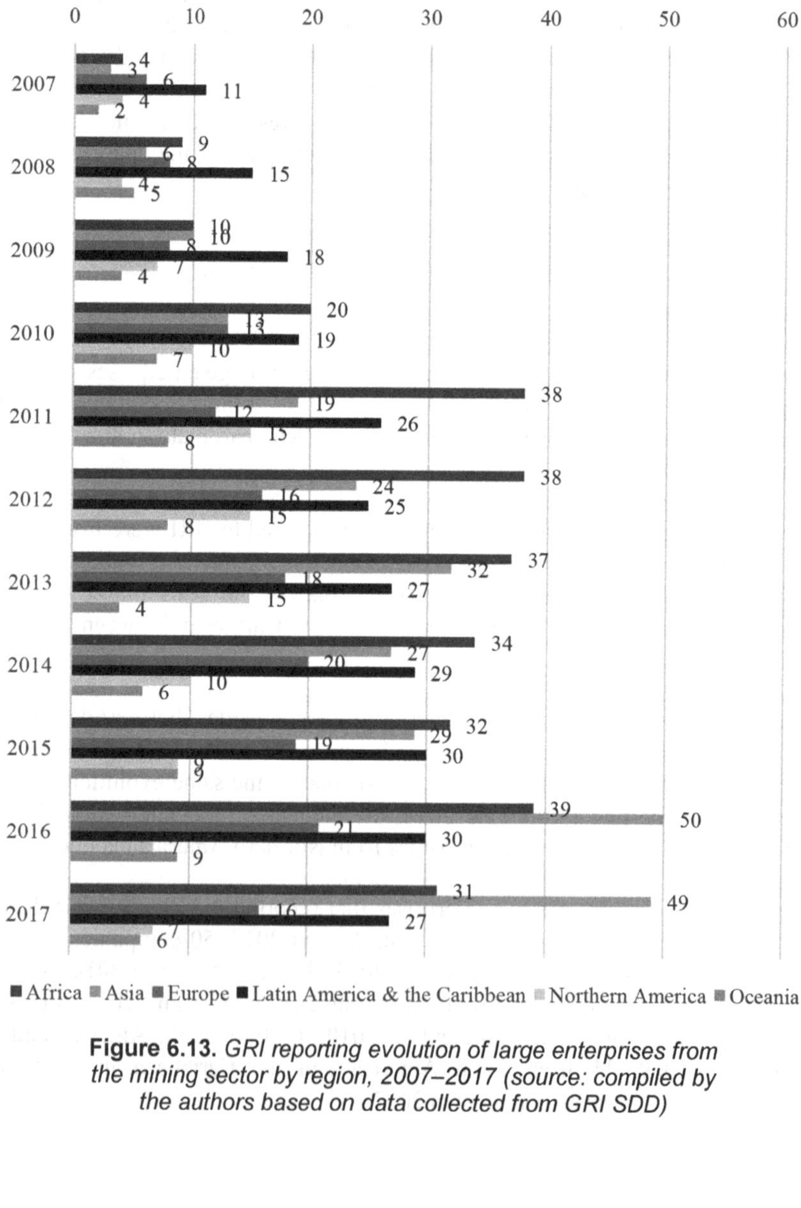

Figure 6.13. *GRI reporting evolution of large enterprises from the mining sector by region, 2007–2017 (source: compiled by the authors based on data collected from GRI SDD)*

With respect to the highest increase in the number of GRI reporting large enterprises from the same continent, there were cases such as: the companies from Oceania in 2008 as compared to 2007 (150%); followed by the companies from Africa in 2008 versus 2007 (125%); those from Asia in 2008 as opposed to 2007 (100%); those from Northern America in 2009 against 2008 (75%); the companies from Europe in 2010 in contrast to 2009 (62.5%); and those from Latin America and the Caribbean in 2008 versus 2007 (36.36%). All of these increases took place in the first third of the analyzed period – that is between 2008 and 2010 – and two-thirds of them were in 2008 against 2007.

Concerning the largest decrease in the number of GRI reporting large enterprises from the same continent, the following cases can be highlighted: the companies from Oceania in 2013 against 2012 (-50%); the companies from Northern America in 2014 versus 2013 (-33.33%); those from Europe in 2017 as compared to 2016 (-23.81%); those from Africa in 2017 as opposed to 2016 (-20.51%); the companies from Asia in 2014 in contrast to 2013 (-15.63%); and those from Latin America and the Caribbean in 2017 against 2016 (-10%). All of these decreases occurred in the second half of the analyzed period, that is between 2013 and 2017, and 50% of these were in 2017 in contrast to 2016.

Figure 6.14 shows the evolution of GRI reporting by MNEs within the mining sector, by region, between 2007 and 2017. The highest numbers of MNEs that reported to GRI were from Northern America, Oceania, and Europe. The number of MNEs from Europe and Oceania was similar throughout the 11 years, with slight differences in half of the analyzed period.

By contrast, the smallest numbers of MNEs that reported to GRI were from Asia, Africa, and Latin America and the Caribbean. There are several years in which the number of MNEs were the same among these three continents, for example: in 2017, 2016 and 2010 for Africa and Asia; in 2014 for all three continents; in 2013 for Africa and Latin America and the Caribbean; and, respectively, in 2007 for Asia and Latin America and the Caribbean.

The highest numbers of MNEs that reported to GRI by year, for the 2007–2017 period were: 22 companies from Northern America in 2017; 20 companies from Northern America in 2016; 20 from Northern America in 2015; 24 from Northern America in 2014; 21 from Northern America in 2013; 19 companies from Northern America in 2012; 13 from Northern America in 2011; 10 from the same continent in 2010; 7 companies from Northern America and Oceania in 2009; 6 from Northern America in 2008; and 3 companies from Northern America and Oceania in 2007.

Conversely, the lowest numbers of MNEs that reported to GRI, by year, were: four companies from Africa and Asia in 2017; three from the same two continents in 2016; four from Asia in 2015; five companies from Africa, Asia, and Latin America and the Caribbean in 2014; four from Asia in 2013; three companies from Asia in 2012; three from Asia in 2011; two from Africa and Asia in 2010; one company from Africa in 2009; one from Africa in 2008; and one company from the same continent in 2007.

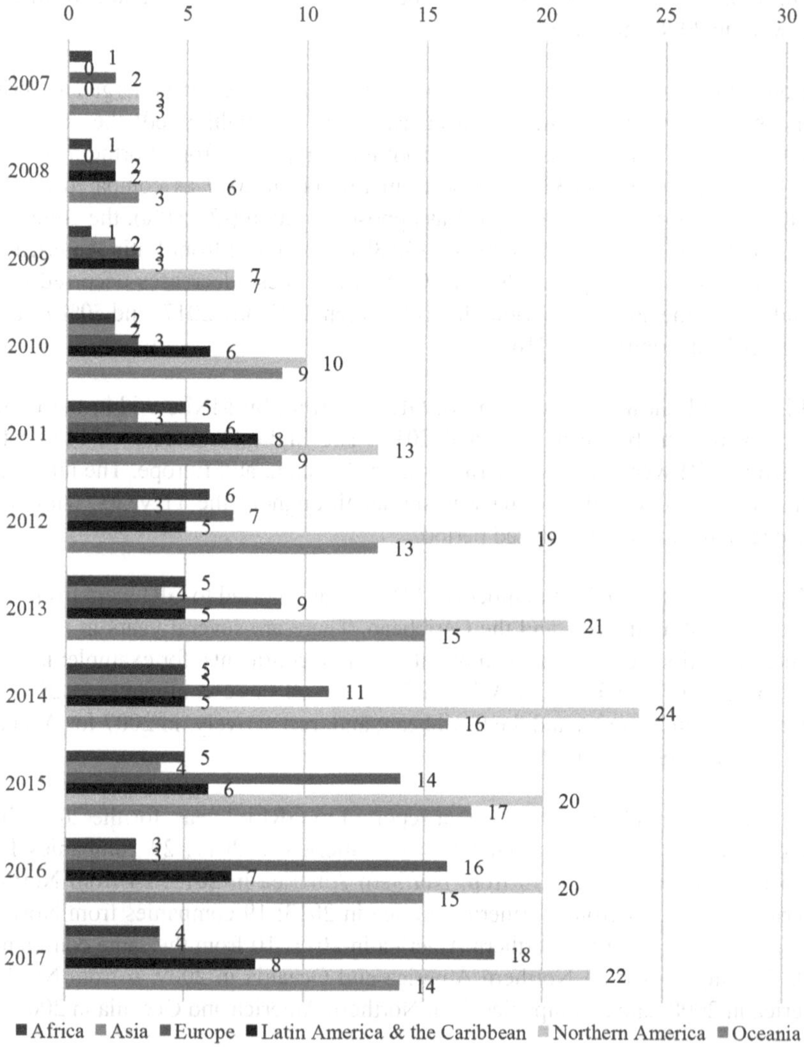

Figure 6.14. *GRI reporting evolution of MNEs from the mining sector by region, 2007–2017 (source: compiled by the authors based on data collected from GRI SDD)*

In terms of the highest increase in the number of GRI reporting MNEs from the same continent, there were cases such as: the companies from Africa in 2011 versus 2010 (150%); followed by the companies from Oceania in 2009 as compared to 2008 (133.33%); the companies from Europe in 2011 in contrast to 2010 (100%); those from Latin America and the Caribbean in 2010 against 2009 (100%); the companies from Northern America in 2008 as opposed to 2007 (100%); and those from Asia in 2011 versus 2010 (50%). These increases occurred in the first half of the analyzed period, and three out of the six increases were in 2011 in contrast to 2010.

With respect to the largest decrease in the number of GRI reporting MNEs from the same continent, the following cases can be highlighted: the companies from Africa in 2016 versus 2014 (-40%); the companies from Latin America and the Caribbean in 2012 against 2011 (-37.5%); those from Asia in 2016 as compared to 2015 (-25%); those from Northern America in 2015 in contrast to 2014 (-16.67%); and the companies from Oceania in 2016 as opposed to 2015 (-11.76%). The MNEs from Europe are not in this ranking because their number has grown throughout the analyzed period. The above-mentioned reductions were at the end of the first and second half of the 11 years, and approximately two-thirds of them took place in 2016 against 2015.

Figure 6.15 shows the evolution of GRI reporting by SMEs within the mining sector, by region, between 2007 and 2017. The highest numbers of MNEs that reported to GRI were from Asia, Latin America and the Caribbean, and Northern America. There are slight differences between all of these continents, each of them led the ranking in different years.

The smallest numbers of SMEs that reported to GRI were from Oceania, Europe and Africa. The latter two continents had similar numbers of companies, for example: between 2007 and 2010; in 2012; between 2013 and 2015; and in 2017. No SMEs from Oceania submitted reports to GRI throughout the 11 years.

The highest numbers of SMEs that reported to GRI, by year, for the 2007–2017 period were: four companies from Asia in 2017; four companies from Asia and Northern America in 2016; three from Northern America in 2015; five from Asia in 2014; four from the same continent in 2013; two companies from Asia, Latin America and the Caribbean, and Northern America in 2012; three from Latin America and the Caribbean in 2011; two from Asia and Latin America and the Caribbean in 2010; two from Asia in 2009; one company from Asia and Latin America and the Caribbean in 2008; and one from Latin America and the Caribbean in 2007.

Conversely, the lowest numbers of SMEs that reported to GRI, by year, were: none from the following continents: Latin America and the Caribbean, and Oceania in 2017; Europe, Latin America and the Caribbean, and Oceania in 2016; Africa, Europe, Latin America and the Caribbean, and Oceania in 2015; Africa, Asia, and Latin America and the Caribbean in 2014; Africa, Europe, and Oceania in 2013; Oceania in 2012; Europe and Oceania in 2011; Africa, Europe, and Oceania in 2010, Africa, Europe, Northern America, and Oceania in 2009; the same four continents in 2008; and Africa, Asia, Europe, Northern America, and Oceania in 2007.

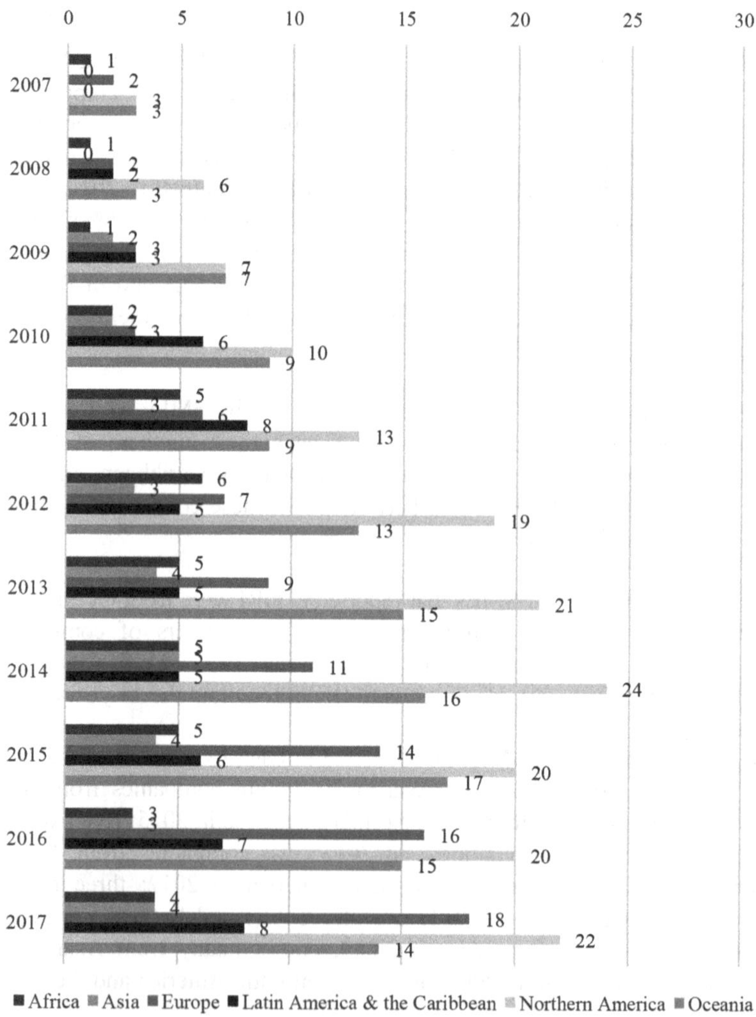

Figure 6.15. *GRI reporting evolution of SMEs from the mining sector by region, 2007–2017 (source: compiled by the authors based on data collected from GRI SDD)*

In terms of the highest increase in the number of GRI reporting SMEs from the same continent, there were cases in which the increase was 100%, such as: the companies from Africa in 2011 versus 2010, and, respectively, 2016 as opposed to 2015; the companies from Asia in 2009 against 2008, 2013 as compared to 2012, and 2016 against 2015, respectively; those from Europe in 2012 in contrast to 2011, and, respectively, 2017 versus 2016; those from Latin America and the Caribbean in 2010 against 2009; and the companies from Northern America in 2012 as opposed to 2011. These increases were scattered throughout the analyzed period and most of them were focused in the latter half of the period.

With respect to the largest decrease in the number of GRI reporting SMEs from the same continent, the following cases can be highlighted: the companies from Africa in 2013 as compared to 2012 (-100%); the companies from Europe in 2013 versus 2012 (-100%); those from Latin America and the Caribbean in 2015 against 2014 (-100%); those from Asia in 2015 as opposed to 2014 (-60%); and the companies from Northern America in 2014 in contrast to 2013 (-33.33%). These reductions occurred in the second half of the analyzed period. A third of the decreases took place in 2013 versus 2012, and another third appeared in 2015 as compared to 2014.

6.4.5. *Analysis of the GRI reporting enterprises from the automotive sector between 2007 and 2017*

Figure 6.16 shows the evolution of GRI reporting by large enterprises within the automotive sector, by region, between 2007 and 2017. The highest numbers of large companies that reported to GRI were from Asia, Europe, and Latin America and the Caribbean. More specifically, the highest numbers of large enterprises that reported to GRI were from Asia in 6 out of the 11 years and from Europe in the remaining 5 years.

On the contrary, the smallest numbers of large companies that reported to GRI were from Oceania, Africa and Northern America. The number of large enterprises from the first two continents had a similar evolution, with slight variations in 6 out of 11 years.

The highest numbers of large enterprises that reported to GRI, by year, for the 2007–2017 period were: 59 companies from Asia in 2017; 45 companies from the same continent in 2016; 35 from Europe in 2015; 32 from the same continent in 2014; 31 from Asia in 2013; 26 companies from Europe in 2012; 23 from Asia in 2011; 17 from the same continent in 2010; 13 from Europe in 2009; 10 companies from Asia in 2008; and 5 companies from Europe in 2007.

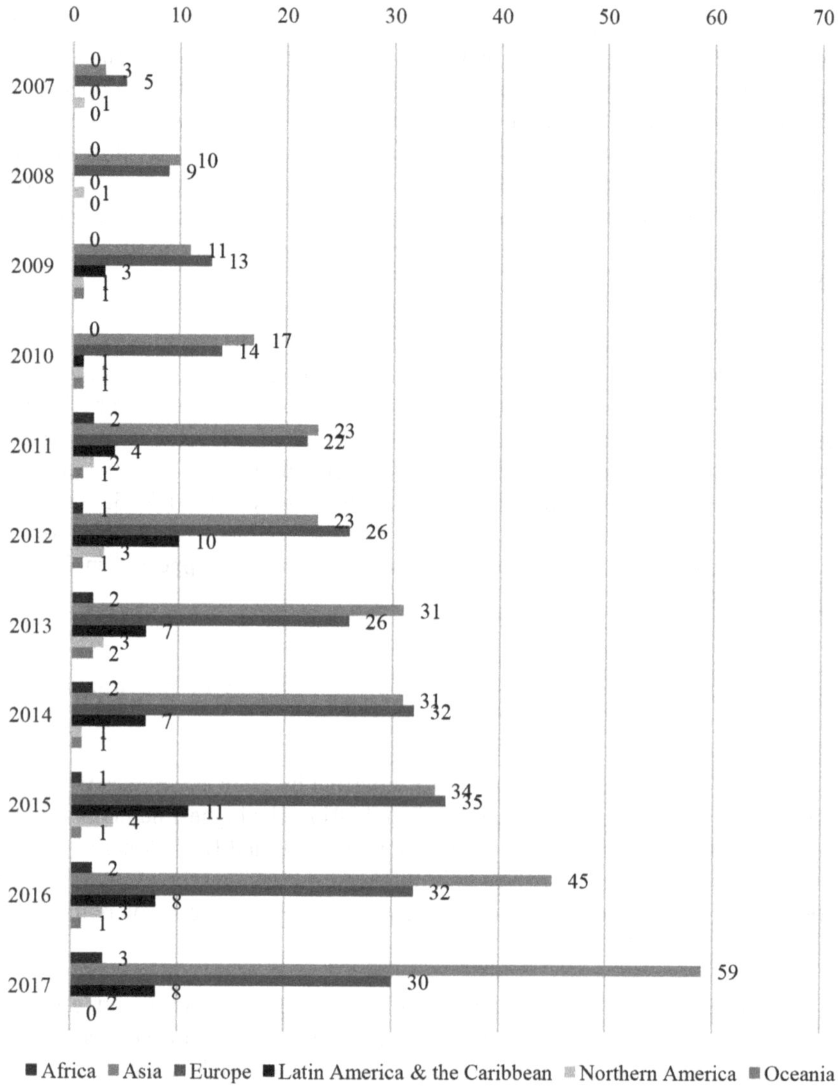

Figure 6.16. *GRI reporting evolution of large enterprises from the automotive sector by region, 2007–2017 (source: compiled by the authors based on data collected from GRI SDD)*

Conversely, the lowest numbers of large enterprises that reported to GRI, by year, for the same period were: none from Oceania in 2017; one company from the same continent in 2016; one from Africa and Oceania in 2015; one from Northern America and Oceania in 2014; two companies from Africa and Oceania in 2013; one from the same continents in 2012; one from Oceania in 2011; none from Africa in 2010; none from the same continent in 2009; none from Africa, Latin America and the Caribbean, and Oceania in 2008; and none from the same continents in 2007.

In terms of the highest increase in the number of GRI reporting large enterprises from the same continent, there were cases such as: the companies from Latin America and the Caribbean in 2011 versus 2010 (300%); the companies from Northern America in 2015 against 2014 (300%); those from Asia in 2008 as opposed to 2007 (233%); those from Africa in 2011 in contrast to 2010 (100%); the companies from Oceania in 2013 as compared to 2012 (100%); and the companies from Europe in 2008 in contrast to 2007 (80%). All of these increases took place throughout the analyzed period. One-third of them were in 2008 versus 2007 and another third were in 2011 in contrast to 2010.

In relation to the largest decrease in the number of GRI reporting large enterprises from the same continent, the following cases can be highlighted: the companies from Oceania in 2017 against 2016 (-100%); the companies from Latin America and the Caribbean in 2010 against 2009 (-66.67%); those from Northern America in 2014 versus 2013 (-66.67%); the companies from Africa in 2012 as opposed to 2011, and, respectively, 2015 versus 2014 (-50%); and the companies from Europe in 2016 as compared to 2015 (-8.57%). Companies from Asia are not part of this ranking because their number increased each year, across the entire analyzed period. All of these decreases were scattered throughout the 11 years and they are not correlated.

Figure 6.17 shows the evolution of GRI reporting by MNEs within the automotive sector, by region, between 2007 and 2017. The highest numbers of MNEs that reported to GRI were from Asia, Europe and Northern America. The number of MNEs from Asia exceeded the number of MNEs from Europe and Northern America, by far, in each of the 11 analyzed years.

The smallest numbers of MNEs that reported to GRI were from Oceania, Africa, and Latin America and the Caribbean. The number of MNEs from Oceania and Africa had an identical evolution in 6 out of the 11 years. By contrast, the evolution in the number of MNEs from Latin America and the Caribbean was independent of the first two continents.

The highest numbers of MNEs that reported to GRI, by year, for the 2007–2017 period were from Europe only: 27 companies in 2017; 26 in 2016; 23 in 2015; 22 in 2014; 19 companies in 2013; 15 in 2012; 12 companies in 2011; 7 in 2010; 7 in 2009; 5 companies in 2008; and 4 in 2007.

The lowest numbers of MNEs that reported to GRI, by year, were: none from Oceania between 2014 and 2017; one company from Africa and Oceania in 2013; two companies from the same continents in 2012; none from Oceania in 2011; and none from Africa and Oceania between 2007 and 2010.

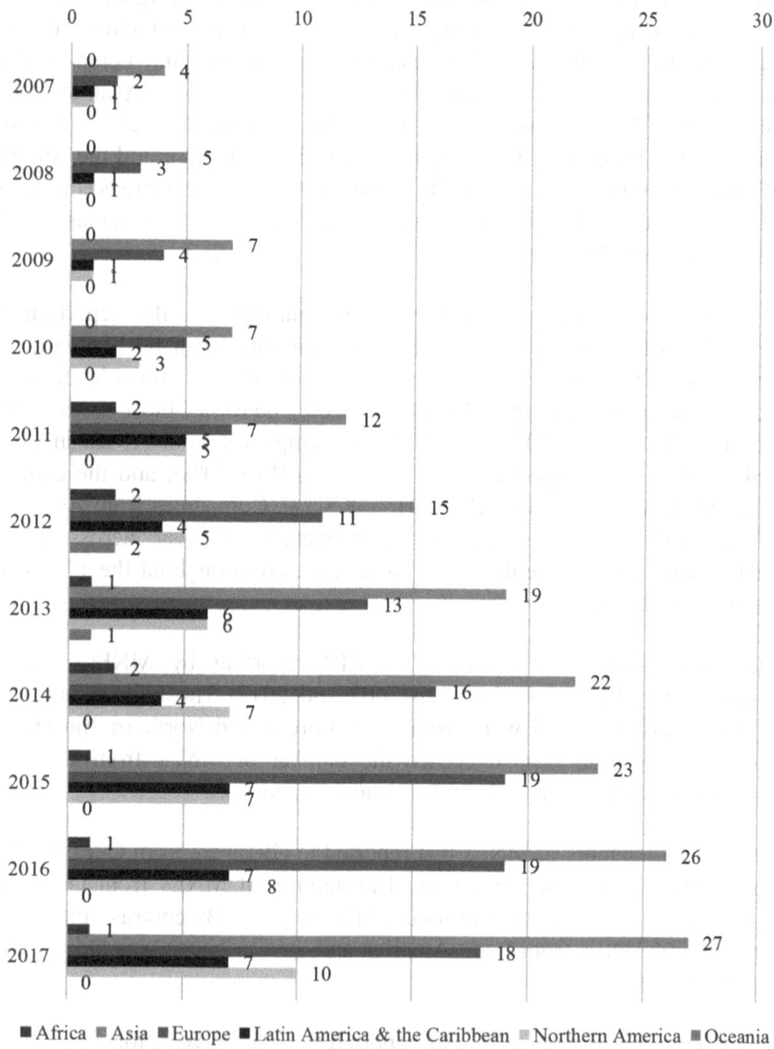

Figure 6.17. *GRI reporting evolution of MNEs from the automotive sector by region, 2007–2017 (source: compiled by the authors based on data collected from GRI SDD)*

In terms of the highest increase in the number of GRI reporting MNEs from the same continent, there were cases such as: the companies from Northern America in 2010 as opposed to 2009 (200%); followed by the companies from Latin America and the Caribbean in 2011 against 2010 (150%); those from Africa in 2011 versus 2010 (100%); those from Oceania in 2012 as compared to 2011 (100%); the companies from Asia in 2011 versus 2010 (71.43%); and those from Europe in 2012 in contrast to 2011 (57.14%). These increases occurred in the first half of the time period analyzed. Half of the six significant increases were in 2011 versus 2010, and one-third of them were in 2012 against 2011.

With respect to the largest decrease in the number of GRI reporting MNEs from the same continent, the following cases can be underlined: the companies from Oceania in 2014 as opposed to 2013 (-100%); those from Africa in 2013 versus 2012, and, respectively, 2015 as compared to 2014 (-50%); the companies from Latin America and the Caribbean in 2014 against 2013 (-33.33%); and the companies from Europe in 2017 in contrast to 2016 (-5.26%). The companies from Asia and Northern America are not part of this ranking as their number increased each year, throughout this period. These decreases began halfway through the 11 years and extended until the end of the period. Half of the decreases occurred in 2014 as compared to 2013.

Figure 6.18 shows the evolution of GRI reporting by SMEs within the automotive sector, by region, between 2007 and 2017. The highest numbers of MNEs that reported to GRI were from Europe, Latin America and the Caribbean, and Asia. Few companies from these three continents submitted reports to GRI and they only began reporting in 2012.

The smallest numbers of SMEs that reported to GRI were from Africa, Oceania, and Northern America. No SMEs from Africa submitted reports to GRI throughout the analyzed period and the number of companies from Northern America is lower than corresponding companies from Asia, by year.

The highest numbers of SMEs that reported to GRI, by year, for the 2007–2017 period were: two companies from Latin America and the Caribbean in 2017; one from Asia, Europe, and Northern America in 2016; seven companies from Asia in 2015; three from Europe in 2014; one company from Europe and Latin America and the Caribbean in 2012; and one company from Oceania in 2011. The ranking does not contain data about the year 2013 as no reporting took place. Furthermore, the ranking is limited to 2011 onwards, since no companies reported between 2007 and 2010.

The lowest numbers of SMEs that reported to GRI, by year, were: none from the following continents: Africa and Oceania in 2017; Africa, Latin America and the Caribbean, and Oceania in 2016 and 2015; Africa, Asia, and Oceania in 2014; all six continents in 2013; Africa, Asia, Northern America, and Oceania in 2012; Africa, Asia, Europe, Latin America and the Caribbean, and Oceania in 2011; and all six continents between 2007 and 2010.

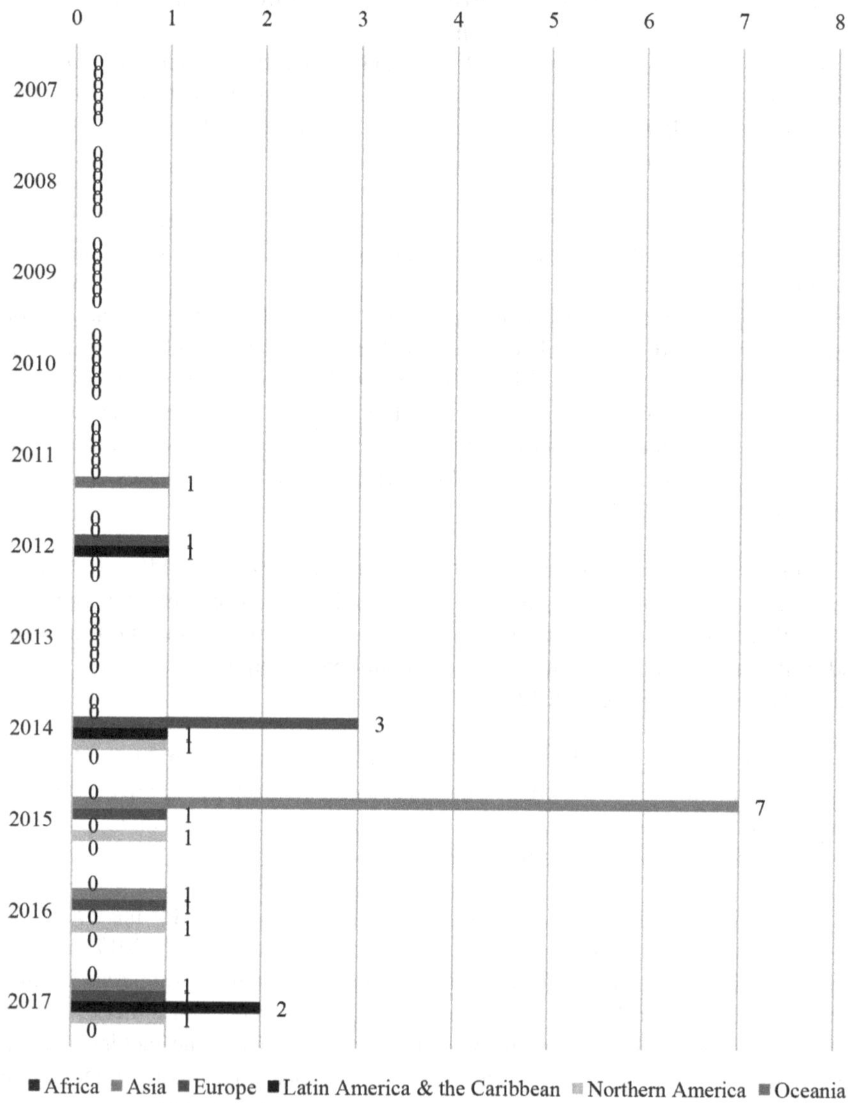

Figure 6.18. *GRI reporting evolution of SMEs from the automotive sector by region, 2007–2017 (source: compiled by the authors based on data collected from GRI SDD)*

With refence to the highest increase in the number of GRI reporting SMEs from the same continent, there were cases such as: the companies from Asia in 2015 against 2014 (700%); the companies from Europe in 2014 in contrast to 2013 (300%); those from Latin America and the Caribbean in 2017 as compared to 2016 (200%); those from Northern America in 2014 as opposed to 2013 (100%); and the companies from Oceania in 2011 versus 2010 (100%). These increases were scattered in the second half of the analyzed period and approximately 40% are in 2014 versus 2013.

Concerning the largest decrease in the number of GRI reporting SMEs from the same continent, the following cases can be highlighted: the companies from Europe in 2013 versus 2012 (-100%); the companies from Latin America and the Caribbean in 2013 against 2012 (-100%); those from Oceania in 2012 as compared to 2011 (-100%); and those from Asia in 2016 as opposed to 2015 (-85.71%). This ranking does not include the companies from Africa as they did not submit reports; nor does it include the companies from Northern America since their number was constant between 2014 (first year of reporting) and 2017. These reductions occurred in the latter half of the 11-year period and 50% are in 2013 in contrast to 2012.

6.5. Conclusion

The problem of CSR in general, and CSR reporting, presents a lot of variables and interpretations that one researcher may choose to study. CSR is an evolving concept with interest for management and policy makers. CSR reporting, in particular, has come a long way and provides a lot of opportunities for reporting standards and report submission.

The quantitative analysis of policy instruments revealed that the number of those instruments has followed an upward trend and, in the few last years, a balance between mandatory and voluntary instruments has become within reach, after a decade of mandatory policy proliferation. Governments are the main issuer of policy instruments followed by financial markets and stock exchanges; as a result, the main type of policy instruments are public law and regulations. Most policy instruments target all companies and a significant share targets large and listed companies. Most of these instruments incorporate more than one ESG component.

Overall, throughout this period of time, the energy sector had the highest number of GRI reporting companies, irrespective of the type of enterprise, that is 3,026 non-unique companies. This value is 2.86 times higher than that of the metal products and automotive sectors and it is, respectively, 1.77 and 1.74 higher than that of the mining and chemicals sectors.

Taking company type into account in the case of large enterprises, the energy sector also had the highest number of GRI reporting companies, that is 2,226 non-unique companies, 3.51 times higher than the automotive sector, 3.13 times higher than the metal products sector, 2.39 times higher than the chemicals sector, and 1.95 times higher than the mining sector. In terms of MNEs, the chemicals sector had the highest number of GRI reporting companies, that is 730 non-unique companies. This value is 2.46 times higher than the metal products sector, 1.84 times higher than the automotive sector, 1.46 times higher than the mining sector, and 1.24 times higher than the energy sector. Concerning the SMEs, the energy sector had the highest number of GRI reporting companies with 215 non-unique companies, 8.6 times higher than the automotive sector, 4.3 times higher than the metal products sector, 3.16 times higher than the mining sector, and 2.68 times higher than the chemicals sector.

With respect to the sector that had the highest number of GRI reporting companies by region, the data were as follows: in the case of Africa, the mining sector had the highest number of GRI reporting companies, that is 334 non-unique companies, 14.52 times higher than the automotive sector, 8.5 times higher than the metal products sector, 8.35 times higher than the chemicals sector, and 7.42 times higher than the energy sector. In Asia, the energy sector had the highest number of GRI reporting companies, that is 926 non-unique companies, 2.89 times higher than the mining sector, 2.04 times higher than the metal products sector, 2 times higher than the automotive sector, and 1.06 times higher than the chemicals sector.

In Europe, the same energy sector had the highest number of GRI reporting companies, that is 1030 non-unique companies. This number of enterprises is 4.12 times higher than the mining sector, 2.79 times higher than the automotive sector, 2.61 times higher than the metal products sector, and 2.44 times higher than the chemicals sector. For Latin America and the Caribbean, the same energy sector had the highest number of GRI reporting companies with 549 non-unique companies, 6.53 times higher than the metal products sector, 5.08 times higher than the automotive sector, 3.47 times higher than the chemicals sector, and 1.67 times higher than the mining sector.

In Northern America, the energy sector had the highest number of GRI reporting companies, that is 371 non-unique companies. This value is 6.87 times higher than the metal products sector, 4.63 times higher than the automotive sector, 1.61 times higher than the chemicals sector, and 1.29 times higher than the mining sector. As for Oceania, the mining sector had the highest number of GRI reporting companies with 189 non-unique companies, 14.53 times higher than the automotive sector, 9 times higher than the chemicals sector, 5.9 times higher than the metal products sector, and 1.8 times higher than the energy sector.

6.6. References

[ACK 76] ACKERMAN R.W., BAUER R.A., *Corporate Social Responsiveness*. Reston Publishing, Reston, 1976.

[AND 14] ANDREI J.V., PANAIT M., VOICA C., "Implication of the CSR and cultural model features in Romanian energy sector", *Industry/Industrija*, vol. 42, no. 4, pp. 115–131, 2014.

[AND 18] ANDREI J.V., PANAIT M., VOICA M., "Challenges and approaches for the corporate social responsibility and human resource management in the financial sector", *Economics, Management and Financial Markets*, vol. 13, no. 3, pp. 415–431, 2018.

[BER 00] BERNSTEIN A., "Too much corporate power", *Business Week*, September 11, 2000.

[BOW 53] BOWEN H., *Social Responsibilities of the Businessman*, Harper, New York, 1953.

[BRE 18] BREZOI A.G., "Ethics and corporate social responsibility in the current geopolitical context", *Economic Insights – Trends and Challenges*, vol. 7, pp. 45–52, 2018.

[BUR 99] BURTON B.K., HEGARTY W.H., "Some determinants of student corporate social responsibility orientation", *Business and Society*, vol. 38, no. 2, pp. 188–205, 1999.

[CAR 79] CARROLL A.B., "A three-dimensional conceptual model of corporate performance", *Academy of Management Review*, vol. 4, no. 4, pp. 498—505, 1979.

[CAR 91] CARROLL A.B., "The pyramid of corporate social responsibility: Toward the moral management of organizational stakeholders", *Business Horizons*, pp. 39–48, 1991.

[CAR 09] CARROLL A.B., BUCHHOLTZ A.K., *Business and Society: Ethics and Stakeholder Management*, 7th edition, South-Western Cengage Learning, Mason, 2009.

[CAR 10] CARROLL A.B., SHABANA K.M., "The business case for corporate social responsibility: A review of concepts, research and practice", *International Journal of Management Reviews*, vol. 12, pp. 85–105, 2010.

[CAR 18] CARROLL A.B., BROWN J.A., "Corporate social responsibility: A review of current concepts, research and issues", in WEBER J., WASLELESKI D. (eds), *Corporate Social Responsibility*, Emerald Publishing, Bingley, 2018.

[CIU 05] CIUTACU C., CHIVU L., PREDA D., "The social responsibility of the company – A challenge for the contemporary world", *The Romanian Economics Magazine*, vol. 20, no. 1, p. 79, 2005.

[CLA 95] CLARKSON M.B.E., "A stakeholder framework for analyzing and evaluating corporate social performance", *Academy of Management Review*, vol. 20, no. 1, pp. 92–117, 1995.

[DAV 73] DAVIS K., "The case for and against business assumption of social responsibility", *Academy of Management Journal*, vol. 16, p. 2, 1973.

[DEI 16] DEIGH L., FARQUHAR J., PALAZZO M. *et al.*, "Corporate social responsibility: Engaging the community", *Qualitative Market Research*, vol. 19, no. 2, pp. 225–240, 2016.

[EHS 18] EHSAN S., NAZIR M.S., NURUNNABI M. *et al.*, "A multimethod approach to assess and measure corporate social responsibility disclosure and practices in a developing economy", *Sustainability*, vol. 10, no. 8, p. 2955, 2018.

[ENE 17] ENE C., PANAIT M., "The financial education – Part of corporate social responsibility for employees and customers", *Romanian Journal of Economics*, vol. 44.1, pp. 145–154, 2017.

[FRE 78] FREDERICK W.C., From CSR1 to CSR2: The maturing of business-and-society thought, Working paper No. 279, University of Pittsburgh, Graduate School of Business, 1978.

[FRI 70] FRIEDMAN M., "The social responsibility of business is to increase its profits", *New York Times Magazine*, p. 126, September 13, 1970.

[GRI 20] GRI-SDD, Global Reporting Initiative: Sustainability Disclosure Database, available at: https://database.globalreporting.org/, 2020.

[HAY 69] HAYEK F.A., "The corporation in a democratic society: In whose interest ought it and will it be run?", in ANSOFF H. (ed.), *Business Strategy*, Penguin Books, Harmondsworth, 1969.

[IBR 93] IBRAHIM N.A., ANGELIDIS J.A., "Corporate social responsibility: A comparative analysis of perceptions of top executives and business students", *The Mid-Atlantic Journal of Business*, vol. 29, no. 3, pp. 303–314, 1993.

[IBR 95] IBRAHIM N.A., ANGELIDIS J.A., "The corporate social responsiveness orientation of board members: Are there differences between inside and outside directors?", *Journal of Business Ethics*, vol. 14, pp. 405–410, 1995.

[LEV 58] LEVITT T., "The dangers of social responsibility", *Harvard Business Review*, September/October, pp. 41–50, 1958.

[KOO 03] KOOIMAN J., *Governing As Governance*, Sage, London, 2003.

[KRA 19] KRAWCZYK P., "CSR reporting standards: Implementation in Polish enterprises", *Journal of Eastern Europe Research in Business and Economics*, vol. 2019, pp. 1–9, 2019.

[MAL 93] MALLOTT M.J., Operationalizing corporate social performance: Managerial perceptions of principles, processes and outcomes, Unpublished doctoral dissertation, University of Pittsburgh, 1993.

[MAT 13a] MATEI M., *Responsabilitatea socială a corporaţiilor şi instituţiilor şi dezvoltarea durabilă a României*, Expert Publishing House, Bucharest, 2013.

[MAT 13b] MATEI M., VOICA M.C., "Social responsibility in the financial and banking sector", *Economic Insights: Trends and Challenges*, vol. 65, no. 1, pp. 115–123, 2013.

[MOO 02] MOON J., "The social responsibility of business and new governance", *Government and Opposition*, vol. 37, no. 3, pp. 385–408, 2002.

[ONE 89] O'NEILL H.M., SAUNDERS C.B., MCCARTHY A.D., "Board members, corporate social responsiveness and profitability: Are tradeoffs necessary?" *Journal of Business Ethics*, vol. 8, pp. 353–357, 1989.

[PAN 14] PANAIT M., VOICA M.C., RADULESCU I., "The activity of capital market actors: Under the sign of social responsibility", *Procedia Economics and Finance*, vol. 8, pp. 522–528, 2014.

[PAN 15] PANAIT M., PETRESCU M.G., "Quality management and social responsibility in the context of sustainable development", *Industrija*, vol. 43, no. 4, pp. 175–189, 2015.

[PIE 00] PIERRE J. *Debating Governance: Authority, Steering and Democracy*, Oxford University Press, Oxford, 2000.

[PIN 96] PINKSTON T.S., CARROLL A.B., "A retrospective examination of CSR orientations: Have they changed?", *Journal of Business Ethics*, vol. 15, pp. 199–206, 1996.

[RHO 97] RHODES R.A.W., *Understanding Governance: Policy Networks, Governance, Reflexivity and Accountability*, Open University Press, Buckingham and Philadelphia, 1997.

[SCH 03] SCHWARTZ M.S., CARROLL A.B., "Corporate social responsibility: A three-domain approach", *Business Ethics Quarterly*, vol. 13, no. 4, pp. 503–530, 2003.

[SMI 01] SMITH W.J., WOKUTCH R.E., HARRINGTON K.V. *et al.*, "An examination of the influence of diversity and stakeholder role on corporate social orientation", *Business and Society*, vol. 40, no. 3, pp. 266–294, 2001.

[STE 10] STEURER R., "The role of governments in corporate social responsibility: Characterising public policies on CSR in Europe", *Policy Sciences*, vol. 43, pp. 49–72, 2010.

[SWA 95] SWANSON D.L., "Addressing a theoretical problem by reorienting the corporate social performance model", *Academy of Management Review*, vol. 20, no. 1, pp. 43–64, 1995.

[SWA 99] SWANSON D.L., "Toward an integrative theory of business and society: A research strategy for corporate social performance", *Academy of Management Review*, vol. 24, no. 3, pp. 521–596, 1999.

[VOL 11] VOLLERO A., SIANO A., PALAZZO M. *et al.*, "Corporate communication and CSR: Comparing Italian and Dutch energy companies on anti-greenwashing strategies", *Proceedings from the 1st International CSR Communication Conference*, 2011.

[WAR 85] WARTICK S.L., COCHRAN P.L., "The evolution of the corporate social performance model", *Academy of Management Review*, vol. 10, pp. 765–766, 1985.

[WOO 91] WOOD D.J., "Corporate social performance revisited", *Academy of Management Review*, October, pp. 691–718, 1991.

[ZAM 20] ZAMAN G., PANAIT M.C., VOICA M.C. *et al.*, "Corporate social responsibility in the agri-food sector: Recent advancements in sustainable entrepreneurship and corporate social responsibility", *IGI Global*, pp. 37–68, 2020.

7

Integrated Management Systems Under the Banner of Sustainable Development: Risks and Opportunities

This chapter focuses on the importance of integrated management systems used by different organizations in order to improve their performances in a dynamic environment with many challenges and opportunities. The authors analyzed the importance of integrated management systems for sustainable development.

7.1. Introduction

7.1.1. *Organizations and sustainable development*

Currently, organizations operate in a complex environment, full of challenges, but also expectations from stakeholders. Operating in a knowledge economy, in which performance evaluation is based on the degree of implementation of new concepts – the promotion of innovation, environmental protection and corporate social responsibility (CSR) – we can note the redefinition of management systems that companies implement. Moreover, economic, social and political instability generate multiple risks that must be identified and managed by organizations. However, there is always the possibility of a black swan [TAL 07, AVE 15]. Permanently, organizations must face challenges, adapt to crisis situations, find solutions and restore the balance between their own interests and those of stakeholders. Currently, consumers, portfolio investors and suppliers are forces that reshapes the activity of companies.

Chapter written by Marius Gabriel PETRESCU, Mirela PANAIT and Hailong FU.

Nowadays, the economy is subordinated to a knowledge society that integrates and promotes the objectives of sustainable development, based on reducing poverty and increasing quality of life, equal opportunities, environmental protection, freedom, improving education and developing innovation, restructuring industry and the business environment. Humanity is in a new stage of civilization, which allows wide access to information, accountability of consumers and companies to the environment and to society, a new way of working and knowledge, amplifying the possibility of economic globalization and increasing social cohesion [NAE 09, CIA 17, MAC 17].

The Sustainable Development Goals (SDGs) adopted in 2015 by the United Nations have led to reactions from organizations that have adapted their work to promote the principles of sustainable development. Thus, all entities try to contribute to achieving these objectives. From this perspective, the main features of the world economy, in terms of the activity of an organization, can be detected:

1) the increasing capacity of the Information and Communication Technology (ICT) sector for the research-development-innovation (R-D-I) activities in order to support the knowledge-based society and economy. Organizations are aware of the importance of fostering innovation in order to build resilient infrastructure and to promote inclusive and sustainable development [IVA 07, CON 14, CAT 16, IAC 17, ALF 19] The current COVID-19 health crisis has demonstrated the importance of digitalizing national economies in the situation of a need for social distance;

2) the increasing technological competence and promotion of the transfer of knowledge and technologies, especially in the field of energy, taking safety into account and respecting the principle of sustainable development. Renewable energy is an alternative to classical energy that not only provides access to affordable, reliable, sustainable and modern energy, especially for populations in developing countries, but also solves problems such as energy poverty that affects certain categories of vulnerable consumers, with consequences on quality of life and environmental pollution [DUS 14, MAC 14, POP 18, NEA 20]. The use of agricultural crops for the production of biofuels has generated discussions about providing food for the population, especially in developing countries. Usually, however, for such crops, less fertile lands are used, which are not used for the production of foodstuffs intended for human consumption [ENE 17];

3) the creation of clean or green products, processes and technologies and the waste recovery and promotion of a circular economy [HYS 20] are imposed by the necessity of promoting sustainable development. According to SDG12 (Responsible Consumption and Production), the population and organizations are encouraged to promote responsible consumption and production [PLA 06, BOC 16, SIM 14, GUR 17, FRO 17];

4) the scientific substantiation and development of technologies for the conservation, reconstruction and consolidation of biological diversity. The United Nations has set distinct goals that consider SDG14 (Life Below Water) and SDG15 (Life On Land) to protect both terrestrial and marine biodiversity given the impact of these biodiversities on reducing pollution and securing resources for productive activity. The importance of marine resources is also demonstrated by the emergence of the blue economy concept, which aims at the sustainable use of these resources and which have a major impact on economic development through various mechanisms such as maritime transport, fisheries, maritime renewable energy and tourism [FRO 17];

5) developing knowledge in the field of spatial planning in a sustainable manner. In order to reduce the impact of human activity on the environment, not only companies must adopt the principle of sustainable development but so must local communities, which is why the concept of inclusive, safe, resilient and sustainable cities is promoted. Close collaboration is needed between companies, public authorities, universities and civil society, so that cities can cope with the particularly complex urban problems they face. In addition to SDG11 (Sustainable Cities and Communities), the Global Compact program was launched by the United Nations for cities, involving a translation of CSR principles from companies to cities [MAT 13, ALL 18, VIS 20];

6) development of biotechnologies with impact on quality of life and economic development. Researchers have become increasingly aware of the positive impact that biotechnologies can have on sustainable development, through the specific targets of food production, renewable materials, waste prevention and bioremediation [ZEC 99, NAS 03].

In the current context, we note the increasing complexity of phenomena and the intensification of interdependencies between economic processes. Therefore, it is increasingly necessity to redefine the managerial profession from "managing resources and human labor" to "managing the application of knowledge". Efficient management of knowledge application can be the tool with which management turns constraints into opportunities (Figure 7.1). At this moment, maximizing the results of the economic activity of the organization is inextricably linked to the scientific research activity and the promotion of sustainable development principles. The effect is appreciated by the market success of the results: new products or new technologies for making products [PET 19].

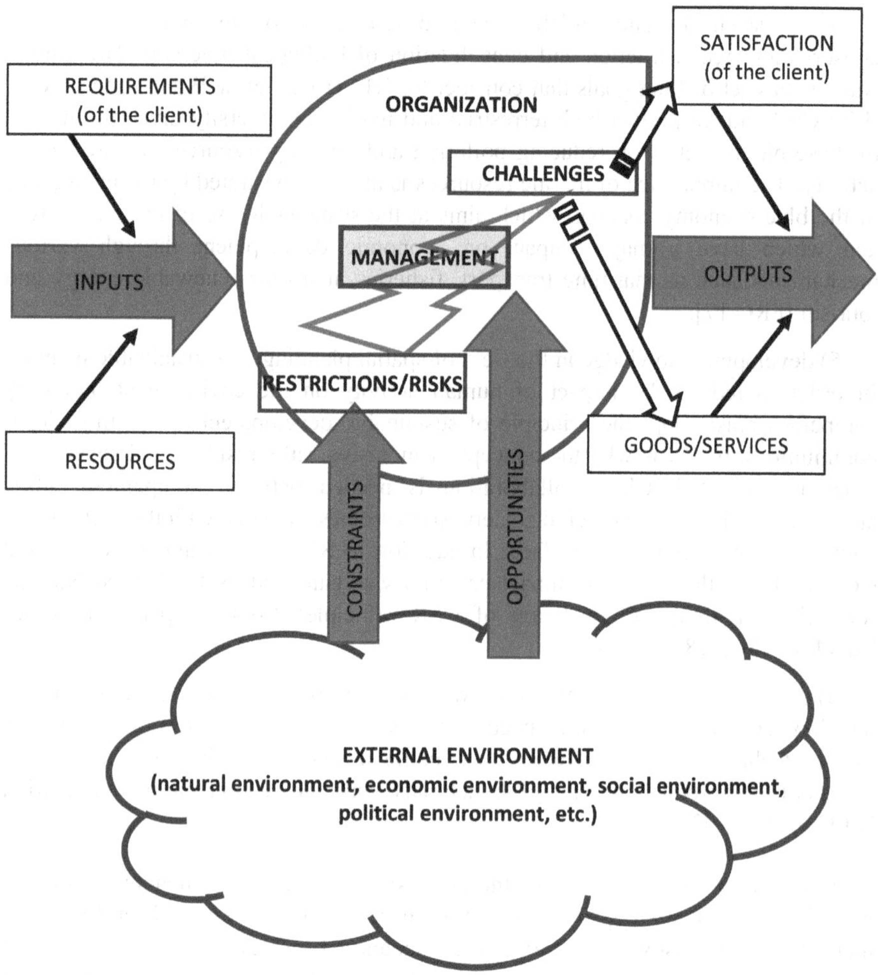

Figure 7.1. *The place and role of management in the current situation. For a color version of this figure, see www.iste.co.uk/machado/sustainable.zip*

There are factors [PET 19] with significant importance on the activity of the organization and influence the formulation and achievement of objectives (Figure 7.1):

– technological factors such as scientific discoveries and inventions, technical progress and changes in the manufacturing processes of products;

– economic factors;

- financial perspectives. The liberalization of capital movements, the integration of national financial markets and the emergence of new products have generated access to financial resources on the international market for more and more companies, thus increasing the interconnections between national economies and the spread of negative effects of financial crises, in the world economy [MAT 13],

- the evolution trend of the lifecycle of products (the consumer society generated a drastic decrease of the lifecycle of all products, but major changes can be observed with the public's growing awareness of the conservation of resources, pollution, etc.). Currently, the lifecycle is differentiated by product classes and, in areas such as, for example, ICT, it continues to be particularly short; this is also the case in the automotive industry, a fact generated by the existence of anti-pollution laws and efforts to reduce specific fuel consumption and environmental impact,

- the future evolution of the markets in terms of demand variation, in terms of quality (structure of demand) and quantity (market size), trends in consumer demand but also in terms of a competitive environment; another determining element of the markets is the speed with which a new demand is answered, a speed that is constantly increasing;

– ecological factors;

- the growing influence of environmental movements, the promotion of the principles of sustainable development as a concern not only of international organizations but also of companies, and environmental conservation efforts being increasingly supported by final consumers and portfolio investors, with effects on the demand of different products or types of services,

- the existence of international cooperation agreements and protocols regarding the use of raw materials, cross-border pollution, etc.;

– cultural, social and political factors, such as the general orientation of the organization, its specific "culture"; the communication and information circulation system within the organization; the level and evolution of the consumer education system that favors social inclusion [ZAM 11, BĂL 15].

The objectives set by the management of the organization must be established according to the economic, social and political context, be realistic and measurable and cover the problems in the short and medium term. When setting the objectives, all the technological options of the organization, corroborated with the available techniques, are taken into account (analyzed from the point of view of cost efficiency and reasoning related to the achievement) and the risks that may affect the activity of the organization. The introduction of an integrated management system is the best opportunity to improve the performance of the organization because there is always a basis for analysis and evaluation [MUZ 19].

7.1.2. *Integrated management systems in the context of sustainable development*

The companies' preoccupations are not strictly limited to production activity and the maximization of the profit for the shareholders. The way in which companies are organized and operated has changed considerably in recent decades by intensifying their concerns about quality, environmental protection, employee health, risks and social responsibility. Management systems have emerged for these segments, through which companies try to face the challenges generated by operating in a particularly complex environment, determined by globalization but also by the intensification of economic, social and political uncertainties.

The ability to face challenges, to resist competition and to develop activity are determined by the implementation of a management system (a quality management system or an integrated management system) that works and that allows the adaptation of activities to the new requirements imposed by sustainable development.

The concept of an "integrated management system" (IMS) refers to the integration of the applicable management system standards in a single documentation [GRY 01], based on which the effective control of the processes within the organization is ensured, in the sense of establishing policies, objectives and the obligations of the organization, in accordance with legal and other applicable requirements [DAR 14].

The emergence of the concept of integration of management systems was generated by the existence of several management systems within the same organization, the presence of several categories of stakeholders with different expectations of the organization, the intensification of mergers and acquisitions as a result of liberalization of capital movements on international markets, but also of the need to consolidate companies by taking over some local enterprises, mainly during crises.

The integration of existing management systems at the level of an organization for quality management, environmental management and occupational health and safety is necessary for improving internal communication, reducing costs [NUN 16] and increasing the efficiency of the activity through reducing "time, bureaucracy" and a better use of "human, technical and financial resources" [ALG 19]. In addition, the activity of an organization is tracked by multiple categories of stakeholders and the solution for their satisfaction is the implementation of management systems through which risks are identified, managed and controlled. Given that the implementation of management systems was generated by the need to improve the company's performance in areas such as health and safety at work, quality or environment [BER 09], the existence of several management systems can lead to the duplication of certain operations, with negative consequences on costs and, implicitly, on the profitability of companies, all reasons for requiring their integration.

The takeovers of companies, made at national and international level, in areas such as the oil and gas industry, the chemical industry or the banking sector, have generated the need to re-assess management systems in newly created entities [HOL 03]. This is due to the existence of numerous procedures that are duplicated, the conflicts that exist between quality management procedures, process safety, risk and environment, safety, health management and the existence of mixed formal and informal systems or semi-formal systems that are not sufficiently documented.

Therefore, specialists have agreed on the importance and benefits of applying an integrated management system. Thus, in a study conducted in Romania, for the northwestern region of the country, the advantages of an integrated management system were identified [MAI 17], such as reducing costs related to system maintenance, cutting time allocated to management systems, better focus on business objectives, increasing innovation capacity, reducing responsibilities conflicts, increasing business profitability, better communication between departments and managers and better balancing between the conflicting objectives of facilitating training and human resource development.

We can see that common ground is needed for all applicable requirements and standards like quality, environment, health and occupational safety, to which can be added those related to information security, food safety and CSR [ROS 09]. Consequently, the management of the organization adopts an integrative vision for: the analyses performed by the management; addressing policy and objectives; internal audits; management system documentation (manuals, procedures and other common documents); addressing the improvement mechanisms (corrective, preventive actions, continuous improvement measures); the approach to risk planning and management.

The idea of integrating management systems has developed relatively recently. The process of integrating management systems is approached differently by specialists, which involves a combination of resources used to achieve a complex goal, loss of unique identities of individual management systems, common practices and harmonization of departmental activity, the goal being to increase organizational efficiency and improve stakeholders' satisfaction [KAR 98].

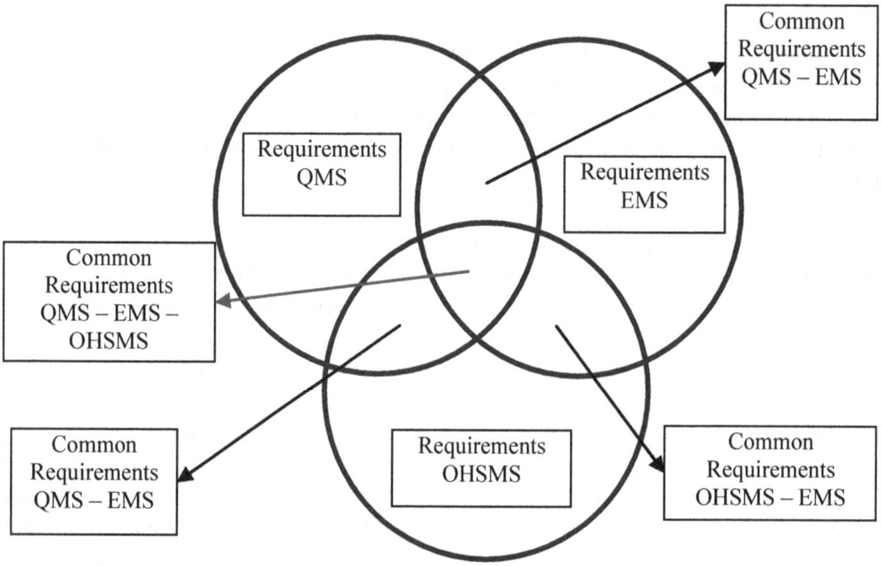

Figure 7.2. *Integrated management systems: QMS – quality management system; EMS – environmental management system; OHSMS – occupational health and safety management system*

As in other fields, the literature retains several definitions relevant to this concept, such as:

– [GRI 99] defined the integrated management system as "the organizational structure, resources and procedures used to plan, monitor and control the quality, environment and security of a project";

– [GAR 91] defined integration as the "degree of alignment or harmony in an organization – whether different departments and levels speak the same language and are tuned to the same wavelength";

– [BEC 03] consider integration as "a process of putting together different function-specific management systems into a single and more effective IMS";

– [KAR 03] says that an integrated management system can be defined as a "set of interconnected processes that share a pool of human, information, material, infrastructure, and financial resources in order to achieve a composite of goals related to the satisfaction of a variety of stakeholders";

– [POJ 06] says that an integrated system "is one that combines management systems using an employee focus, a process view, and a systems approach, that makes it possible to put all relevant management standard practices into a single system";

– [BER 09] say that “integration is a process of linking different standardized MSs into a single MS with common resources aiming to improve stakeholders’ satisfaction”.

The Integrated Management System (IMS) is a complex management system that is built by combining the requirements corresponding to each system adopted, according to a model like the one shown in Figure 7.2 (most often integrated management systems are formed by co-opting the three management systems: QMS – quality management system; EMS – environmental management system; OHSMS – occupational health and safety management system).

The 2009 edition of ISO 9004 has a new approach to organization management in the form of: “leading an organization to sustained success – an approach through quality management”. This standard introduced a new concept, that of “sustained success”, defined as “[meeting] the needs and expectations of its customers and other interested parties, over the long term and in a balanced way”. This concept can assimilate with sustainable development and corporate sustainability. ISO 9004 defines “sustained success” as the result of an organization’s ability to meet and maintain long-term goals, regardless of the standards used as a reference in the IMS.

The complexity of the aspects specific to current management – as previously presented – is an additional argument in favor of the development of integrated management systems that have the capacity of systemic monitoring of the organization in correspondence with changes in the environment it operates in. The association of the two notions – success and, respectively, sustainability – is not only a form of marketing but, moreover, attracts the obligation of the organization to design strategies capable of guaranteeing the right of future generations to develop.

In addition, since the establishment of the Sustainable Development Goals by the United Nations, ISO has become very involved in promoting them, given that the standards developed have a significant impact on the three pillars of sustainable development [ISO 18a]:

– economic sustainability is supported by ISO standards by promoting sustainable business practices that dramatically reduce costs, risks, fraud and facilitate business transactions;

– social sustainability is ensured by ISO standards through the development of local communities, the promotion of social inclusion, the health and well-being of citizens;

– environmental sustainability is ensured by adopting the ISO environmental standard through which organizations try to reduce their impact by reducing greenhouse gas emissions and by promoting responsible production and consumption.

Therefore, the integration of management systems can be achieved in two architectural variants: (1) full integration, in which the targeted systems lose their identity and (2) partial integration, which is limited to aligning the objectives, processes and resources of the management systems taken into consideration. There are also different approaches to integrating management systems. Most organizations proceed to the sequential integration of management systems, in the sense that a management system is applied for legal reasons, usually the quality management system, after which other systems are integrated. A less used method is the simultaneous application and integration of several management systems and the creation of an integrated management system [MOH 06]. The sole objective of all implemented management systems, regardless of the method chosen in an organization, must be "sustained success", thus ensuring the coherence of management actions.

7.2. Evolution of approaches for management systems

7.2.1. *Quality and quality management system*

The intensification of competition between companies, both nationally and internationally, has generated the need to reflect on ways to stay in the market, to improve their position and to develop their business, including by strengthening partnership relations.

At the beginning of the emergence of human communities and the diversification of human relationships, the appreciation of quality was done through the senses, and the criteria for assessing it were subjective, in the sense that they were generated by the needs of the direct user. The first concerns were for well-done things, and the achievements of the ancient world are dominated by the involvement of people for quality assurance [CHA 09]. Subsequently, the industrial revolution generated the intensification of the engineers' preoccupations with increased production and quality of the products, registered in notorious initiatives on a technical level but also on managerial habits, both in Europe and in the USA.

The emergence and development of production processes generated by the industrial revolution brought to the attention of organizations concrete concerns for ensuring the quality of products, which were based on scientific approaches. The results being improved production and increased quality of goods created. Thus, the literature retains the initiative of Frederich Winslow Taylor (1856–1915), in US industrial organizations, to detect defects by inspection, which aimed to increase the efficiency of the organization by scientific design of the tasks of all employees and by separating the planning function from the function of products execution [GIA 11, RAH 12].

Henry L. Gantt aimed to improve the systems developed within organizations by innovating task planning, introducing a specific chart (now recognized in both academia and business as the GANTT chart and frequently used under a software program called Microsoft Project). This chart summarizes the information on the activities planned and carried out but also the responsibilities of the people who carry out these activities.

Another important step in crystallizing the concept of quality control is that made by Ford Motor Co., which introduced conveyor-type assembly lines and conveyor-type transport lines, mechanized production flows, placed machines and equipment in a certain way to allow conveyor-type manufacturing and the use of standardized automobile components. In addition, the company performed the final inspection of the products, initially, piece by piece, so that later it developed inspection techniques and procedures that laid the foundations of quality control. The implementation of these technical innovations, but also new management methods, led to increased product quality, productivity and reduced production costs.

The verification of product quality went to a higher level when the engineer Walter Andrew Shewhart began to use statistics in 1931. The use of statistical methods in this field increased during the Second World War due to the large number of controls that had to be initiated for different categories of weapons. Shewhart is known as the father of statistical quality control [SHE 86]. Another notable contribution is the proposal of a schematic control chart consisting of a diagram and the essential principles and considerations for process quality control. The recognition of the importance of this chart is its adoption by the American Society for Testing and Materials in 1933. His most important contributions are summarized in the book published in 1931 entitled *Economic Control of Quality of Manufactured Product* [SHE 31].

In 1945, Dr. Armand Vallin Feigenbaum published the book *Quality control: Principles, practice and administration; An industrial management tool for improving product quality and design and for reducing operating costs and losses.* The book is based on the practical experience that Feigenbaum gained as an engineer at General Electric. Moreover, he launched the concept of Total Quality Control, which inspired Total Quality Management, this being one of the basic concepts of modern management and which proved its reliability by being practiced in organizations in different fields of activity and in many countries [WAT 05].

In 1956, Feigenbaum wrote the paper "Total Quality Control" which proposes an effective system for integrating efforts in all departments of a company (marketing, design-development, production and services) to achieve, maintain and improve quality. In Feigenbaum's view, the quality approach must be done on three levels: (1) consumer requirements that generate a certain "quality standard" that must be met by the organization, (2) the responsibilities of managers and employees on product quality, and (3) quality, which is a concern for all departments of the organization, each with a specific contribution to its achievement. Another significant contribution of Feigenbaum focused on quality costs.

Juran had similar concerns, and considered it necessary to separate avoidable costs (scrap, retouching expenses, commercial damages, etc.) from unavoidable costs (expenses to prevent them). This cost approach allows the identification and application of preventive actions, in the form of quality control procedures at all levels of the manufacturing process, in all stages of product development [JUR 86, JUR 99].

The resumption and intensification of industrial activity after the Second World War generated the intensification of the preoccupations of the specialists for quality problems. The Japanese miracle had many positive effects ideologically, economically and politically. Thus, the exchanges of ideas between Ishikawa and JUSE, on the one hand, and Deming, Juran and Feigenbaum, on the other, led to the implementation of new quality techniques in Japanese industry [DES 15]. In China, product quality concerns are very old, but the implementation of the quality management system took place only in 1978, with the economic opening of the country and the initiation of economic reforms [LI 03].

Gradually, associations were established in developed countries and these brought together quality specialists (e.g. The American Society for Quality Control and the French Association for Industrial Quality Control), and later, as the collaboration between European entities intensified, the European Organization for Quality Control was set up.

In 1961, starting from Philip B. Crosby's idea of "zero defects", the Martin Company (supplier of the American army) implemented this concept, taking into account the economic aspect along with the motivation of the personnel. Thus, in achieving quality, the company's activity must be organized on the basis of four basic principles [CRO 79, CRO 96]: ensuring compliance with requirements; quality assurance through prevention "quality must not be controlled, it must be achieved"; promoting the concept of "zero defects" and the measure of quality being represented by the costs due to the non-satisfaction of the requirements (quality does not cost – "quality is free").

The Japanese specialists also had significant contributions in the field of product quality assurance. In 1968, Ishikawa launched the concept of "Company Wide Quality Control (CWQC)" which is based on three requirements: (1) quality assurance, (2) quality control and (3) control of costs, quantities and delivery times. We can note the evolution of the "Quality Assurance" concept, observing the transition from the quality of the finished product to the "quality assurance of all activities and processes" regarding the costs, the requested quantities and the established delivery terms.

Moreover, Ishikava gives a new dimension to the principle of customer orientation. The customers of an organization can be divided into two categories: internal customers (persons involved in the process of making products from different departments of the company) and external customers (final beneficiaries of products). This principle (the next process is your customer) will become one of the basic principles of total quality management [MAR 98, NEY 17].

The process of quality assurance is based on the idea of a personal commitment of all employees to research quality improvement and lead to the formation of a problem-solving group (Table 7.1).

Stage	Objective	Responsibility
1	Product quality	Technical quality controllers (on the production flow and at the end)
2	Sectoral quality	All people involved in making the product
3	System quality	All persons involved in the design, manufacture, verification, and approval of the product
4	Preventive quality	The entire staff of the organization is responsible for meeting customer requirements

Table 7.1. *Main stages, objectives and responsibilities in the field of quality*

The contributions of Genichi Taguchi must be understood in the specific context of the Japanese economy, which after the Second World War went through a stage of survival and rebirth under conditions of scarce resources. Therefore the revolution of the production process was based on the concepts of cost savings and detection of outside influences. Noise was essential in that period. Moreover, Taguchi proposed "methods of identifying those noise sources, which have the greatest effects on product variability" [KAR 12]. The viability of his ideas is demonstrated by their adoption by manufacturers from different countries who have improved the quality of products and the production process and reduced costs, developed statistical methods and found applicability, not only in engineering, but also in other fields, such as biotechnology, marketing and advertising. Genichi Taguchi defines the quality of the product during its exploitation stage as "quality is the amount of losses a product imparts to society from the moment of shipment" due to the improper fulfillment of the skills to be used [MAG 04].

Globalization and the intensification of economic activity have brought the attention of specialists to new concerns that address issues such as real environmental protection, occupational health and safety, food security and information security. In addition, it is noted a series of changes in economic and political life, such as the diversification of the companies' offer, the increase of the clients' exigencies towards the quality of the products and services, but also towards the activity of the organizations in terms of social involvement and environmental protection, legislative changes and financial and technical innovation. Thus, all these transformations generate the need to move to integrated management systems. The concept of quality has increased in complexity, in the sense that for quality assurance it is important to know how to design, fine-tune and maintain processes and how to package and deliver products. Therefore, the designed quality, manufactured quality and delivered quality can be different, which is why all the economic and technical processes from the moment of designing the product or service until the moment of consumption are essential to ensure the satisfaction of the final consumer.

The existence of a quality management system in an organization is proof of the existence of performance management, which considers quality an important factor for increasing the organization's performance, for improving competitiveness in a tough environment and for meeting the requirements of various categories of stakeholders. The implementation of the quality management system implies a change of mentality at the level of the organization, the practice demonstrating the manifestation of some obstacles that the managers must manage and overcome. In this sense, overcoming cultural barriers and implementing an organizational culture are essential, especially in transnational corporations that have many branches and employees from different countries.

The International Organization for Standardization (ISO) developed the first standards for SMC in 1987 (known as the ISO 9000: 1987 series of standards). This event marked the transition from the concept of quality to the concept of quality assurance. The incorporation of the concept of quality assurance in a quality management system has been achieved since 1994. These standards have been periodically revised to take into account the problems which faced organizations in their implementation and the changes generated by economic, social and technical progress, and, moreover, considering the general character of these standards, which have applicability regardless of the form of organization of the entity in which they apply or the field of activity.

7.2.1.1. *Risk and risk management*

The managers of an organization must show skill in taking and managing risks. Considering the complexity of the economic processes, the interdependent relations between the national economies and also the economic instability, the risks make their presence felt in the activity of any entity. In the case of companies, beyond the production costs, the profit and, implicitly, the success depends on the ratio between the coverage costs and those generated by the appearance of the risks, and depends on the contribution of the costs associated with the risks to the total cost. Moreover, in addition to economic aspects, risks can have social, technological, cultural, political, environmental or security consequences. For these reasons, organizations must identify, analyze, evaluate and control risks. Risk identification is a complex process, which requires good knowledge of the organization's activity and its internal and international links.

Risk analysis involves not only determining the consequences and probabilities of their occurrence but also the ways in which one's own objectives may be affected. Risk management procedures have diversified as new risks arise or new crises break out. In the case of financial risks (interest, price or currency), companies use hedging techniques – eliminating risk exposure by taking a clearing position; use of financial instruments – forward contracts, futures contracts, options contracts; in the case of portfolio investments, the economic agents consider reducing the risk by diversifying the portfolio, which implies the acquisition of different types of financial assets whose incomes are not correlated. Frequently, companies use different types of insurance, available on the financial market, through which the transfer of risks is made for protection against possible loss-making situations, using an insurance contract by paying an insurance premium [MAT 08]. The risks appear in all socio-economic activities, each of them taking particular forms, depending on their type, how they manifest and their size.

Despite the existence of these internal or external risk hedging techniques, the international financial crisis launched in 2008 demonstrated the fragility of large economic giants in the face of risks and the failure of executive management in the efficient management of risk factors. 2009 marked a special event in the activity of the International Organization for Standardization, namely the launch of a specific standard for risks ISO 31000: 2009 – *Risk management*. This standard establishes principles and processes for managing any form of risk in any field of application and in any context. Organizations are encouraged to have their own approach to risk management given the field of activity, the managers' and shareholders' risk appetite and the economic environment in which they operate (national/international). Moreover, each entity must create and develop a risk management framework, which is considered an integral component of the management system.

Risk must be accepted and integrated into the management process, and risk management decisions are found at different levels or within different components of an organization's policies or activities. Given the evolution of the international economic system, the ISO 31000 standard was revised and republished in 2018, given the new challenges and risks that are generated by new phenomena such as the digitalization of the economy. Thus, risk management is considered a continuous process, which must be achieved by involving stakeholders and taking into account human and cultural factors [ISO 18b].

The effectiveness of a risk management program is expressed by framing hazardous situations and their severity within the limits set by the security objectives. To determine, report and improve the effectiveness of a risk management program, it must include a planned and structured evaluation of its activities and processes. In addition, the implementation of the risk management program allows companies to identify opportunities and negative consequences associated with risk, which allows them to better allocate resources and thus increase economic performance.

7.2.2. The environment and the environmental management system

The liberalization of trade and capital movements that fueled the globalization of the world economy have also generated the intensification of organizations' concerns for environmental protection. The increase of industrial production, generated by the intensification of trade by domestic companies, but also by large transnational companies, has brought a new approach to assessing the impact of economic activity on the environment [MAT 13, PAN 15, GUI 19]. An important first step was in 1972, when, at the Stockholm Conference, coherent collaboration programs were adopted between the countries of the world in order to reduce the negative ecological phenomena, which had become worrying (acid rain, greenhouse effect, etc.). On this occasion, the United Nations Environment Program was also initiated. Over time, a new concept has crystallized, namely, sustainable development. Next we can look at 1987, when the Brundtland Report entitled "Our Common Future" was published. This report promoted the need for sustainable development, defined as the development that meets the needs of the present, without compromising the ability to meet the needs of future generations and their own needs.

More and more organizations are concerned with improving environmental performance, a fact generated by the emergence of regulations in the field of environmental protection and increasing pressures from consumers who, in a diversified and dynamic offer, make the purchase of products or services not only for reasons of price and quality but also the attitude of the manufacturing company towards the environment. However, the literature draws attention to greenwashing practices, generally used by heavily polluting companies in areas such as the oil and gas industry that try to promote a green image of the organization among consumers and other categories of stakeholders, but who actually have a negative impact on the environment [MAT 13, VOL 16, PAL 19].

Environmental management is the management of those activities of an organization that have or may have an impact on the environment. The environmental management system is a tool for identifying and solving environmental problems which helps companies to meet legal obligations and established environmental performance, but is also a managerial tool that aims to achieve established environmental objectives and targets.

The large-scale implementation of the ISO 14001 standard is promoted by its characteristics. Thus, this standard has a character:

– generic, being applicable to any organization and not including absolute requirements for environmental performance;

– proactive, generated by an anticipatory and preventive approach which involves a commitment that results in the prevention of pollution and compliance with legal and other requirements governing the activity of an organization;

– continuously involving implementation and then continuous improvement. This standard is based on the principle of continuous improvement, which involves a process of developing the environmental management system to achieve improvements in overall environmental performance in accordance with the environmental policy of the organization;

– systematic, based on documented methods and procedures, on an environmental policy with objectives, actions of planning, implementation, verification and continuous improvement.

The establishment of the environmental policy is based on the following considerations: the organization's objectives related to the business process, the impact of the organization's activities on the environment, the organization's products/ services, the requirements imposed by law or other regulations, the organization's past and present performance related to EMS, the necessary resources, the opportunities and needs for continuous improvement and the employee contribution.

Legal regulations play an important role in the design of environmental policy, because there may be laws that challenge the obligation to implement ISO 14000 environmental management certification standards. However, the ISO 14001 certification of the environmental management system does not imply that the company's products are "environmentally friendly", but only that the manufacturer is concerned with reducing its own impact on the environment. Other companies voluntarily adopt an environmental standard given the advantages of implementing such a system.

The benefits of implementing an environmental management system are multiple and consist of increasing employee involvement and motivation, recording cost savings (reducing waste management costs or costs generated by energy and material consumption), increasing the confidence of customers, insurance companies and public institutions, improving the company's image and economic performance. For example, state institutions establish, among the eligibility criteria for participation in tenders, the existence of a certified Environmental Management System.

The companies that have implemented such a system have the possibility of winning the tenders organized by the local or central public administration, which also generates the increase of the turnover. In the case of companies that have a negative impact on the environment, the implementation of such a system considerably increases the chances of obtaining a loan on advantageous terms, because more and more financial institutions have become trendsetters, in the sense that they promote sustainable development principles, but also require a certain principle of environmental protection or the CSR of debtor companies. The most well-known principles used in the banking sector are the Equator Principles [MAT 13]. Internationally, the existence of such a system, implemented by more and more companies, generates the intensification of trade and the reduction of trade barriers [MEL 03].

Moreover, studies have been conducted [FEL 96] that demonstrate the positive impact of EMS implementation on the financial performance of listed companies. Even though the implementation of an environmental management system may involve costs [ALB 00, WAT 04], in the long run, organizations that adopt such a system register the improvement of their economic situation. However, there are major differences depending on the type of property – with majority state-owned or private companies [DAR 06].

The company that implements an EMS must go through certain steps and take into account certain aspects that concern:

– elaboration of a procedure regarding the identification of environmental aspects and the implementation of control measures. For this reason, an initial analysis of the processes within the organization is necessary in order to identify significant environmental aspects created by activities, products or services. This must be done in normal and abnormal working conditions and in potential emergencies, taking into account costs, available data and evaluating feedback from investigating previous incidents and emergencies. Thus, there must be procedures for periodic monitoring and measurement of the main characteristics of activities with significant impact on the environment, but also procedures for periodic assessment of compliance with legal requirements and other applicable requirements;

– the accomplishment actions must be established for each objective and target, as must the persons responsible for their accomplishment, the necessary resources, the necessary trainings, the accomplishment term and the way of communicating the observations;

– internal and external communication with stakeholders, a process that must be documented in the procedure. Thus, it is necessary to establish the method of registration and solution of the requests, the communication mechanism of the employees with responsibilities in the field with the management so that the information is understood, is viable and presents an exact image of the performance;

– establish and maintain information (on paper or in electronic format) describing the main elements of the EMS and the interaction between them, and ensuring access to related documentation. This documentation consists of: the environmental policy, management objectives and programs, a description of the main elements of the EMS and the interaction with related documents, internal standards and operating procedures and contingency plans.

Organizations in sensitive areas of environmental impact, such as those in the oil and gas sector (oil equipment manufacturers, oil and gas extraction and processing and transport) are interested in implementing and certifying an environmental management system to demonstrate their concerns in the field of environmental protection and sustainable development and to improve their image among stakeholders.

At the European level, a standard entitled "Eco-management and Audit Scheme" (EMAS) has been developed. EMAS and the ISO 14001 series are similar in many ways, but there are differences in approach and some details. These differences stem from the fact that the EMAS regulation and ISO 14000 standards have been developed in different fora.

Environmental management has become a challenge due to the complexity of environmental protection legislation. The substantiation of environmental management is the understanding of the laws and regulations that apply in companies. However, simple compliance with the law is not enough and many companies have opted for "beyond compliance" strategies.

The occurrence of EMAS or ISO 14001 has transformed environmental management from a local to a global requirement. In the future, the environmental performance of companies around the world will be compared to the use of environmental management tools, and the ability of companies to meet these standards may affect how accepted their products are on the market.

EMAS	ISO 14001
Legislative regulation applicable only within the EU	International standard applicable worldwide
It is restrictive to locations specific to industrial activity	It is applicable to activities, products and services, including non-industrial activities
Requires an initial environmental analysis	The initial environmental analysis is not mandatory, it is only suggested in the informative annex of the standard
Continuous improvement of environmental performance is required	The continuous improvement of the environmental management system, reflected by the increase of the environmental performance, is requested
A public environmental statement is required. It allows access to environmental management policy and programs	It involves external communication, but it is up to the organization to decide the content of the information; imposes public access only to environmental policy
The frequency of the environmental audit is of a maximum three years. Requires mandatory publication of the result after the audit	Does not specify the frequency of the environmental audit. It does not require the publication of the audit result
Records of environmental effects are required	No environmental effects records required

Table 7.2. *Some differences between EMAS and ISO 14001*

The factors that generate the need to document and implement an environmental management system are [DIM 04, IVA 16]:

– the existence of EU regulations on the voluntary participation of organizations in the effort to reduce significant environmental impacts based on their own criteria for verifying environmental performance;

– the adoption, at EU level, of the concept of "sustainable development", which generates responsibilities for organizations for economic growth and environmental protection;

– implementation of the best technologies, viable from an economical point of view, taking into account the cost efficiency of such technologies. These technologies become an integral part of a management system that contributes to the prevention of environmental pollution.

Analyzing the context, three situations are possible:

– the integrated management system (by requirements) is under the conditions of sustainable development. Proof of the existence and implementation of IMS can provide a competitive advantage to the organization but does not prove the sustainability of the organization. IMS cannot be a guarantee of the management's concerns in order to ensure existential equity. It is possible to discuss, simply, a conjunctural situation in which the management is based on a momentary advantage obtained on considerations of management system documentation and certification;

– the management has multiple options. The advantage offered by IMS should not be neglected, because in this situation, it can ensure the sustainability of the organization. It is dependent, however, on the extent to which management understands the need to invest in the direction of transforming constraints into opportunities;

– the management's investment in technological development proves to be inspired and efficient, creating the premises for achieving "sustained success".

The organization enjoys sustainable economic performance and profitability over time as the external environment shows security and stability, which, in the long run, translates into promoting sustainable development.

To the three situations, which derive from the logic of the manifestation of an economic environment without major disturbances, crisis situations, more or less predictable, more or less possible to be intuited by analysts, can be added. Such situations are considered as challenges of the external environment of the organization, subject to risk. They can be exemplified by the states of uncertainty created by pandemics. Such a situation calls for the adoption of strategies outside the patterns of risk response plans. In such situations, the adaptability of the organization to the risk situation is essential for its sustainability. This translates into technological and design flexibility and adaptation to newly created environmental conditions. In pandemic situations, the organizations most likely to survive are those that ensure the satisfaction of primary needs (physiological: food and clothing) and security (shelter, hygiene, health). Other organizations may choose to transfer the risks (if this was initiated in advance, they may prove too expensive during the crisis) or to adapt their activity to the new situation (for example: garment companies orient their production towards the creation of sanitary equipment, alcoholic beverage companies focus their production on the manufacture of disinfection products, etc.).

Companies and other types of organizations or entities, such as universities, scholarships or public authorities, have become increasingly interested in their societal involvement. They seek to maximize the positive impact on the environment, societies and communities in which they operate. Over time, a new concept crystallized – corporate social responsibility, which was later transferred to other entities, such as universities or portfolio investors [MAT 13, PAL 19]. The interest in SR and the promotion of the principles of sustainable development by various entities has resulted in the emergence of numerous initiatives that have been classified [LLA 15]:

1) standards or general principles for sustainable behavior, such as the UN Global Compact Principles or the OECD Guidelines;

2) certification standards, such as SA8000;

3) reporting standards, such as GRI;

4) process standards that define processes to enable the creation of management system around sustainability, such as ISO 26001. We can see that it addresses all aspects of CSR and provides guidelines for the integration of CSR into the management process [HAH 15], even if it is not a standard management system.

7.2.3. *Occupational safety and health management system*

The topic of health and safety at work has appeared at the international level since the 1950s, and at the level of the European Union, social policy also addresses this issue. Moreover, an important goal of the European Union, set at the Lisbon European Council in March 2000, was to create more and better jobs. In this context, health and safety are key elements in terms of the quality of work and are among the indicators adopted following the Commission Communication "Investing in Quality".

The legal requirements that have emerged in recent decades cannot fully cover the dangers and risks arising from the continuous evolution of the labor market. Public authorities, employers and employees have begun to be concerned with the implementation and development of an occupational health and safety management system as it contributes decisively to reducing hazards and risks and increasing labor productivity, while reducing the costs associated with ensuring an adequate level of occupational safety and health and a clean environment.

Statistics from the International Labor Organization (ILO) demonstrate the economic and social impact of accidents at work and occupational diseases. Thus, in one year, occupational accidents or work-related diseases generate more than 2.78 million deaths and 374 million non-fatal injuries and illnesses. In addition to the emotional impact on the people concerned, families and local communities, accidents at work and occupational diseases involve considerable costs for companies and national health systems, so they generate negative externalities that companies must try to compensate for.

The solution to these problems is provided by ISO, which has launched ISO 45001 – *Occupational health and safety management systems – Requirements with guidance for use*, the first international standard for this field. In order to support the organization that has already implemented other management standards, ISO designed this standard in a similar manner to ISO 9001 (quality management) and ISO 14001 (environmental management). It has the same high-level structure, identical core text, terms and definitions. Moreover, the standard was created based on similar national and international standards, such as OHSAS 18001 – *Occupational health and safety management*, the International Labor Organization's ILO-OSH 2001 guidelines.

Occupational health and safety (OHS) management is a complex process that must take into account the specifics of the production activity, the technological process and the equipment used, the employment policy, the policy applied to people with disabilities and the preventive or curative health policy in general. Occupational safety and health are major elements in the employment strategy, given the importance of staff quality, the use of productive potential in achieving the profitability objectives of companies. Implementing an organizational culture is important for creating a relaxed work environment in which employees can express their opinions without fear, come to the company with pleasure and even be happy at work. In this way, the emotional health of employees is ensured, which is becoming increasingly important in an increasingly complex economic and social environment, with more and more challenges.

Top management must establish, document, implement and maintain an OHS policy that sets out overall health and safety objectives and a commitment to improving performance.

The policy must be in line with the nature and extent of the organization's OHS risks, include a commitment to injury and disease prevention and continuous improvement, include a commitment to comply with legal and other applicable requirements to which the organization subscribes, be documented, implemented and maintained, be communicated to all staff working under the control of the organization, be available to stakeholders, be periodically reviewed and provide the framework for setting and analyzing OHS objectives [DAR 17, MAD 20].

The organization must establish, implement and maintain procedures for the continuous identification of hazards, the assessment of risks and the determination of the necessary controls. These should include:

– routine and non-routine activities of all staff who have access to the workplace (including subcontractors and visitors);

– behavior, capabilities and other human factors;

– identification of hazards generated outside the workplace that may affect the health and safety of persons working under the control of the organization, hazards created near the workplace to work activities under the control of the organization;

– infrastructure, equipment and materials used at work, provided by the organization or others;

– changes or proposed changes within the organization (activities, materials, of the OHSAS system), including temporal changes;

– any applicable legal obligation regarding the risk assessment and the implementation of the necessary controls;

– designing work areas, processes, installations, machines, equipment, work procedures and work organization.

The organization must establish and maintain procedures to ensure that staff working for or on its behalf are aware of:

– the importance of compliance with OHS policy, procedures and requirements;

– the real or potential consequences on OHS of the activities they carry out and the benefits brought by the improvement of individual performance;

– their attributions, responsibilities and importance in achieving compliance with OHSAS policy, procedures and requirements, including with requirements regarding emergency preparedness and response capacity;

– possible consequences of deviations from the specified procedures.

The organization must establish, implement and maintain a procedure to ensure that relevant OHS information is communicated to, and from, staff and other stakeholders for internal communication between the various levels and functions of the organization, as well as communication with contractors and site visitors. The procedure should contain the responsibilities for receiving, documenting and responding to communications with stakeholders.

A procedure for employee participation/consultation on hazard identification, risk assessment and determination of controls, appropriate involvement in incident investigation, involvement in the development and analysis of OHS policy and objectives consultation of staff and other stakeholders must be established, implemented and maintained with relevant OHS issues.

Determining the level of performance, over time, of the occupational health and safety management system is essential for verifying a continuity aiming at the processes related to the elimination of work-related injuries and occupational diseases.

Management at the highest level should review the occupational health and safety management system at planned intervals to ensure that it is appropriate,

appropriate to the objectives pursued and effective. The analysis performed by management has, as input data, the results of internal audits, assessment of compliance with legal and other requirements, communication with stakeholders (including complaints), the results of participation and consultation, OHS performance, the extent to which objectives were achieved, stage of incident investigation, corrective and preventive actions, follow-up actions from previous analyses performed by management and statistics related to accidents and a change of surroundings (including developments of legal requirements).

The implementation of an occupational health and safety management system requires the involvement of the entire staff of the organization and the engagement of a dynamic and cyclical process of continuous improvement and self-assessment of risks and dangers [DAR 17, MAD 20].

The success of the occupational health and safety management system is generated by the benefits it brings to the company, namely the reduction of individual absenteeism and, implicitly, the increase of labor productivity, the reduction of costs with accident insurance premiums, the improvement of mood and of employee morale, improving the organization's reputation among the employees.

7.3. Conclusion

Documentation and implementation of an integrated management system is a logical and systematic managerial approach that allows for optimal strategic and operational decisions that take into account all the essential aspects that lead to the efficient functioning of an organization in terms of quality, the environment and occupational health and safety. This system must be integrated into the general management system of the organization which involves three action plans (normative plan, strategic plan and operational plan). Integrated management systems (quality, the environment and occupational health and safety) are different from one organization to another, the differences given by their organization and functioning, management vision, group policy, sectoral interests and the influence of external stakeholders.

Even if there are no generally valid rules on establishing relationships in which these management systems should be put, some recommendations can still be made to those who want to implement an integrated management system within the organization:

– the organization must establish an objective relationship between the importance of the quality of the products/services provided, the identified environmental aspects and the aspects regarding the occupational health and safety;

– making the decision to achieve an integrated management system (quality, environmental or occupational health and safety) must be based on the analysis of the essential reasons that were the basis for the decision to implement each of the three management systems;

– consulting a certification body from the outset.

The concept of an "integrated management system" includes the integration of applicable management system standards into a single documentation which ensures effective control of the processes within the organization by establishing the organization's policies, objectives and obligations (according to legal requirements and other applicable requirements).

An integrated management system has a number of elements in common for all applicable standards (quality, environment and occupational health and safety, to which may be added those relating to information security, food safety, etc.), namely: analyses performed by management; integrated approach to policy and objectives; internal audits; documentation (manuals, procedures and other common documents); integrated approach to improvement mechanisms (corrective, preventive actions and continuous improvement measures); an integrated approach to planning and a risk management approach for the entire business of the organization.

7.4. References

[ALF 19] ALFARO E., YU F., REHMAN N.U. *et al.*, "Strategic management of innovation", in CHEN J., BREM A., VIARDOT E. *et al.* (eds), *The Routledge Companion to Innovation Management*, Routledge, pp. 107–168, 2019.

[ALG 19] ALGHERIANI N.M., KIRIN S., SPASOJEVIC BRKIC V., "Risk model for integrated management system", *Tehnički vjesnik*, vol. 26, no. 6, pp. 1833–1840, 2019.

[ALL 18] ALLAM Z., NEWMAN P., "Redefining the smart city: Culture, metabolism and governance, *Smart Cities*, vol. 1, no. 1, pp. 4–25, 2018.

[AVE 15] AVEN T., "Implications of black swans to the foundations and practice of risk assessment and management", *Reliability Engineering & System Safety*, vol. 134, pp. 83–91, 2015.

[BĂL 15] BĂLAN M., VASILE V., "Cultural determinants of economic performance in Romania", *Procedia – Social and Behavioral Sciences*, vol. 188, pp. 290–296, 2015.

[BEC 03] BECKMERHAGEN I., BERG H., KARAPETROVIC S. *et al.*, "Integration of management systems: Focus on safety in the nuclear industry", *International Journal of Quality and Reliability Management*, vol. 20, no. 2, pp. 209–227, 2003.

[BER 09] BERNARDO M., CASADESUS M., KARAPETROVIC S. *et al.*, "How integrated are environmental, quality and other standardized management systems? An empirical study", *Journal of Cleaner Production*, vol. 17, no. 8, pp. 742–750, 2009.

[BOC 16] BOCKEN N.M., DE PAUW I., BAKKER C. *et al.*, "Product design and business model strategies for a circular economy", *Journal of Industrial and Production Engineering*, vol. 33, no. 5, pp. 308–320, 2016.

[CĂT 16] CĂTĂLIN V.M., "Changes of EU industrial policy and its effects on Romania's industrial paradigm", *Industrija*, vol. 44, no. 4, pp. 197–210, 2016.

[CHA 09] CHANDRUPATLA T.R., *Quality and Reliability in Engineering*, Cambridge University Press, New York, 2009.

[CIA 17] CIASULLO M.V., MAIONE G., TORRE C. *et al.*, "What about sustainability? An empirical analysis of consumers' purchasing behavior in fashion context", *Sustainability*, vol. 9, no. 9, p. 1617, 2017.

[CON 14] CONSTANTINESCU A., FRONE S., "The role of technological innovation in sustainable economic development", *Journal of Knowledge Management, Economics and Information Technology*, vol. 4, pp. 1–15, 2014.

[CRO 79] CROSBY P.B., *Quality is Free: The Art of Making Quality Certain*, McGraw-Hill, New York, 1979.

[CRO 96] CROSBY P.B., *Quality is Still Free: Making Quality Certain in Uncertain Times*, McGraw-Hill, New York, 1996.

[DAR 14] DARESTANI S.A., TADI A.M., TAHERI S. *et al.*, "Development of fuzzy U control chart for monitoring defects", *International Journal of Quality & Reliability Management*, vol. 31, no. 7, pp. 811–821, 2014.

[DAR 17] DARABONT D.C., ANTONOV A.E., BEJINARIU C., "Key elements on implementing an occupational health and safety management system using ISO 45001 standard", *MATEC Web of Conferences*, EDP Sciences, vol. 121, 2017.

[DES 15] DESHMUKH K., "Remembering Kaoru Ishikawa – A great practical philosopher", *Auto Tech Review*, vol. 4, no. 10, pp. 12–13, 2015.

[DIM 04] DIMIAN M., "Atenţie la mediul înconjurător", *Revista Jurnalul de Petrol şi Gaze*, Editura USI România SRL, Ploieşti, 2004.

[DUS 14] DUSMANESCU D., ANDREI J., SUBIC J., "Scenario for implementation of renewable energy sources in Romania", *Procedia Economics and Finance*, vol. 8, pp. 300–305, 2014.

[ENE 14] ENE C., VOICA M.C., PANAIT M., "Green investments and food security: Opportunities and future directions in the context of sustainable development", in MIEILA M. (ed.), *Measuring Sustainable Development and Green Investments in Contemporary Economies*, IGI Global, pp. 163–200, 2014.

[FRO 17a] FRONE S., *The Role of Eco-innovation for Promoting a Green Economy*, Lambert Academic Publishing, Saarbrucken, 2017.

[FRO 17b] FRONE S., CONSTANTINESCU A., "Industrial symbiosis for promoting the green economy in Romania", *Cleaner Production and Green Economy, Proceedings of the International Conference "Information Society and Sustainable Development"*, p. 34, 2017.

[GAR 91] GARVIN D., "How the Baldrige award really works", *Harvard Business Review*, vol. 69, no. 6, pp. 80–93, 1991.

[GIA 11] GIANNANTONIO C.M., HURLEY-HANSON A.E., "Frederick Winslow Taylor: Reflections on the relevance of the principles of scientific management 100 years later", *Journal of Business Management*, vol. 17, pp. 7–10, 2011.

[GRI 99] GRIFFITH A., Developing an integrated management system for quality, safety and environment, Construction Papers, 1999.

[GRY 01] GRYNA F.M., *Quality Planning and Analysis*, McGraw-Hill, New York, 2001.

[GUI 19] GUIJARRO F., "A multicriteria model for the assessment of countries' environmental performance", *International Journal of Environmental Research and Public Health*, vol. 16, no. 16, p. 2868, 2019.

[GUR 17] GURTU A., SEARCY C., JABER M.Y., "Sustainable supply chains", in KHAN M., HUSSAIN M., AJMAL M.M. (eds), *Green Supply Chain Management for Sustainable Business Practice*, IGI Global, pp. 1–26, 2017.

[HOL 03] HOLDSWORTH R., "Practical applications approach to design, development and implementation of an integrated management system", *Journal of Hazardous Materials*, vol. 104, nos 1–3, pp. 193–205, 2003.

[HYS 20] HYSA E., KRUJA A., REHMAN N.U. *et al.*, "Circular economy innovation and environmental sustainability impact on economic growth: An integrated model for sustainable development", *Sustainability*, vol. 12, no. 12, p. 4831, 2020.

[IAC 17] IACOVOIU V., STANCU A., "An empirical analyses of the correlation between innovation performance and economic development", *The USV Annals of Economics and Public Administration*, vol. 17, no. 25, pp. 45–51, 2017.

[ISO 18a] ISO, Contributing to the UN SDGs with ISO standards, available at: https://www.iso.org/files/live/sites/isoorg/files/store/en/PUB100429.pdf (accessed May 21, 2020), 2018.

[ISO 18b] ISO, ISO 31000, Risk management, available at: https://www.iso.org/files/live/sites/isoorg/files/store/en/PUB100426.pdf (accessed May 21, 2020), 2018.

[IVA 09] IVAN M.V., IACOVOIU V., "Innovation and research and development important factors related to the nations competitiveness. The case of European economies", *Communications of the IBIMA*, vol. 10, pp. 110–118, 2009.

[IVA 16] IVANOVA D., HARADINOVA A., VASILEVA E., "Environmental performance of companies with environmental management systems in Bulgaria", *Calitatea*, vol. 17, no. 152, p. 61, 2016.

[JUR 86] JURAN J.M., "The quality trilogy", *Quality Progress*, vol. 19, no. 8, pp. 19–24, 1986.

[JUR 99] JURAN J.M., BLANTON GODFREY A., *Juran's Quality Handbook*, McGraw-Hill, New York, 1999.

[KAR 98] KARAPETROVIC S., WILLBORN W., "Integration of quality and environmental management systems", *TQM Magazine*, vol. 10, no. 3, pp. 204–13, 1998.

[KAR 03] KARAPETROVIC S., "Musings on integrated management systems", *Measuring Business Excellence*, vol. 7, no. 1, pp. 4–13, 2003.

[KAR 12] KARNA S., "An overview on Taguchi Method", *International Journal of Engineering and Mathematical Sciences*, vol. 1, pp. 11–18, 2012.

[LI 03] LI J.H., ANDERSON A.R., HARRISON R.T., "Total quality management principles and practices in China", *International Journal of Quality & Reliability Management*, vol. 20, no. 9, pp. 1026–1050, 2003.

[MAC 14] MACHADO C., DAVIM J.P., *Human Resource Management and Technological Challenges*, Springer International Publishing, New York, 2014.

[MAC 17] MACHADO C., DAVIM J.P (eds), *Green and Lean Management*, Springer International Publishing, New York, 2017.

[MAD 20] MADSEN C.U., KIRKEGAARD M.L., DYREBORG J. *et al.*, "Making occupational health and safety management systems 'work': A realist review of the OHSAS 18001 standard", *Safety Science*, vol. 129, p. 104843, 2020.

[MAG 04] MAGHSOODLOO S., OZDEMIR G., JORDAN V. *et al.*, "Strengths and limitations of Taguchi's contributions to quality, manufacturing, and process engineering", *Journal of Manufacturing Systems*, vol. 23, no. 2, pp. 73–126, 2004.

[MAI 17] MAIER D., SVEN-JOACHIM I., FORTMÜLLER A. *et al.*, "Development and operationalization of a model of innovation management system as part of an integrated quality-environment-safety system", *Amfiteatru Economic*, vol. 19, no. 44, pp. 302–314, 2017.

[MAR 98] MARTÍNEZ-LORENTE A.R., DEWHURST F., DALE B.G., "Total quality management: Origins and evolution of the term", *The TQM Magazine*, vol. 10, no. 5, pp. 378–386, 1998.

[MAT 13] MATEI M., *Responsabilitatea socială a corporaţiilor şi instituţiilor şi dezvoltarea durabilă a României*, Expert Publishing House, Bucharest, 2013.

[MOH 06] MOHAMMAD M., OSMAN M.R., YUSUFF R.M. *et al.*, "Strategies and critical success factors for integrated management systems implementation", *Conference on Computers and Industrial Engineering*, vol. 35, pp. 1391–1396, 2006.

[MUZ 19] MUZAIMI H., HAMID S.R., ISA S. *et al.*, "Integrated management system: The converging of key quality standards into single standard", *International Journal of Human and Technology Interaction*, vol. 3, no. 1, pp. 75–82, 2019.

[NAE 09] NAE I., PETRESCU M.G., LUPU F., *Managementul cercetării-dezvoltării-inovării*, Editura ILEX, Bucharest, 2009.

[NAS 03] NASIM A., "Biotechnology for sustainable development", *Commission on Science and Technology for Sustainable Development in the South Science Vision Quarterly*, no. 1–2, 2003.

[NEA 20] NEACSA A., PANAIT M., MURESAN J.D. *et al.*, "Energy poverty in European Union: Assessment difficulties, effects on the quality of life, mitigation measures, some evidences from Romania", *Sustainability*, vol. 12, no. 10, p. 4036, 2020.

[NEY 17] NEYESTANI B., Principles and contributions of total quality management (TQM) gurus on business quality improvement, available at: http://behynamneyestani.pbworks.com/w/file/fetch/117028989/Principles%20and%20Contributions%20of%20Total%20Quality%20Mangement%20%28TQM%29%20Gurus%20on%20Business%20Quality%20Improvem.pdf, 2017.

[NUN 16] NUNHES T.V., MOTTA L.C., DE OLIVEIRA O.J., "Evolution of integrated management systems research on the Journal of Cleaner Production: Identification of contributions and gaps in the literature", *Journal of Cleaner Production*, vol. 139, pp. 1234–1244, 15 December, 2016.

[PAN 15] PANAIT M., PETRESCU M.G., "Quality management and social responsibility in the context of sustainable development", *Industrija*, vol. 43, no. 4, pp. 175–189, 2015.

[PET 19] PETRESCU M.G., *Managementul Tehnologiilor Industriale*, Petroleum-Gas University of Ploiești, Ploiești, 2019.

[PLA 06] PLATON V., *Dezvoltare Durabilă şi Reciclarea Materialelor*, Editura Expert, Bucharest, 2006.

[POJ 06] POJASEK R., "Is your integrated management system really integrated?", *Environmental Quality Management*, vol. 16, no. 2, pp. 89–97, 2006.

[POP 18] POPESCU G.H., MIEILA M., NICA E. *et al.*, "The emergence of the effects and determinants of the energy paradigm changes on European Union economy", *Renewable and Sustainable Energy Reviews*, vol. 81, 768–774, 2018.

[RAH 12] RAHMAN M.H., "Henry Fayol and Frederick Winslow Taylor's contribution to management thought: An overview", *ABC Journal of Advanced Research*, vol. 1, no. 2, pp. 32–41, 2012.

[ROS 09] ROSAM I., PEDDLE R., *Understanding ISO 9001:2008 and Process-based Management Systems*, 2nd edition, BSI, London, 2009.

[SHE 31] SHEWHART W.A., *Economic Control of Quality of Manufactured Product*, Macmillan and Co Ltd, London, 1931.

[SHE 86] SHEWHART W.A., DEMING W. E., *Statistical Method from the Viewpoint of Quality Control*, Courier Corporation, Chelmsford, 1986.

[SIM 14] SIMA V., "Green policies – Determinant vector for competitiveness enhancement", *Economic Insights – Trends & Challenges*, vol. 66, no. 1, pp. 1–15, 2014.

[TAL 07] TALEB N.N., *The Black Swan: The Impact of the Highly Improbable*, Random House, New York, 2007.

[VIS 20] VISVIZI A., LYTRAS M.D., "Sustainable Smart Cities and Smart Villages research: Rethinking security, safety, well-being, and happiness", *Sustainability*, vol. 12, no. 1, pp. 1–4, 2020.

[VOL 16] VOLLERO A., PALAZZO M., SIANO A. *et al.*, "Avoiding the greenwashing trap: Between CSR communication and stakeholder engagement", *International Journal of Innovation and Sustainable Development*, vol. 10, no. 2, pp. 120–140, 2016.

[WAT 05] WATSON G.H., "Feigenbaum's enduring influence", *Quality Progress*, vol. 38, no. 11, p. 51, 2005.

[ZAM 11] ZAMAN G., VASILE V., "Cultural-creative industries (CCI) – Economic and social performances", *The USV Annals of Economics and Public Administration*, vol. 10, no. 3, pp. 63–77, 2011.

[ZEC 99] ZECHENDORF B., "Sustainable development: How can biotechnology contribute?", *Trends in Biotechnology*, vol. 17, no. 6, pp. 219–225, 1999.

8

Mentoring… Really? And Why Not?

The pressures and competition faced by organizations to attract talent and retain "brains" who hold valuable information and knowledge, increases the need to adopt innovative human resource practices. Mentoring programs are one of these practices, which aim to potentiate the transmission of knowledge from more experienced employees for newcomers' employees to an organization. Therefore, the implementation and formalization of mentoring as an organizational process and practice aims above all to meet the needs of reception and integration of human resources, and at the same time, serve as a strategy to attract new employees. This chapter aims to contribute to a better understanding of the concept of mentoring, especially in more technological and emerging areas of management. The study highlights that mentoring processes can assume an important role in terms of human resource management, enhancing greater and better interaction between different professional groups. Moreover, the success or failure of this type of practice is a function of factors of varying nature and involves all those who directly or indirectly have responsibilities in organizations.

8.1. Introduction

Due to the high demand for highly qualified human resources and the scarce availability of it, organizations are in fierce competition to attract talent and retain "brains" who hold valuable information and knowledge. It is in this context that

---

Chapter written by Bruna ROCHA, João Leite RIBEIRO and Delfina GOMES[1].

1 Financial Support: Delfina Gomes has conducted the study at the Research Center in Political Science (UIDB/CPO/00758/2020), University of Minho/University of Évora and was supported by the Portuguese Foundation for Science and Technology (FCT) and the Portuguese Ministry of Education and Science through national funds.

mentoring programs often appear. These are aimed at the transmission of knowledge from more experienced employees – mentors – for newcomers' employees to an organization, a job, a project – mentees.

The implementation and formalization of mentoring as an organizational process and practice aims above all to meet the needs of reception and integration of human resources, and at the same time, to serve as a strategy to attract new employees. To accommodate this growth and make it sustainable, it is necessary to adopt policies that welcome, retain and develop these same human resources. However, it is not always easy. In some areas of activity these human resources are highly sought after, for example in technological companies where the turnover rate at an international level is high [PIK 14].

If there are sectors of activity where certain levels of turnover are strategically and operationally desirable, it is also true that the management paradigm based on competitiveness with quality can lead to a greater awareness that the loss of certain workers may have several implications, namely economic, financial and psychological [YAN 17]. Such losses can be translated, respectively, into productivity losses during the replacement period, discrediting from external customers with possible financial losses and possible loss of cohesion and a weakening of individual, group and organizational identity [YAN 17].

A context of rapid and discontinuous changes and an environment of great volatility influence the dynamics of the teams, which are formed and reformed at an accelerated pace in response to business developments and changes in human resources [KUM 16]. In these situations, processes such as reception and integration and mentoring can be, if properly contextualized and integrated into the organization's values and strategy, relevant contributions.

Mentoring processes, as long as they are not carried out according to some passing trend, can assume an important role in terms of human resource management, enhancing greater and better interaction between different professional groups. In the case of workers with management responsibilities at different levels – strategic, tactical and operational – mentoring that is properly framed, contextualized and implemented can contribute to organizational performance. In particular, mentoring can contribute so that in the development of organizational responsibilities, holders of management positions have more sustained actions, promoting organizational empathy and a greater commitment to the establishment and construction of a stronger and more positive organizational identity [KUM 16, RIB 16].

Despite being a very old practice, it is also true that mentoring, especially in more technological and emerging areas, needs more studies and research. These areas are constantly changing, and this can lead to the establishment of structures and untraditional working relationships. Thus, mentoring, as it is known, may have lesser-known outlines that need more attention on the part of future research on the complex nature of relationships that this process can create [RÉG 06, KAL 02]. Therefore, this chapter aims to contribute to a better understanding of the concept of mentoring in these technological and emerging areas of management. The theoretical framework presented in this chapter also aims to serve as a basis for a research project developed in a Portuguese subsidiary of a technological multinational to defining a practical mentoring plan. The main objective is to develop a mentoring project based on theoretical assumptions that would enhance the advantages of onboarding processes and the development of workers in the organization's sustainability policies.

The chapter is structured as follows. First, the concept on mentoring is contextualized and characterized. Next, the different types of mentoring are identified, and this is followed by the analysis of the main objectives of mentoring. The participants of a mentoring process are identified and analyzed. Next, the advantages and disadvantages of mentoring are described. The next section provides an analyses of the facilitators and of the obstacles in a mentoring process. Finally, we draw some conclusions.

8.2. Concept of mentoring

8.2.1. *Development of the mentoring concept*

Mentoring is a concept that has spread to management and humanities schools as a career development tool [HIG 01]. Around the 1980s, it also appeared in the business world as an organizational phenomenon [JAK 16]. However, the term "mentor" is already quite old, originating from Greek mythology, inspired by a character in Homer's *Odyssey* named Mentor [COL 01]. When Ulysses leaves for the Trojan War, he leaves his son, Telemachus, in the care of Mentor, who later accompanies, gives support, inspiration and guidance to Telemachus on his journey to find Ulysses. This 3,000-year-old Greek myth has been universally recognized as the conceptual source of mentoring [COL 01].

However, since Ancient Greece right up until today, mentoring has always been present in the history of humankind, in the various strata of ancient society. The nobility, at the time when there were counselors and educators, took charge of the education and training of the youngest [SAN 07]. In the clergy, priests were disciples of someone in the religious hierarchy [BRO 11]. The people, at the base of the pyramid of a stratified society, had artisans who took up a trade after being welcomed for years by an artisan as apprentices [BRO 11].

Currently, during all stages of our life, we are constantly in contact with some form of mentoring, whether at school, at home, or in the group we belong to (namely in the professional group) [ANI 17]. With the rise of large organizations in the last century, mentoring has left its educational sphere [COL 01] to extend itself to the business environment as well [SAN 07]. Initiatives related to mentoring began to proliferate, and with very positive results, which in turn attracted the attention of organizations [TAL 14a].

Authors such as Watts and Dynamics [WAT 96] state that mentoring was always present in organizations even before formal references were made to this concept. However, mentoring as a conscious and more systematic process emerged in the USA, between the 70s and 80s, after it was observed that several successful executives had received support from informal mentors, having progressed in their careers faster than others who did not benefit from this. From then on, more research and studies on this phenomenon began to emerge, which served as a basis to extrapolate this knowledge on the development of formal mentoring programs [DOU 97, THO 16, ANI 17].

As such, in the 1980s, according to Douglas [DOU 97], there was a rapid growth in mentoring programs resulting from the appreciation of the positive impacts of mentoring relationships. In addition, some factors influenced the emergence of mentoring programs, such as: the increasing competitiveness of companies, the increase in business mergers, the focus on new technologies and innovations, attention to the diversity of the workforce and the progression of collaborators [DOU 97]. Watts and Dynamics [WAT 96] also add that, during the 80s and early 90s, many companies had to reduce costs and proceed with restructuring, and mentoring emerged as a tool for regeneration and support for change as well as a retention tool of employees. The issue was that losing important workers could jeopardize an organization's own growth [BRI 17].

In addition to the question of what the purpose of mentoring is and the subject of its appearance in organizations, one also questions who it was intended for. According to the Talent Management Staff [TAL 14a], in the 80s and 90s, mentoring was seen as exclusive and designed only for those with great potential, those seen as being able to one day reach a leadership position. It was a relationship established between a more experienced mentor and a more novice mentee, where the focus was on career progression.

In addition to all the changes that occurred between the 70s and 90s, at the turn of the 20th Century to the 21st Century, drastic transformations occurred in organizations [BAU 05] as new technologies took on a central role in these organizations. These technological changes established contact with new ways of communicating and new forms of relationships, with an emphasis on virtual communication. This led to the introduction of virtual mentoring relationships and facilitated collaboration between peers [TAL 14a].

Due to the influx of new technologies, globalization and the growing diversity of people and forms of work also appeared. Thus, paradigms were broken and the relationships between people and organizations led to new challenges. The dissemination of knowledge has become important; it forces organizations to adopt methods such as mentoring [BRI 17]. Another associated issue is the globalized market, which makes the supply of talented people scarce, which forces companies to compete with each other to attract and retain the best workers, because it is expensive to recruit, select, train and then retain good workers [JON 17].

8.2.2. *Mentoring, the concept*

Mentoring is increasingly a trend and attracted a lot of interest from academics and professionals in the areas of psychology and human resource management [BAU 05, MEI 14]. Despite the numerous researches already carried out, for example, on the impacts of mentoring (direct and indirect), there is still much to explore and understand in the different aspects of mentoring [BAU 05, THO 16]. In addition to opening up for more future research on the different aspects of mentoring, there is also some difficulty in finding a unique concept. For Galluci, Van Lare, Yoon and Boatright [GAL 10], the difficulty in finding a single definition of mentoring stems from the fact that it is ambiguous, flexible and adaptable to the circumstances in which it is applied. The same authors also state that the more research on the subject is done, the more and different definitions of mentoring arise. For Haggard *et al.* [HAG 11], the lack of clarity regarding the definition of the concept, both by researchers and those who build and apply mentoring programs, makes each one use their own concept of mentoring. As for the ambiguity of the concept, Bhatta and Washington [BHA 03] stated that this is a broad concept, as it involves areas beyond the organizational area, the work itself, such as career and work-life balance, as well as other areas of personal life.

For Cuerrier [CUE 01], the concept of mentoring should be particularly centered on the development issues of the mentee's career and not on debating other dimensions of their life, as this would be confusing the concept of mentoring with a different concept: counseling. According to Baugh and Sullivan [BAU 05], the definition lacks precision and focuses mainly on the phases of development of relationships as well as the levels of involvement experienced by individuals.

From a professional perspective, in the organizational field, efforts have been made to define the functions and results of mentoring and to create programs or define guidelines to develop mentoring relationships that positively benefit a worker's career and the results of an organization [BAU 05, NOW 17]. Although it is known that, as in all organizational practices, there are beneficial and other, less positive, aspects that require an equal amount of attention from academics, researchers and professionals in the area, according to Baugh and Sullivan [BAU 05], the majority of research on the subject presented an optimistic perspective on mentoring.

Still at the organizational level, mentoring was defined, in the past, in a long-term perspective, focusing on the development of the mentee [BAU 05] – this development was done through a relationship based on a hierarchical dyad [BAU 05]. Currently, this time horizon is no longer commonly accepted since the volatile and frantic nature of careers and the organizational environment make this type of relationship a short-term, temporary one [BAU 05, IVA 19]. In addition to the changes in time duration in the concept of mentoring, the frequency of occurrence also varied. Once, it was believed that mentoring relationships happened sporadically and that they were relatively rare, however, currently the opposite is believed – mentoring relationships happen sequentially and/or simultaneously [BAU 05, MUR 17].

Despite the various definitions presented in the literature in the area, it is Kram's 1988 definition of mentoring that is considered the most classic and has the most citations [BRI 17]. According to Kram [KRA 80, KRA 85a], mentoring is defined as a relationship between two individuals, where one – older, experienced, expert and respected, called the mentor – transmits knowledge, suggestions and guidance to a second individual – younger, less experienced and with an ambition to learn, called the mentee [KRA 88, BRI 17]. From this concept come many similar ones, which only have different names in relation to the actors in the mentoring relationship – often the mentor is also designated as the tutor, the advisor, the buddy, etc. and the mentee as the protégé the mentored, the one undergoing mentoring, the apprentice, etc.

It is not only in relation to the mentoring players that synonyms arise. In the objective/action resulting from the relationship between the players in the mentoring relationship, it is common to find in the literature verbal forms such as guide, support, facilitate, teach, prepare, show, help, assimilate, develop, transmit, supervise, encourage, win, train, favor, progress, etc. Table 8.1 presents some definitions of mentoring chronologically.

By analyzing Table 8.1, it is easy to find similarities between the various definitions and at the same time realize that the concept, in essence, has not changed much over the years.

Author	Year	Definition of *mentoring*
Kram	1980	Strong interpersonal relationship between a senior employee, with more experience, and another, junior, less experienced.
Kram & Isabella	1985b	Relationship created between an inexperienced person – the mentee – and another more experienced – the mentor – who assumes the role of tutor and trainer of the first, preparing him for new challenges and favoring his recognition before the organization, aiming for his professional progress.
Kram	1988	Relationship between two individuals, one of whom is older, expert, understood, respected – the mentor – who passes on knowledge, suggestions and guidance to the mentee – younger, with less experience, willing to learn.
Clutterbuck & Megginson	1999	Support given from one person to another, where there is a transfer of knowledge/learning.
MacLennan	1999	Process in which a senior, more experienced manager is available to establish an unspecified relationship with a beginning manager, committing to help in the search for information; to behave as a model; to build feedback and opinions; explaining any aspect that may be important for the learner's performance in his organizational context.
Center for Health Leadership & Practice, Public Health Institute	2003	Mentoring is a process in which an experienced individual helps another to develop his or her goals and skills through a series of limited, confidential activities, one-to-one conversations and other learning activities.
Eby & Lockwood	2004	Interpersonal relationship where a more experienced individual (mentor) provides guidance and support to a younger organizational member (mentee).
Santos	2007	Mentoring presupposes the participation of a more experienced person (mentor) who will teach and try to prepare another person (mentee), less experienced or knowledgeable of a certain area/topic.
Crisp & Cruz	2009	Formalized medium where a person, with greater experience and wiser, supports and supervises, encourages reflection and gaining knowledge, another person with less experience with the aim of developing the latter personally and professionally.
Erlich	2015	Mentoring is a partnership between an individual with certain knowledge and/or experience who voluntarily transmits it and allows the development of another person.
Anitha & Chandrasekar	2017	Mentoring is a professional relationship where an experienced person (mentor) supports another (mentee) in developing certain skills and gaining knowledge, and will make the less experienced person develop professionally and personally.

Author	Year	Definition of *mentoring*
Brito *et al.*	2017	The mentor shares their knowledge and assistance with an inexperienced employee in order to teach them something that it would be difficult to learn otherwise. Mentoring is the act of helping others to assimilate knowledge.
Environmental Careers Organization of Canada	2017	Mentoring is the guidance provided by a mentor, especially to an inexperienced person in an organization.
Jones	2017	Mentoring happens when new employees are paired with more veteran employees who can show them the way forward.
Rodrigues	2018	It consists of an experienced employee helping a less experienced one.

Table 8.1. *Definitions of mentoring*

After the presentation of the concept of mentoring and the mentoring relationship, it is important to understand what the practice of mentoring implies for human resource management and for the organization. According to Brito *et al.* [BRI 17], mentoring can be considered a human resource management tool that is, in a traditional way, under the coordination of an organization's development department. Still according to the same authors, mentoring can also be considered as: a method of integrating new employees; a method of developing entrepreneurial careers; a feedback collection strategy; a succession plan; a continuous learning strategy; a method for the development of interpersonal skills; a method of disseminating knowledge; a social inclusion strategy and a method to develop management skills. Rodrigues [ROD 18] agrees with Brito *et al.* [BRI 17], stating that mentoring is a human resource development tool in an organization. In addition to being considered a development tool, for Eby and Lockwood [EBY 04], mentoring is also a tool for socialization and on-the-job training, corroborating the idea of Brito *et al.* [BRI 17]. The authors consider that mentoring has career functions (related to the development of human resources) and psychosocial functions (related to the socialization part, for example) [EBY 04, BRI 17].

In addition to the traditional definitions of mentoring shown above, some variants of the original concept of mentoring have begun to emerge, as described in the next section.

8.2.3. *Types of mentoring*

8.2.3.1. *Formal versus informal mentoring*

This dichotomy of the original concept of mentoring is the oldest and most addressed in the literature. Thus, for authors like Hegstad [HEG 99], mentoring can be formal or informal. As for informal mentoring, it can be said that it is a relationship that arises naturally, the result of a chemistry between two people, without any preparation or prior programming [CEN 03, ELR 15].

Chao [CHA 97] states that informal mentoring is not created, managed or formally recognized by the organization – these are relationships that exist intrinsically in any organization, arise spontaneously and are the result of mutual attraction processes. As for this process of mutual attraction, Kram [KRA 80] states that it happens because, unconsciously, mentees seek mentors who want to follow as a model, who they consider to be a source of access to information, networks, influence and even protection, and the mentors choose minds with characteristics that mirror their own. The key to this type of relationship is the feeling of sharing the same identity, both having a similar background. There are usually two situations contributing to the occurrence of informal mentoring. On the one hand, someone with more knowledge and/or experience is willing/happy to help another individual to evolve and feels useful thanks to this collaboration. On the other hand, someone who needs knowledge and/or experience approaches someone who has it [ERL 15].

As for formal mentoring, it is a process/program that is pre-planned and implemented by the organization itself, where there are well-defined objectives for the creation of alliances between less experienced employees, in order to meet certain organizational objectives [HEG 99, BRI 17]. Kram [KRA 80] also presents his own definition of formal mentoring, stating that these are programs structured and managed by organizations, and that are standardized by the pursuit of certain standards. Murray and Owen [MUR 91] corroborate Kram [KRA 80], and reiterate that formal mentoring consists of structural processes created to form effective relationships and orientations. Thus, formal mentoring translates the organizational effort to pair mentors and mentees – this process is traditionally called the match process [EBY 04]. As for participation in formal programs, it is up to the organization itself to grant the participation of all workers so that they can assume one of the roles (mentor or mentee) or designate criteria for that purpose, such as performance, appointment of third parties or type of job [EBY 04]. After the participants are chosen, organizations usually offer preparatory activities, such as guidance and training, so that mentors and mentees understand their role and obligations and feel comfortable with the entire mentoring process [EBY 04]. In short, formal mentoring is characterized by its intentionality. The relationship members (mentor and mentee) offer/ask for guidance, set goals and agree on the nature of the relationship to be established [CEN 03].

Regarding the differences between these two types of mentoring, Chao [CHA 97] affirms that the main difference lies in the way the relationship is born. Meanwhile, Eby and Lockwood [EBY 04] argue that in addition to the way the mentoring relationship begins – spontaneous approach or a match by third parties – the concepts also differ in relation to the structure of the relationship, in terms of its duration and level of formality. For Hunt and Michael [HUN 83], the main differences between formal and informal mentoring are found in view of two distinct variables: the focus of the objective and the social intensity. Thus, in informal relationships the focus is on the individual and there is a strong social intensity, while in formal mentoring the focus is on organizational objectives and the social intensity is only moderate [HUN 83].

8.2.3.2. *Reverse mentoring*

After the concept of formal and informal mentoring, the most prominent type of mentoring in the literature and that is more recent as well, is so-called reverse mentoring.

According to Brito *et al.* [BRI 17], reverse mentoring happens when younger employees teach and transmit new learning to older employees. This type of mentoring stimulates older collaborators, to keep the younger ones committed to helping others to progress, thus allowing the development of intergenerational relationships [ANI 17]. Reverse mentoring is very common in organizations in the areas of new technologies [BRI 17].

8.2.3.3. *Peer mentoring*

According to Anitha and Chandrasekar [ANI 17], mentoring relationships can arise between junior and senior members, as well as between peers. The Talent Management Staff [TAL 14b] suggests that peer mentoring (internationally known as "peer mentoring" and even "buddy mentoring") is mainly the bond and dialogue between peers that not only allows information to be exchanged, but also allows feedback and common problems, emotional and personal support and companionship to be shared. This bond is created with employees who do not show much difference in terms of level of experience. According to Tjan [TJA 11], this type of mentoring focuses more on learning than on mentoring itself. The author explains that, particularly in an organization's onboarding processes, what really benefits the new employee is the "buddy"/"peer" system that aims to accelerate the individual's learning curve. It mainly consists of help with certain more specific skills, explanations of certain organizational practices and demonstrations of how things are done in that organization. The buddy's interaction with the new employee must be constant from day one [TJA 11].

8.2.3.4. *Other mentoring types*

Santos [SAN 07] considers that there are different types of mentoring depending on the organizational objective that is intended to be achieved. Thus, Santos proposes four types of mentoring:

– *Integration mentoring*: when the organization aims to promote and integrate minority groups or integrate people in very specific careers [SAN 07].

– *Succession mentoring*: when the organization aims to develop workers in order to reduce the turnover of human capital. It is about preparing workers for career growth and attracting new workers with these development policies [SAN 07].

– *Entrepreneurship mentoring*: when an organization intends to sponsor and guide new entrepreneurs who are starting their business in order to develop attitudes and the culture of a successful entrepreneur [SAN 07].

– *Career mentoring*: when the organization wants to develop a worker in order to obtain the skills necessary for their growth and adaptation to the function, such as leadership, communication, conflict resolution, among others [SAN 07]. Tjan [TJA 11] adds that this type of mentoring arises after an employee's integration period, where another more senior professional in the organization assumes the role of their career counsellor. The senior professional should show the mentee how the mentee contributes to the organizational purpose, what their impact is and how far they can go. This will make the mentee feel motivated, satisfied and fulfilled [TJA 11]. Tjan [TJA 11] also points out that in this situation the mentee's superior should not be the mentor.

8.2.4. *Mentoring objectives*

Before presenting the advantages and disadvantages of mentoring and its programs in organizations, it is important to know for what purpose organizations use this tool. The literature points to numerous and diverse objectives of mentoring programs, but Douglas [DOU 97] managed to group them into two large groups: development of organizational objectives and development of organizational members. In what concerns the development of organizational objectives, it is related with the objectives that focus the interests of the organization, mainly related to productivity, such as:

– attract and recruit qualified employees, develop and retain them [DOU 97, EBY 04, GRA 17];

– plan successions [DOU 97, LEU 17];

– rapid integration of new employees and transmission of knowledge to them [ROD 18], as well as their introduction to important contacts and resources [ANI 17]; and

– creating challenging tasks and goals [ANI 17].

In what concerns development of organizational members, the focus is on the interests and benefits for the organization's workers, mainly related to personal satisfaction and development. These include:

– provide a rapid development of employees appointed by the organization as having strong potential [DOU 97, FIN 18]. The development is done both professionally and personally [CLU 12];

– to serve as a tool to develop the career of its workers [EBY 04, CLU 12];

– stimulate learning, knowledge and skills development on both sides [EBY 04, CLU 12, ERL 15];

– serve as an emotional support and as a form of socialization in relation to the environment in which the employee needs to act [ERL 15];

– give visibility and recognition, as well as sponsoring and protecting workers [ANI 17].

This division of objectives made by Douglas [DOU 97], is based mainly on the division that exists in Kram's mentoring function model. This model resulted from research carried out in the late 1970s by the American professor Kathy Ellen Kram and is still currently the most widely used model of organizational mentoring functions [KRA 80]. Thus, the career functions according to Kram's model [KRA 80] are divided into two groups:

– *Job and/or career functions*: promote career development within the organization through the sharing of professional experiences and mentor knowledge [SAN 07]. It consists of aspects of the relationship that guarantee the learning of the roles that the employee must assume at a professional level and that prepare him/her for the evolution of their career within the organization [GUE 09].

– *Psychosocial (or behavioral) functions*: improve the skills and identity of the mentee as well as their behaviors and attitudes, promoting the spirit of leadership and vision of the future [SAN 07]. Since mentoring is mainly an interpersonal relationship, where emotions occupy a central place, psychosocial functions focus mainly on emotional and relational aspects that can help the mentee improve their level of competence, identity and efficiency in a professional role [KRA 88, GUE 09, ERL 15].

It should also be noted that these two types of functions are not dissimilar and asynchronous, that is, the mentor can provide their mentee with a career function and, at the same time, a psychosocial function [GUE 09].

8.2.5. *Mentoring participants*

In a mentoring relationship, there are at least three actors: the mentor, the mentee and the organization itself. Each of them plays a different role and benefits from this process in a different way. Thus, it is important to know each one individually to understand the interaction that may arise between them.

8.2.5.1. *Mentor*

For Fouché and Lunt [FOU 10], a mentor is a kind of trusted advisor or guide. Kumar *et al.* [KUM 16] adds that the mentor is an experienced guide and transmitter of knowledge and know-how. Daniel *et al.* [DAN 06] considers that the mentor is an experienced person, capable of helping their mentee to develop professionally. In addition, the mentor also has psychosocial functions, as they serve as a role model and support for the mentee, while assuming the role of their defender [DAN 06, TAL 13]. Finally, according to Kram [KRA 80], the main function of the mentor is to discover all the potentialities of their mentee.

Since mentoring programs are often designed with emphasis on the mentor's knowledge [CLU 12], it is important that, in order for the mentor to help the mentee to develop specific skills and leadership skills, the mentor has these same characteristics [CEN 03]. If they don't have them, mentors must acquire these skills, techniques or tools in order to transmit knowledge better [ROD 18].

In addition to technical knowledge and skills, mentors must be highly committed and involved in understanding their role in the mentoring process/relationship and the role of their respective mentee [TAL 13]. For this there are formations/trainings called pre-mentoring that can be an option for those who have lesser social skills, in order to establish basic skills so that they can become effective mentors [CLU 12].

Regarding the relationship that the mentor should maintain with their mentee, Rodrigues [ROD 18] says that mentors must be found and chosen to assume this role according to the needs of the mentees. According to Clutterbuck [CLU 12], given that the mentor sees in their mentee a version of himself/herself in the past, the relationship should focus on the mentee, on their needs and rhythms. The mentor should question what their mentee thinks about certain projects/challenges and should encourage them to think as their superiors would think in order to prepare the mentee for possible future management and/or leadership positions [TAL 13].

As for who can be a mentor, as previously mentioned, this decision is up to the organization itself. It may be someone with more or less experience in the organization; they may be direct superiors, peers from the same organization or outside, subordinates among many other options [BAU 05]. For Baugh and Sullivan [BAU 05] the options are endless to the point of stating that mentoring relationships do not necessarily need to be in pairs. However, the Talent Management Staff [TAL 14a] points out that a mentor who is "peer" to the mentee, that is, who has a level of experience just above the latter, understands better and creates greater empathy with the mentee's problems. If the mentor was or is in a similar situation, this allows for better communication, greater mutual and collaborative support than if they were a traditional mentor, that is, much more experienced. Going beyond the question of experience, the Association of Legal Administrators [ASS n/d], through its "ALA Guide to Cross-Functional Mentoring"[2], believes that there are certain ideal characteristics that a mentor should present – the "3 C's". First, competence, through professional experience, knowledge, respect and interpersonal skills. Second, confidence, observed through the sharing of resources and the sharing of the network, the fact of allowing the mentee to establish their own rules, by showing initiative, giving credit and taking risks. Third, commitment, by investing time, effort and energy in the mentoring relationship and by sharing professional experiences.

8.2.5.2. *Mentee*

The mentee, also known as the "mentored", the "protégé" or the "apprentice", among other terminologies is the one who receives mentor guidance [MIN 14, ROD 18]. Rodrigues [ROD 18] states that mentees are the ones who need and want to learn and develop in a certain area, so they are relatively easy to find. Thus, it can be concluded that it is usually someone who is starting a career in a new organization and who is in a more fragile position, as they do not yet feel completely integrated, so he/she will be the one who typically, in comparison with the mentor, will be most interested in the mentoring relationship [ROD 18]. However, Clutterbuck [CLU 12] recalls that, in the case of formal mentoring programs, there may be two main reasons for mentees to participate in this relationship: either they are genuinely interested in developing a relationship with another more experienced employee, in order to gain knowledge, or they participate only because their organization appoints them.

It should also be noted that the benefits of a mentoring relationship are much more evident to the mentee than to other players and that this type of relationship is often born and/or is built based on the mentee's needs. Although the following section presents the benefits of mentoring for mentees in detail, a small preview of

2 https://www.alanet.org/docs/default-source/diversity/mentoringguide.pdf?sfvrsn=65e348ab_4, accessed 2 July 2020.

some of them is presented. Minnick *et al.* [MIN 14] argue that through the support of a mentor, the mentee feels greater security and help, for example, in preventing errors, due to the past experience of their mentor. Minnick *et al.* also add that, compared to those workers who did not receive any mentoring, those who had help from the mentor have a higher rate of promotion, salary and career success [MIN 14]. However, one cannot think that the mentee is simply present passively in the relationship to receive advice and teachings from the mentor. The mentee must be an active player, shaping and leading the relationship itself [ZER 09]. Thus, ideally the mentee should seek in a mentoring relationship to make a self-assessment, to be receptive, to take initiative, to show responsibility and honesty towards the mentor [ZER 09]. According to the proposal by Zerzan *et al.* [ZER 09], the most productive position that a mentee can adopt in order to optimize the mentoring relationship is "managing up". Zerzan *et al.* argue that this is a management concept that characterizes the form of relationship between an employee and a supervisor, in this case applied to mentoring relationships, in which the mentee conducts and appropriates the relationship, allowing the mentor to know what he/she needs and in what way he/she prefers to learn. The mentee can do this by planning and setting the meeting agenda, by asking questions, by actively listening and carrying out tasks and requesting feedback [ZER 09]. Regardless of how it arises or how it is conducted, mentoring, according to Zachary [ZAC 05], is always a relevant tool for the mentee, both at a personal and a professional level, as their personal and professional skills are developed simultaneously. Clutterbuck [CLU 12] corroborates this position and states that, contrary to what happens with the mentor during mentoring relationships, whose skills remain relatively constant, those of the mentee, on the contrary, evolve continuously throughout the different phases of the relationship [ROD 18].

Another variable to be aware of in the case of mentees is the fact that most of them are from the millennial generation [TAL 13]. This generation has relatively peculiar characteristics in relation to other generations, as they want to be part of a mentoring relationship but not a traditional mentoring [TAL 12a, TAL 12b, TAL 13]. Millennials like to learn through different collaborations and see mentoring as a learning process that takes place through different relationships – through managers, colleagues, customers, among others – instead of the traditional one-to-one format. In addition, they expect to be told from their first day on the job what they are supposed to do, although they prefer to work with collaborative mentors who are close, who listen to them and who are not authoritarian [TAL 13].

8.2.5.3. *Organization*

The organization consists of the environment in which mentoring relationships are inserted and developed. The organization must provide the necessary conditions (such as resources, time, etc.) so that both mentors and mentees can benefit from the mentoring relationship [MAS 15]. As mentors and mentees both benefit from this type of relationship, it creates a general atmosphere of satisfaction in the organization and makes it more agile, more conducive to change. The implementation of this organizational practice will allow the organization to take more risks in hiring new workers, reducing costs and training time that these same employees would need to adapt to the organization and start producing value [POW 10].

In this third element of the mentoring relationship, the literature points out two fundamental elements for mentoring relationships with regard to the organization: the head/management/supervision of the mentor and the mentee [TAL 13] and the team responsible for management mentoring programs [MAN 12].

As for the manager/leadership of the mentor–mentee pair, it must provide a structured plan with the mentoring activities for both parties; it must schedule check-ins to ensure that the mentees are learning properly and feel comfortable with the mentoring relationship, and understand how mentors are developing the relationship and how they are developing themselves [TAL 13]. The manager must adopt an open and welcoming attitude from the beginning, thus communicating that they want to develop mentoring work with the team and, at the same time, develop a relationship with both the mentor and the mentee. The manager should also question the mentor and the mentee about ideas and feedback, so that they understand that their contributions are taken into account [TAL 13].

As for the mentoring program management team, as Penim and Catalão [PEN 18] claim, organizational mentoring programs are often linked to other development strategies such as competency management, which shows that the mentoring management is usually the responsibility of the Human Resource Management Department or the Development Department. Penim and Catalão also recognize and emphasize the indispensability of the management team for the success of mentoring programs, even stating that their constitution is a prerequisite for this type of organizational initiative. This team is responsible for designing/creating the program and is also responsible for its implementation and management [PEN 18]. Mentoring program managers also benefit from their involvement through: strengthening their management and leadership skills; creating opportunities to put certain skills into practice, such as conflict management, for example; and for learning to work with different personalities and at different stages of their careers [MAN 12].

8.2.6. *Advantages and disadvantages of mentoring*

Mentoring, in the form of organizational mentoring programs, naturally presents advantages for the organization and for those involved, just like any other tool used by human resource management. According to Baugh and Sullivan [BAU 05], when the mentoring programs are well designed and work well, they can generate positive effects for both mentors and mentees, as well as for the organization itself.

However, it is also necessary to know its potential disadvantages and/or organizational problems that may arise with its implementation, in order to prevent and actively combat them. Thus, and although the literature focuses mainly on the positive aspects of mentoring, with the analysis of cases of successful programs, mentoring can both benefit the organization and its human resources, as well as contribute to the occurrence of organizational errors [BAU 05].

8.2.6.1. *Advantages for the mentee*

Thus, starting with the mentee, who is usually at the center of the research's attention on this subject, according to Eby and Lockwood [EBY 04] the benefits that mentoring can provide can be divided into four areas: learning, coaching, career planning, and psychosocial support.

According to Penim and Catalão [PEN 18], mentoring contributes to the mentee's learning process and accelerates their adaptation to the organization. The mentee, by having someone to learn with, will be more available to assimilate information and knowledge and transfer them to reality and professional context. As for the greater adaptation to the organization, it may come from the fact that the mentor had previously considered what the mentee would need to know and how to do to adapt. Mentoring helps the mentee learn about the organization's culture as well as its intrinsic norms [DOU 97, MAN 12]. According to Clutterbuck [CLU 12], with the mentoring relationship, three different types of learning are transmitted to the mentee. First, the mentee learns directly from the mentor through their experience and wisdom. Second, the mentee learns from the dialogue they maintain with the mentor, by challenging their beliefs, which in turn makes them more self-confident, and they obtain an opinion on their behavior and the behavior of others, while also learning how to acquire knowledge. Thirdly, the mentee learns from their own reflection on the mentoring sessions.

Concerning coaching, having a mentor from day one in an organization increases the productivity of the mentee, as the mentor will help identify the necessary resources and some cultural norms that they would have difficulty identifying without the mentor's help [TAL 13]. With mentoring, the mentee is taught to know how to speak and be heard, as well as how to accept feedback [MAN 12]. In addition, both support and feedback are personalized [DOU 97]. With a mentor, mentees feel safer with their work and, consequently, perform better [ENV 17].

Another area is career planning. Employees who participated in mentoring programs as mentees show greater satisfaction with their work [PEN 18], and in turn, according to some studies, satisfied employees stay longer in the organization and work more and better [GRA 17]. Douglas [DOU 97] states that mentees have greater opportunities for career advancement. These opportunities result from the mentees receiving concrete support from the mentor along the road to progress and in the respective decision-making made by them [PEN 18].

Finally, the fourth area is psychosocial support. According to the Talent Management Staff [TAL 12a], the period in which an employee joins a new company is always a moment of great vulnerability for them, especially if they recently left university to enter the job market. Uncertainty and fear take a back seat when the employee knows they will be able to rely on someone – their mentor. According to Erlich [ERL 15] and Douglas [DOU 97], mentoring provides greater security and self-confidence to the mentee, as they know they will not be alone [PEN 18]. The mentee benefits from the reduction of stress levels, as they will be helped both in recognizing the challenges that they will have to go through, as well as the skills that the mentee possess to face the challenges [DOU 97, PEN 18]. With mentoring, the mentee expands the network of relationships [MAN 12] by benefiting from the mentor's own networking [PEN 18]. Mentoring helps the mentee to develop and/or improve their interpersonal skills [MAN 12].

8.2.6.2. *Advantages for the mentor*

The benefits of mentoring are for both parties and not exclusively or mainly for the mentee [BAU 05]. For Clutterbuck [CLU 12], the most common benefit for mentors is that they can be challenged. However, a mentoring relationship can present many other benefits for the mentor, such as those listed and grouped into categories by Eby and Lockwood [EBY 04]: learning, development of a personal relationship, personal qualification, and improvement of management skills.

Concerning learning, mentoring programs often contribute to the acquisition of knowledge, serve as a source of inspiration for the mentor and help to evolve their own way of thinking, more or less consciously for the mentor themselves [CEN 03]. The generational difference that often occurs between the mentor and the mentee provides a great exchange of knowledge between both parties [PEN 18]. The mentor learns through the mentoring relationship and gets used to using active listening instead of passive listening.

Another benefit results from the development of a personal relationship. The mentor, through a mentoring relationship, has the opportunity to share wisdom and experiences [CEN 03]. In addition, there is also personal qualification. Participation in mentoring programs gives the mentor an energetic boost to their career and a revitalization at work that leads to greater satisfaction and personal fulfilment as well as their own career [DOU 97, MAN 12]. Through the contacts established to increase the network of their mentee, the mentor, in turn, increases and/or reactivates their own network [CEN 03, ERL 15, PEN 18]. The feeling of contribution, of leaving a legacy and greater visibility, prestige and recognition are also considered benefits that contribute to the motivation and self-esteem of the employee who is or was a mentor [DOU 97, MAN 12, PEN 18]. This situation is even more critical and essential when working in an organization that focuses heavily on youth and young employees, since in this type of organizational environment, older employees can easily feel useless and undervalued, leading to demotivation [PEN 18]. For this reason, the mentor is able to increase their self-confidence [DOU 97]. According to Penim and Catalão [PEN 18], mentoring provides mentors with the development of some skills that they acquire either through preparation to assume their role or during the mentoring process itself. These skills may already be previously intrinsic to the mentor; however mentoring is an excellent opportunity to put them into practice. According to Clutterbuck [CLU 12], personal development is common to the vast majority of mentors, especially with regard to interpretation skills.

Another benefit results from improvement of management skills. One of the most recognized management skills of employees in leadership positions is empathy and interpersonal communication. Thus, the mentor, when developing their interpersonal communication skills for assuming the role of mentor, is also developing their management skills [MAN 12]. The mentor, having to show and contact the different areas of their organization because of their mentee, will acquire more organizational knowledge about the different areas and thus have a global perspective that they would hardly have if they simply focused on their own tasks and did not have the opportunity to participate in a mentoring relationship [MAN 12]. Knowing the organization well makes the job of any manager more efficient because it allows them to gain knowledge on how it works and where to go for help on a given subject.

In addition to these main benefits pointed out by Eby and Lockwood [EBY 04], others can also be highlighted, such as:

– employees who have taken on or take on the role of mentors receive more promotions than other employees and perform better, due to the reinvigoration with the mentoring experience [GRA 17];

– participation as a mentor in mentoring programs provides an opportunity to thank and return the support of the organization and the mentoring itself that may have been received in the past [MAN 12].

8.2.6.3. *Advantages for the organization*

As previously mentioned, the organization itself also benefits from the implementation of mentoring programs, if not for the benefits felt by its employees (both mentors and mentees), since co-learning is the most common benefit in relationships between mentoring pairs. As mentioned earlier, benefits appear at a more subjective level – such as through job and career satisfaction – or at an objective level – potential salary increases, promotions, etc. [EBY 04]. According to Hegstad [HEG 99], when organizations are able to create formal mentoring programs, they are also able to create strategies for the development of employees. Thus, some of the organizational benefits of mentoring include, among others: human resources input/output management, career management, learning/knowledge, image.

Regarding human resources input/output management, the organization benefits result from employee involvement [GRA 17], increased engagement [DOU 97, JON 17] and increased loyalty [MAN 12]. It benefits also from the creation of a more solid contributory culture with a focus on diversity [ASS n/d]; the creation of a good organizational environment based on cooperation between employees [MAN 12, ENV 17]; and, from the reduction of turnover, which in turn increases retention rates and decreases costs with the loss of workers and talent [JON 17, GRA 17, ENV 17]. According to O'Brien and Allen [OBR 06] mentoring is particularly interesting for organizations that aspire to growth and that want to attract and retain talent. According to the Association of Legal Administrators [ASS n/d], mentoring can serve as an organizational tool that simultaneously attracts and retains the best employees, because, for many, the existence of a mentoring program may be more relevant than a better remuneration offer, when they have to decide to stay in the organization or accept a job offer.

Another benefit results from career management. According to Grayless [GRA 17], top executives have attributed their career success to their mentors. Mentoring helps to create succession plans [DOU 97], to form future leaders [JON 17] and works on the development of leadership skills [MAN 12, ERL 15]. In addition, mentoring relationships provide increased networking for the people involved [ERL 15]. Thus, according to Erlich [ERL 15], mentoring provides the organization with feasibility in terms of more functional career development processes.

The organization also benefits in terms of learning and knowledge, since it is in mentoring relationships that 80% of learning takes place in the workplace, and is the most cost-effective form of learning for the organization [DOU 97, GRA 17], which in turn allows for cost savings with training and development. Jones [JON 17] presents an example of a mentoring program for new teachers where, for every $ 1 spent on the program, there was a return of $ 1.50. Mentoring relationships also speed up the organizational learning process as well as the adaptation of new employees, which in turn contribute to greater productivity [ERL 15] as well as create a better and more informed workforce [ENV 17]. Mentoring relationships allow both parties involved (mentors and mentees) to develop soft skills, especially those related to interpersonal relationships [ENV 17]. According to the Association of Legal Administrators [ASS n/d], mentoring, through its role model, can be more effective than certain training actions, as mentoring is a good leadership model that allows the learning of skills difficult to achieve with training in a classroom environment. The same association adds that mentoring encourages excellence for mentors and mentees, since the mentee learns and gains knowledge from a good mentor and, in turn, the mentor has the opportunity to recapitulate knowledge and rethink while explaining things to the mentee.

Also, the image of the organization can benefit from mentoring. With the development and implementation of mentoring programs, organizations internally convey the idea that management is committed to investing in its employees [MAN 12]. At the same time, organizations transmit to their external environment the idea that they value their human resources [MAN 12].

8.2.6.4. *Disadvantages of mentoring*

Despite the scarcity of studies dedicated to the disadvantages of mentoring [COL 01, BUR 10], it is important to note that dysfunctional mentoring relationships can lead to very harmful results for all parties involved [BAU 05]. According to Eby and Lockwood [EBY 04], these problems are more likely to occur when it comes to formal mentoring, since the relationship may not be voluntary and always depends on the involvement of a third element external to the relationship: the organization. Another situation that can contribute to the emergence of problems in terms of mentoring, according to Clutterbuck [CLU 12], is the dispersion and lack of a clear definition of the end of the relationship and consequent lack of recognition of the contribution made by both parties.

Next, the disadvantages for each of the mentoring members will be addressed.

8.2.6.5. *Disadvantages to the mentee*

One disadvantage or problem that may result from mentoring to the mentee is related with carelessness with work. According to Douglas [DOU 97], the fact of assigning a mentor to a worker can, wrongly, make the latter relax and feel more comfortable to unravel small details, since the mentee believes that the mentor will supervise and filter their mistakes. Another possible problem may emerge from a conflict between mentor–boss. If there is a conflict between the mentor and the boss of a worker, the worker can be harmed, since the boss can interfere and damage the relationship with the person who has the most contact and who protects them – their mentor. The boss may be influenced by the fact that the mentee may be somewhat the mirror of their mentor, and unfairly harm the mentee [DOU 97].

Differently, but which may also result in a problem, is excessive expectations of promotion. According to Douglas [DOU 97], the mentee can naively feel that by being protected and sponsored by their mentor, they can more easily achieve an ascendancy in their career. Another problem may arise from dependency. Douglas

[DOU 97] and Clutterbuck [CLU 12] point to the danger of the mentee creating such a state of dependence on their mentor that results in them being unable to develop their own autonomy. There is also a possibility that the mentee will not create other relationships or be in isolation. The mentee, by spending a lot of time and depending a lot on their mentor, may be discouraging other socialization opportunities that they could have with other colleagues, who are also willing to help them [DOU 97].

A possible disadvantage emerges from less positive experiences and "bad" mentors. Douglas [DOU 97] and Broder-Singer [BRO 11] claim that worse than a worker not having a mentor is having a mentor who is not committed to their role. This can disturb the mentee's morale and their intention to stay in the organization [BRO 11]. Colley [COL 01] also points out that there is a danger that the mentor will be interpreted as the most powerful member of the relationship and the mentee as incapacitated or powerless. Thus, in the transmission of knowledge, the mentor's knowledge may be reinforced, overlapping the established practice and nullifying the importance of new knowledge brought by the mentee [COL 01].

In addition to the mentioned disadvantages, Colley [COL 01] goes further and points out that, in extreme cases, mentoring can be considered a tool for controlling and manipulating minds, in order to do what the organization or even the mentors want.

8.2.6.6. *Disadvantages to the mentor*

Mentors do not only benefit from mentoring, their participation in a mentoring relationship also has some disadvantages. First, less time and availability – a worker with a mentee in charge, if they want to play an active role as a mentor, will be left with more tasks to do than they had before making that commitment [DOU 97, KAR 16]. In turn, this increase in the workload is not usually reflected proportionally in the reduction of the usual tasks under their responsibility or in an extension of deadlines [KAR 16]. Second, unclear benefits – the poor definition and presentation of the benefits of mentoring to the mentor may prevent the mentor from being able to take full advantage of them [DOU 97]. Third, pressure to be a mentor – there is sometimes pressure on workers to assume the role of mentors, mainly by their managers [DOU 97]. This can lead to the fact that, from the perspective of the mentors, the denial of participation in a mentoring relationship can be seen as a limitation and a disillusionment for their leadership. Fourth, lack of skills – as it is difficult to ensure that mentors have all the key skills necessary to perform their role well [JOH 03]. Thus, mentors who do not have them, may be playing a less positive role in mentoring relationships, which may also bring them a little personal and professional frustration [DOU 97].

8.2.6.7. *Disadvantages to the organization*

As with the advantages, mentoring can also have direct disadvantages for the organization. First, failure due to the lack of organizational support – Douglas [DOU 97] and Jones [JON 17] consider that a poor or weak execution of a mentoring program can translate into negative feelings about a certain organization. Second, an environment of favoritism and resentment from those who have been left out – when organizations choose to limit access to mentoring programs to certain workers, feelings of injustice may arise from those who were not included in this group, regardless of the role they could possibly play – mentor or mentee [DOU 97]. Third, difficult coordination – coordinating a mentoring program requires time, dedication, resources and constant and professional monitoring. In a highly competitive environment where this type of initiative is still not seen as a priority, there may be a certain neglect in monitoring mentoring relationships [DOU 97].

In addition to the disadvantages presented above, Jones [JON 17] adds that any negative experience regarding mentoring causes more intense emotional and behavioral responses compared to positive situations. It is therefore extremely important to prevent this type of situation.

8.2.7. *Mentoring: facilitators and obstacles*

As with many human resource management policies and practices, mentoring is no exception in the sense that those responsible for its implementation, management and supervision must take into account certain factors that contribute to the success of the organizational policy and practice in question. In other words, due attention should be given to facilitating factors, but also to factors that limit it or that may raise some difficulties – understood from now on as obstacles.

Thus, the successes and respective factors most commonly presented in the mentoring literature are presented in a generic way, as well as the problems and possible causes. Then, it addressed more specifically certain factors that mentoring program managers should take into account when planning, implementing, managing or supervising their programs.

8.2.7.1. *Success of mentoring programs*

Eby and Lockwood [EBY 04] state that the facilitators of successful mentoring programs are: assertive communication of program objectives; a good match between mentor and mentee; presentation of targets regarding participation in the mentoring program; better and greater monitoring/management of mentoring programs.

Cuerrier [CUE 01] points out five premises and three essential conditions for the success and sustainability of a mentoring program: the program should focus on the mentor and the mentee; the match process must establish criteria for selection and participation; the program must include a coordination and management team; the program must contain pre-mentoring training to clarify the roles to be developed; and, the program must include a process for evaluating the results (based on comparison with the pre-established objectives) and collect feedback on the satisfaction and quality of the program.

According to Cuerrier [CUE 01], the three necessary conditions are: ensure the exchange of knowledge between the parties; guarantee the resources and conditions necessary for the development of the program's activities; recognition by management and promotion of the program's importance to the organization's strategic vision.

Finally, the Environmental Careers Organization of Canada [ENV 17] only point out four basic considerations for the success of a mentoring program, namely:

– *Compatibility*: the success of the program will largely depend on how good the mentor–mentee match is. It is necessary for them to be able to communicate easily and to be genuinely interested in each other.

– *Double contribution*: mentoring must flow through both parties. The mentees must feel that they are also making a significant contribution to the relationship and not just waiting for advice from the mentor.

– *Clear expectations*: having realistic expectations and goals helps to guide the partnership in a good way.

– *Objectives of the relationship*: defining objectives for the mentoring relationship is essential for its success. Both parties must be taken into account as well as how they can work to achieve something concrete together.

8.2.7.2. *Problems with mentoring programs*

As for the problems identified in the mentoring programs, it is possible to distinguish between the problems identified by the main players in the relationship (mentor and mentee) and also the different problems that occur in formal and informal mentoring. These problems can provide valuable clues about some obstacles that can be overcome by mentoring program managers, which will be presented in detail later.

Thus, Clutterbuck [CLU 12] identified three problems simultaneously identified by mentors and mentees: first, incompatibility in the formation of mentor–mentee pairs; second, difficulty in scheduling meetings and poor availability of the other; third, geographic distance (which happens in cases of virtual mentoring).

Eby and Lockwood [EBY 04] are able to distinguish the problems identified by both mentors and mentees. Thus, the main problem identified by the mentors is the feeling of not being personally suited to the role, of not feeling like the best person to take on someone else's mentoring. As for the mentees, the problems most pointed out by them are: negligence of the mentor; unmet expectations; and structural separation (at organizational level) from the mentor.

Regarding the formal mentoring and informal mentoring dichotomy, Eby and Lockwood [EBY 04] argue that the most common problems identified in formal programs in comparison with informal programs are: greater mentor disinterest and less interpersonal competence on their part, greater selfishness and neglect on both sides.

8.2.7.3. *Planning, creating and implementing mentoring programs*

Jones [JON 17] explains that competition between companies is growing and fierce, especially when it comes to talent recruitment. In order to face this pressure, management feels the need to offer something different to its employees to attract and retain them, and often the option is mentoring. One consequence of this pressure is the decrease in the quality of organizational mentoring as well as the mentoring programs seeming fictitious and devoid of scientific validity. Jones [JON 17] thus stresses that any mentoring program is unique and cannot be simply copied to another organization. The specificities and objectives of each organization must be taken into account.

However, for Broder-Singer [BRO 11], mentoring programs are extremely difficult to design and implement. Jones [JON 17] adds that in order to create these programs, a deep reflection is necessary when planning the different phases and they have to stop being seen as band-aids of the organization. Mentoring programs must stop being made by people who are very busy and overworked, who had never even built any type of program of this kind, or by workers who have never had contact with any type of mentoring role [JON 17]. According to Jones [JON 17], one of the obstacles found for the success of mentoring programs is the low investment in their construction and implementation, because while the organization hires a specialist consultant to provide training, the same investment is not applied to mentoring. According to the same author, organizations have a habit of placing employees with little training or availability at the forefront of the development of these mentoring programs without setting clear expectations for them. It is essential to have a well thought out planning of the program's objectives as well as for each of its phases, as mentoring has different needs and requires different skills in its different phases [TJA 11, ROD 18].

Another dimension to be taken into account when building mentoring programs is the organizational complexity itself. The Talent Management Staff [TAL 14a] recalls that organizations currently work with multidisciplinary teams – narrowing the interconnections between research and development areas and production and commercial areas in order to provide more flexible business strategies – which requires equally flexible processes by the organization. Broder-Singer [BRO 11] supports this idea, remembering that overly structured and rigid mentoring programs can lead to interpersonal relationships not developing as they should.

Finally, the Association of Legal Administrators [ASS n/d] proposes a series of measures for organizations to be successful with their mentoring programs: have a support structure for both parts of the relationship; have a mechanism that provides constant feedback; have evaluation mechanisms; and, have a benchmarking routine.

8.2.7.4. *Supervision of mentoring programs and feedback*

For Rodrigues [ROD 18], it is extremely important for the success of mentoring programs to define who will supervise them, who will manage them and monitor the interactions between mentor and mentee.

In addition, Tjan [TJA 11] states that some organizations do not reflect, as they should, in their mentoring programs or collect feedback, they simply have the basics to be able to claim that they implement it. However, this proves to be an obstacle to the success of these programs at the organizational level, as it is difficult to correct and change mentoring programs if the organization, for example, does not collect feedback to know what employees think, what is not going well and how it can be improved [JON 17].

8.2.7.5. *Mentor–mentee pair*

As mentioned earlier, the mentor–mentee pair may be the result of a spontaneous process (informal mentoring) or a process created by the organization (formal mentoring). Regarding the latter, the fact that the formed pair results in the vast majority of a match process, can cause less comfort and interpersonal identification between them, and create an obstacle in building a close relationship, supported by trust [EBY 04].

However, when talking about the match process, it should be noted that this does not necessarily mean that the participation of workers is mandatory. Broder-Singer [BRO 11] states that organizations should not make participation in mentoring programs mandatory, but rather they must make sure that all workers understand the objectives and benefits of their participation, and how these objectives are connected with organizational objectives. Moreover, they should only participate if from that moment they demonstrate willingness to participate voluntarily.

8.2.7.6. *Mentor–mentee relationship*

For a mentoring relationship to work well it is necessary to have a series of conditions that facilitate its functioning. There are facilitators of the mentor–mentee relationship, but that is not enough, it is necessary that both mentor and mentee present a series of characteristics and situations in order to contribute to common success.

Thus, in relation to the mentor–mentee relationship, Eby and Lockwood [EBY 04] state that there are certain factors that can influence the benefits obtained in a mentoring relationship, such as the way the relationship is initiated, the structure of the relationship and the characteristics of the relationship. In addition to these facilitators, there are also factors which, according to Eby and Lockwood, can emphasize possible relational problems, such as the existence of a weak interpersonal adjustment between mentor and mentee or the perceived lack of commitment of some part in the relationship [EBY 04]. Clutterbuck [CLU 12], in addition to stating that there are certain personal qualities that can facilitate the success of the relationship, such as having behaviors that promote rapport, proposes two types of factors that facilitate the relationship resulting from the contract established between both. First, internal factors in the relationship: the establishment of expectations regarding the frequency of meetings and the way in which concepts and problems of the respective roles will be explored [CLU 12]; external factors to the relationship: the level of support of the organization and logistical issues related to the meetings [CLU 12].

Other authors also present their perspective on relationship facilitators such as Higgins and Kram [HIG 01], who stress that empathy between mentor and mentee is the key factor for a successful mentoring relationship. For the Talent Management Staff [TAL 14b], some of the essential characteristics for the success of mentoring relationships are the establishment of an authentic relationship, the sharing of the same perspectives and the fact that mentoring is relevant for both parties. Eby and Lockwood [EBY 04], however, conclude that the organizational characteristics and consequent characteristics of the mentoring programs themselves, especially the formal ones, can influence both the type and amount of mentor assistance and the receptivity of the mentee.

However, Clutterbuck [CLU 12] also recalls that, for example, difference can become an obstacle in the creation of affinity, which is essential and one of the first steps in the mentoring process. Another obstacle pointed out by the same author is the fact that the power in the relationship is on the side of the mentor. Nevertheless, Clutterbuck [CLU 12] also states that both participants tend to take steps to reduce the gap at this level, such as:

– an agreement of the learning objectives for both;

– establishing and recognizing that power should be used to influence and not to be authoritarian;

– the mentee should always be encouraged to give their opinion before the mentor. There must be respect for the views of both parties;

– mentoring meetings in places that demonstrate the mentor's power (e.g. the mentor's office) should be avoided;

– one should have an equality discourse and avoid being imperative;

– the mentee should be allowed to be responsible for managing the relationship and to learn from it;

– a regular review to identify situations in which the mentee felt an imbalance of power should be established.

Regarding the mentor, it can be said that they should have certain characteristics that must be developed and worked on in order to obtain successful mentoring relationships. Phillips-Jones [PHI 01], expert in mentoring and author of the book "The New Mentors and Protégés: How to Succeed with the New Mentoring Partnerships among other publications in the area, points out four key skills in mentoring, mainly for mentors:

– Active listening: creates empathy, a positive and accepting environment that in turn allows for open communication. Thus, the mentor will be able to assist the mentee according to the mentee's interests and needs. The mentor should: show interest in what the mentee says and reflect on it in order to show that they understand the mentee's opinion; use body language, such as looking into the mentee's eyes, showing that they are paying attention; reduce background noise and limit any interruption in order to give the mentee full attention; and wait for the mentee to express their ideas and thoughts first.

– Building trust: a time-consuming process. To do this, the mentor may: maintain confidentiality, honor their commitments to the mentee, show interest and ongoing support, and be honest.

– Define objectives and build capacities: the mentor can help the mentee to develop capacities and to identify and achieve their objectives by: helping the mentee find resources (people, tools, etc.); share knowledge through explanations, examples, demonstrations and rhetorical questions; and discuss actions the mentor has taken throughout their career and explain why.

– Encourage and inspire: being encouraging is the mentor's most valued skill. So, the mentor should: comment favorably on the achievements of the mentee; communicate to the mentee how much they believe in the mentee's growth and their ability to achieve their goals; counteract the frustrations of the mentee with positive words of support, understanding and encouragement; talk about the mentor's own achievements, challenges and mistakes and how they overcame them; talk about people who motivated and inspired them and introduce the mentee to people who can help them.

Having employees with mentoring skills is difficult to guarantee, especially in the case of complex organizations, with different competitive priorities and an unstable workforce [JON 17]. However, Clutterbuck [CLU 12] proposes an easy and inexpensive solution for the mentor: sharing their experience of personal discovery, since the influence of the mentor is central to the relationship. The mentor must use their "authority" to make introductions, protect and defend the mentee, and promote the name of the mentee.

Mentors' motivations for participating in formal mentoring programs vary, especially if they do not result from voluntary entry into a formal mentoring process. The mentor may not be motivated to help the mentee to grow and develop [EBY 04]. Mentors can only be concerned with obtaining organizational recognition or participate simply because they are required to do so [EBY 04].

Regarding the mentee, little information is provided by the literature, but it is known that the mentees will feel more comfortable sharing their ideas with someone who shows openness and receptivity from the beginning [TAL 13]. Currently, employees are no longer used to waiting for information or answers to their questions. Thus, if the mentor is not very active, the mentee's proactivity will lead to them seeking out other people, which can become an obstacle to the creation of a strong relationship between them. It is also known that younger workers are more receptive to aligning their behaviors with a respected mentor in the organization [TAL 12a].

8.2.7.7. *Management support*

Nowadays, in the job market where another job offer from another company is easily found, companies have invested in more benefits for employees, such as mentoring programs, especially if those same organizations cannot compete with others that offer higher wages [JON 17]. But, according to Jones [JON 17], creating a mentoring program is not an easy task, and programs often fail. One of the reasons cited for this failure is the fact that there is no due support from management – often because Management believes that mentoring programs are meaningless [JON 17].

Thus, after realizing the potential benefits of mentoring programs, according to Tjan [TJA 11], the organization should take the first step in establishing that this program is part of the strategy for developing and valuing its human resources. According to the same author, it does not need to be something complex, but it is essential that all organizational members know that the organization adopts mentoring as part of its organizational culture [TJA 11]. Broder-Singer [BRO 11] argues that the support and recognition of Management in relation to mentoring programs is extremely important, since this type of programs consumes a lot of time, for both the mentor and the mentee. They will only dedicate the necessary time to the relationship if Management supports it. The Talent Management Staff [TAL 14b] states that the organization must support the mentoring programs, and its importance must be corroborated by Management, by establishing the time and space necessary to facilitate the relationship between mentors and mentees.

It is therefore important to reaffirm that a mentoring program can be very well designed and planned, but it will only succeed if Management becomes a facilitator, being committed to mentoring as well [BRO 11]. Broder-Singer [BRO 11] suggests that organizations create clear incentives for these programs as systems of evaluation and incentives and rewards.

8.3. Conclusion

The objective expressed in the introduction to this chapter was aimed at promoting a theoretical approach to the mentoring process, but without simultaneously failing to create points of connection and interaction with the organizational reality at each point. The concept of mentoring is not new, and it must be seen from the perspective of the development of organizations and those who constitute it. The success or failure of this type of practice is a function of factors of varying nature and involves all those who directly or indirectly have responsibilities in organizations.

We also emphasized that the very reinvention that this concept must have in a world agitated by rapid, permanent and discontinuous changes where the conceptions of management, organization, worker, work and values and of the person is in reformulation and reflection, in evolution and revolution.

This chapter also helps show that human resource management practices must be framed and adapted to the organization's vision and mission; consistent with the values and principles defended and assumed by the organization. Additionally, one must understand that regardless of the formal or informal mentoring processes that are established, there is a whole set of relationships that must be enhanced. A whole set of interactions, relational experiences, learning possibilities in terms of knowing-knowing, knowing-doing, knowing-being and knowing-evolving allow those who lead organizations to find other matches, other commitments and other reciprocal and systemic learning desires that favor the growth of each and every one.

Such learning needs to be enhanced and presented in a way that everyone understands that an organization must sustainably contribute in order to assume its central objective: to be the place where people feel that their dignity is fulfilled and respected. There are more human relations within an organization than those that arise from many formal and informal human resource management practices and from the objectives and responsibilities of those whose mission is to motivate and develop their people and teams.

Therefore: mentoring... really? And why not?

8.4. References

[ANI 17] ANITHA A., CHANDRASEKAR K., "Impact of mentoring on employees of Indian bluechip IT companies", *Global Journal for Research Analysis*, vol. 6, no. 11, pp. 262–266, 2017.

[ASS n/d] ASSOCIATION OF LEGAL ADMINISTRATORS, ALA guide to cross-functional mentoring, available at: https://www.alanet.org/docs/default-source/diversity/mentoringguide.pdf?sfvrsn=65e348ab_4 (accessed July 2, 2020), n/d.

[BAU 05] BAUGH S., SULLIVAN S., "Mentoring and career development", *Career Development International*, vol. 10, no. 6/7, pp. 425–428, 2005.

[BHA 03] BHATTA G., WASHINGTON S., "'Hands up': Mentoring in the New Zealand public service", *Public Personnel Management*, vol. 32, no. 2, pp. 211–227, 2003.

[BRI 17] BRITO L., SILVA A., CASTRO A. *et al.*, "Programa de mentoria: uma estratégia seminal de compartilhamento do conhecimento em uma empresa pública de energia", *RACE – Revista de Administração, Contabilidade e Economia*, vol. 16, no. 3, pp. 209–234, 2017.

[BRO 11] BRODER-SINGER R., "Why mentoring matters", in *Business Miami*, University of Miami School of Business Administration, fall, 2011.

[BUR 10] BURK H.G., EBY L.T., "What keeps people in mentoring relationships when bad things happen? A field study from the protégé's perspective", *Journal of Vocational Behavior*, vol. 77, no. 3, pp. 437–446, 2010.

[CEN 03] CENTER FOR HEALTH LEADERSHIP & PRACTICE, PUBLIC HEALTH INSTITUTE, Mentoring guide – a guide for mentors, available at: https://www.rackham.umich.edu/downloads/more-mentoring-guide-for-mentors.pdf (accessed July 19, 2018), 2003.

[CHA 97] CHAO G.T., "Mentoring phases and outcomes", *Journal of Vocational Behaviour*, vol. 51, no. 1, pp. 15–28, 1997.

[CLU 99] CLUTTERBUCK, D., MEGGINSON, D., *Mentoring Executives and Directors*, Routledge, London, 1999.

[CLU 12] CLUTTERBUCK D., "Understanding diversity mentoring", in CLUTTERBUCK D., POULSEN K., KOCHAN F. (eds), *Developing Successful Diversity Mentoring Programmes: An International Casebook*, McGraw-Hill Education, UK, pp. 1–17, 2012.

[COL 01] COLLEY H., "Righting re-writings of the myth of mentor: A critical perspective on career guidance mentoring", *British Journal of Guidance and Counselling*, vol. 29, no. 2, pp. 177–198, 2001.

[CRI 09] CRISP, G., CRUZ I, "Mentoring college students: A critical review of the literature between 1990 and 2007", *Research in Higher Education*, vol. 50, no. 6, pp. 525–545, 2009.

[CUE 01] CUERRIER C., *Mentoring and the World of Work*, Edition de la Fondation, Quebec, 2001.

[DAN 06] DANIEL J.H., APONTE J.F., CHAO G.T. *et al.*, *Introduction to Mentoring – A Guide for Mentors and Mentees*, American Psychological Association, 2006.

[DOU 97] DOUGLAS C.A., *Formal Mentoring Programs in Organizations: An Annotated Bibliography*, Center for Creative Leadership, Greensboro, North Carolina, 1997.

[EBY 04] EBY L., LOCKWOOD A., "'Protégés' and mentors' reactions to participating in formal mentoring programs: A qualitative investigation", *Journal of Vocational Behavior*, vol. 67, no. 3, pp. 441–458, 2004.

[ENV 17] ENVIRONMENTAL CAREERS ORGANIZATION OF CANADA, Top 5 Reasons Why Mentoring Matters, available at: https://www.eco.ca/blog/top-5-reasons-why-mentoring-matters/ (accessed June 16, 2018), 2017.

[ERL 15] ERLICH P., O poder do mentoring nas organizações, available at: http://www.erlich.com.br/e-book_o_poder_do_mentoring/ (accessed July 20, 2018), 2015.

[FIN 18] FINKELSTEIN L.M., COSTANZA D.P., GOODWIN G.F., "Do your high potentials have potential? The impact of individual differences and designation on leader success", *Personnel Psychology*, vol. 71, no. 1, pp. 3–22, 2018.

[FOU 10] FOUCHÉ C., LUNT N., "Nested mentoring relationships: Reflections on a practice project for mentoring research capacity amongst social work practitioners", *Journal of Social Work*, vol. 10, no. 4, pp. 391–406, 2010.

[GAL 10] GALLUCI C., VAN LARE M.D., YOON I.H. *et al.*, "Instructional coaching: Building theory about the role and organizational support for professional learning", *American Educational Research Association*, vol. 47, no. 4, pp. 919–963, 2010.

[GRA 17] GRAYLESS R., Bottom line stats about employee mentoring programs, Gloo Blog, available at: https://blog.gloo.us/employee-mentorship-stats (accessed July 19, 2018), 2017.

[GUE 09] GUEIROS M.M.B., "As funções de mentoria como um instrumento de apoio ao desenvolvimento profissional dos dirigentes de faculdade de ensino superior", *Proceedings of the XXXIII EnANPAD – Encontro Nacional de Pós-Graduação em Administração (EnANPAD 2009)*, São Paulo, Brazil, 2009.

[HAG 11] HAGGARD D.L., DOUGHERTY T.W., TURBAN D.B. *et al.*, "Who is a mentor? A review of evolving definitions and implications for research", *Journal of Management*, vol. 37, no. 1, pp. 280–304, 2011.

[HEG 99] HEGSTAD C., "Formal mentoring as a strategy for human resource development: A review of research", *Human Resource Development Quarterly*, vol. 10, no. 4, pp. 383–390, 1999.

[HIG 01] HIGGINS M., KRAM K., "Reconceptualizing mentoring at work: A developmental network perspective", *Academy of Management Review*, vol. 26, no. 2, pp. 246–288, 2001.

[HUN 83] HUNT D.M., MICHAEL C., "Mentorship: A career training and development tool", *Academy of Management Review*, vol. 8, no. 3, pp. 475–485, 1983.

[IVA 19] IVANOVA O.E., RYABININA E.V., TYUNIN A.I., "Pragmatic constructivism as a soft-methodology of the HRM concept", *International Transaction Journal of Engineering, Management, & Applied Sciences & Technologies*, vol. 10, no. 2, pp. 245–253, 2019.

[JAK 16] JAKUBIK L.D., ELIADES A.B., WEESE M.M., "Part 1: An overview of mentoring practices and mentoring benefits", *Pediatric Nurse*, vol. 42, no. 1, pp. 37–38, 2016.

[JOH 03] JOHNSON W.B., "A framework for conceptualizing competence to mentor", *Ethics & Behavior*, vol. 13, no. 2, pp. 127–151, 2003.

[JON 17] JONES M., "Why can't companies get mentorship programs right?", *The Atlantic*, available at: https://www.theatlantic.com/business/archive/2017/06/corporate-mentorship-programs/528927/ (accessed July 19, 2018), 2017.

[KAL 02] KALBEISCH P.J., "Communicating in mentoring relationships: A theory for enactment", *Communication Theory*, vol. 12, no. 1, pp. 63–69, 2002.

[KAR 16] KARAKOSE T., YIRCI R., UYGUN H. *et al.*, "Post-graduate students' perceptions regarding effectiveness of mentoring relationship at universities", *Revista de Cercetare si Interventie Sociala*, vol. 52, p. 252, 2016.

[KRA 80] KRAM K.E., Mentoring at work: Developmental relationships in managerial careers, Doctoral Thesis, Yale University, 1980.

[KRA 85a] KRAM K.E. "Improving the mentoring process", *Training & Development Journal*, vol. 39, no. 4, pp. 40–43, 1985.

[KRA 85b] KRAM K.E., ISABELLA L., "Mentoring alternatives: The role of peer relationships in career development", *Academy of Management Journal*, vol. 28, pp. 110–132, 1985.

[KRA 88] KRAM K.E., *Mentoring at Work: Developmental Relationships in Organizational Life*, University Press of America, Lanham, Maryland, 1988.

[KUM 16] KUMAR S., WALLACE C., YOUNG M., "Mentoring trajectories in an evolving agile workplace", *Proceedings of the 38th International Conference on Software Engineering Companion*, Austin, Texas, pp. 142–151, May 2016.

[LEU 17] LEUZINGER J.A., ROWE J., "Succession planning through mentoring in the library", *Library Leadership & Management*, vol. 31, no. 4, pp. 1–22, 2017.

[MAC 99] MACLENNAN N., *Coaching and Mentoring*, Gower, Aldershot, Hants, 1999.

[MAN 12] MANAGEMENT MENTORS, "25 benefits of mentoring", *Corporate Mentoring*, available at: https://www.management-mentors.com/resources/benefits-of-mentoring (accessed July 19, 2018), 2012.

[MAS 15] MASALIMOVA A.R., NIGMATOV Z.G., "Structural-functional model for corporate training of specialists in carrying out mentoring", *Review of European Studies*, vol. 7, no. 4, p. 39, 2015.

[MEI 14] MEIRINHOS V., RODRIGUES A.C., *Gestão e desenvolvimento de recursos humanos: Tendências e boas práticas*, Vida Económica Editorial, Porto, 2014.

[MIN 14] MINNICK W., WILHIDE S., DIANTONIIS R. *et al.*, "Onboarding OSH professionals: The role of mentoring", *American Society of Safety Engineers*, vol. 59, no. 12, pp. 27–33, 2014.

[MUR 91] MURRAY M., OWEN M.A. *Beyond the Myths and Magic of Mentoring: How to Facilitate an Effective Mentoring Programme*, Jossey Bass, San Francisco, 1991.

[MUR 17] MURRELL A.J., BLAKE-BEARD S., *Mentoring Diverse Leaders: Creating Change for People, Processes, and Paradigms*, Taylor & Francis, New York, 2017.

[NOW 17] NOWELL L., NORRIS J.M., MRKLAS K. *et al.*, "Mixed methods systematic review exploring mentorship outcomes in nursing academia", *Journal of Advanced Nursing*, vol. 73, no. 3, pp. 527–544, 2017.

[OBR 06] O'BRIEN K., ALLEN T., "Formal mentoring programs and organizational attraction", *Human Resource Development Quarterly*, vol. 17, no. 1, pp. 43–58, 2006.

[PEN 18] PENIM A.T., CATALÃO J.A., *Ferramentas de Mentoring*, Lidel, Lisbon, 2018.

[PIK 14] PIKE K.L., "New employee onboarding programs and person-organization fit: An examination of socialization tactics", *Seminar Research Paper Series*, University of Rhode Island, p. 24, 2014.

[PHI 01] PHILLIPS-JONES L., *The New Mentors & Protégés: How to Succeed with the New Mentoring Partnerships*, Coalition of Counseling Centers, Ontario, 2001.

[POW 10] POWELL K.S., YALCIN S., "Managerial training effectiveness: A meta-analysis 1952–2002", *Personnel Review*, vol. 39, no. 2, pp. 227–241, 2010.

[RÉG 06] RÉGIS H., DIAS S., MELO P., "Redes informais de mentoria no ambiente de incubadoras de base tecnológica: o apoio ao desenvolvimento da carreira empreendedora", *Journal of Technology & Innovation*, vol. 1, no. 5, pp. 40–52, 2006.

[RIB 16] RIBEIRO J.L., GOMES D., "Other organizational perspectives on the contribution of human resources management to organizational performance", in MACHADO C., DAVIM J.P. (eds), *Organizational Management: Policies and Practices in a Global Market*, Palgrave MacMillan, England, pp. 63–106, 2016.

[ROD 18] RODRIGUES L., "Como montar um programa de mentoring?", *Voitto Blog*, available at: https://www.voitto.com.br/blog/artigo/programa-de-mentoring, (accessed September 4, 2018), 2018.

[SAN 07] SANTOS N., "Programas de mentoring: aprendendo com a realidade canadense", *Interfaces Brasil/Canadá*, vol. 7, no. 1, pp. 251–265, 2007.

[TAL 12a] TALENT MANAGEMENT STAFF, "Mentoring and on-boarding: Two peas in a pod", *Talent Management*, available at: https://talentmgt.com/2012/10/26/mentoring-and-on-boarding-two-peas-in-a-pod__trashed/ (accessed July 19, 2018), 2012.

[TAL 12b] TALENT MANAGEMENT STAFF, "Next-generation mentoring", *Talent Management*, available at: https://talentmgt.com/2012/06/27/next-generation-mentoring__trashed/ (accessed July 19, 2018), 2012.

[TAL 13] TALENT MANAGEMENT STAFF, "Mentoring gets millennials on board", *Talent Management*, available at: https://talentmgt.com/2013/07/17/mentoring-gets-millennials-on-board__trashed/ (accessed July 19, 2018), 2013.

[TAL 14a] TALENT MANAGEMENT STAFF, "Mentoring in a millennial world", *Talent Management*, available at: https://talentmgt.com/2014/10/03/mentoring-in-a-millennial-world__trashed/ (accessed July 19, 2018), 2014.

[TAL 14b] TALENT MANAGEMENT STAFF, "How to develop a peer mentoring program", *Talent Management*, available at: https://talentmgt.com/2014/08/12/how-to-develop-a-peer-mentoring-program__trashed/ (accessed July 19, 2018), 2014.

[THO 16] THOMPSON A.E., GREESON J.K., BRUNSINK A.M., "Natural mentoring among older youth in and aging out of foster care: A systematic review", *Children and Youth Services Review*, vol. 61, pp. 40–50, 2016.

[TJA 11] TJAN A., "Keeping great people with three kinds of mentors", *Harvard Business Review*, available at: http://blogs.hbr.org/tjan/2011/08/keeping-great-people-with-thre.html (accessed July 19, 2018), 2011.

[WAT 96] WATTS L., DYNAMICS D., A guide to mentoring. A project of the National Staff Development Committee for the Australian National Training Authority, Guide, National Staff Development Committee, Australia, 1996.

[YAN 17] YANG J., The onboarding process in agile software development teams: An empirical study, Master Thesis, Auckland University of Technology, New Zealand, 2017.

[ZAC 05] ZACHARY, L., *Creating a Mentoring Culture: The Organization's Guide*, Jossey Bass, San Francisco, 2005.

[ZER 09] ZERZAN J.T., HESS R., SCHUR E. *et al.*, "Making the most of mentors: A guide for mentees", *Academic Medicine*, vol. 84, no. 1, pp. 140–144, 2009.

9

Stop Camouflaging it in Green: Do Not Confuse Corporate Social Responsibility with Sustainable Management

Reviewing the literature, this chapter exposes the concepts of Ecological Economics, Sustainable Management and Corporate Social Responsibility (CSR) in order to verify the conceptual confusion between the latter two. The debate has been marked by conceptual unclarity with both terms being frequently used as synonyms, even though clear distinctions can be highlighted. The first mismatch lands on the historical tradition surrounding both concepts, as CSR has mainly been concerned with the social dimension of organizational impact, marginalizing the environmental length. The second mismatch refers to the reasons why organizations opt for the adoption of CSR strategies or a Sustainable Management paradigm, having a more discretionary decision-making power in the adoption of CSR policies and practices, once historical tradition and empirical evidence shows that some organizations may only choose to be socially responsible in special fields, but may not be fully committed into a Sustainable Management paradigm. The third mismatch arises as these concepts imply a different commitment towards society because the complexity of each is distinct. CSR represents the microeconomic dimension of the macroeconomic concept of Sustainable Management, being a precondition for Sustainable Management. This work provides a useful input as it stresses that these two concepts may be considered as "intrinsically linked" and CSR can be seen as the business contribution to sustainable development. To the best of our knowledge this work is the first so far to directly compare the concepts of CSR and Sustainable Management, exposing their correspondent and opposing points based on a literature review, providing a useful input to bring forth more rigor to fill in the gap of the overlapping and blurred discussion around this topic.

Chapter written by Diana FERNANDES and Carolina Feliciana MACHADO.

9.1. Introduction

As pointed out by de Groot [GRO 92], the life-support function of ecosystems is connected to their physical, chemical and biological role on the overall system. However, since the 18th Century and with more vigor since the 20th Century, that vital function has been continuously harmed. Indeed, the rapid growth of economic activity, fostered by the analogous increasing growth of the world population, has decisively impacted all socio-economic systems, leading to an urgency in debating the clear symptoms of environmental unsustainability. Indeed, the real economy works as an open system, which, in order to function effectively and efficiently, must extract resources from the environment and place large amounts of waste back into it [KNE 15, AYR 69]. Hence, the awareness of actual and potential conflicts between economic growth and environment conservation originated the debate around the concept of Sustainable Management, aiming at Sustainable Development.

Sustainable Development refers to the process of meeting the needs of the present generation without compromising the ability of future generations to meet their own, ensuring a global and lasting conservation of the environment as well as the development and stabilization of economic and social behavior, balancing nature preservation with economic growth at a planetary scale. To achieve Sustainability, the global community must deal with refined problems, these being cross-scale, transcultural, transdisciplinary, transversal to present and future generations [MAR 06b], operating in an holistic spectrum, as the foundation for the concept of Sustainability is founded on the intertwining of environmental, social, political and economic spheres, whose development should be harmonious [ELK 94]. Such problems are calling out for innovative and inclusive research approaches, interconnecting different fields of study and action, as well as new social institutions as they are increasingly threatening the future existence and well-being of *Homo sapiens* [BER 00b, GOL 94, HOL 94, VIE 94, COM 92, COS 87].

It is important to highlight that, while classical economists namely Malthus [MAL 98], Ricardo [RIC 17], Mill [MIL 57] and Marx [MAR 67] clearly advocated in their models that economic activity is bounded by the environment, neo-classical economics completely overlooked this central characteristic of real world economics until the 1970s, when the debate had started around the urgency of social and environmental limits to economic growth. Indeed, considering the economy as a system in which firms sell goods and services and then remunerate the production factors (land, labor and capital), traditional neo-classical economics examines the process of price formation conceiving economics in this closed system logics. We see here a “reductionist” paradigm on traditional neo-classical economics, once it assumes the world is divided and separable into relatively isolated units, which, by their end, are possible to examine on their own and then reassemble to provide a picture of the whole complex, summing up the several fragments. As complexities in science increased, this turned to be understood as a very useful approach, given the fact that it enabled the whole problem to be divided into smaller, more tangible, simpler and manageable fragments that could be dissected intensively [COS 96]. In economics, this fostered a rising isolation from the natural resources component of the classical triad of land, labor and capital, as well as a growing segregation from the natural sciences, progressively drifting away from the fruitful outcomes of interdisciplinary approaches. At the same time, economics was becoming absorbed into professionalization. This trend had been profoundly present through until the middle of the 20th Century, and was only put into question around the 1970s, by the time of the renewed environmental awareness.

Ecological Economics has grown in importance ever since, not only in academic research, but also in political debates and in civil society, as it addresses the connections between ecosystems and economic systems in a comprehensive logic, as a means to develop a more intense and rigorous understanding of the entire system formed by the interdependence between humans and nature as a root for the design and execution of effective policies towards sustainability [COS 91]. Indeed, few organizational topics are as broadly reaching as those regarding society and the environment, so that societal and environmental responsibility is increasingly assumed to be a core business issue [ORL 03, WAL 03]. Subsequently, it has gained momentum as a strong approach to address the issues around Sustainable Management and Sustainable Development.

Through a literature review, this chapter aims to expose the concepts of Ecological Economics, Sustainable Management and CSR, in order to verify the conceptual confusion and overlap between the latter two, based on the argument that the conceptual proliferation and the theoretical approaches so far available in the literature have often been presenting and operationalizing such concepts as if they are synonymous, which we do not consider to be accurate. So, this is a descriptive work, mapping the terrain for a conceptual discussion and clarification around CSR and Sustainable Management, framing it on the basis of the theoretical background of Ecological Economics. The remainder of the work is the following: we start by explaining the concept of Ecological Economics, and on the basis of which, we expose the concepts of Sustainable Management and CSR. Based on such argumentation, we then intricate these two concepts, comparing them in order to verify their conceptual common and distinct points and how these then reflect into implications with regards to organizational strategies, management approaches, academic research, political agenda definition and civil society debates towards the sustainability imperative.

We conclude that the debate has indeed been marked by conceptual unclarity in both the terms and their conceptual umbrella frequently used as if they were synonymous. A primary reason for this is due to their relative recency, given the fact that we have only seen a more intense discussion on the topic only since the 1990s. Nevertheless, clear distinctions between both concepts can be highlighted, which we present as mismatches when comparatively analyzing both conceptual structures and their preconized approaches. We have distinguished three such mismatches, which are interconnected even though different from one another. The first mismatch is based on the historical tradition surrounding both concepts, CSR by tradition was once only concerned with the social dimension of organizational impact, marginalizing the environmental dimension. The second mismatch refers to the reasons why organizations opt for the adoption of CSR strategies or for a Sustainable Management paradigm. We argue that organizations have a more discretionary decision-making power in the adoption of CSR policies and practices, in other words they have a more casuistic decision-making approach with regards to CSR, as they casuistically opt for which CSR strategies they wish to implement, in which time frames and with which operative methods to achieve the desired outcomes. Historical tradition and empirical evidence show that some organizations may only choose to be socially responsible and active in special fields, but they may not be fully committed to a Sustainable Management paradigm. So, we suggest that the adoption of CSR strategies is mainly based on the organizations' self-interest, either to comply with the law (normative case) and/or to achieve competitive advantage, as organizations often understand that the adoption of CSR may provide them with valuable resources, offering them the opportunity to achieve an additional input to incorporate in their value chain. The third mismatch arises as these concepts imply a different commitment towards society, taking into consideration that the complexity of each concept is markedly distinct. Hence, we suggest that a micro analysis is more the case for CSR, but Sustainable Management consists of a holistic approach, requiring a macro analysis [MAR 03]. We argue that CSR represents the microeconomic dimension of the macroeconomic concept of Sustainable Management, thus, CSR acts only as a precondition for Sustainable Management: business sustainability is a consequence of the application of CSR strategies. To fulfil their purpose, CSR strategies must be integrated into the overall business strategy, embedded across the organization horizontally and vertically [FRA 01].

This chapter provides a useful input as it stresses that these two concepts may be considered as "intrinsically linked" and CSR can be understood as the business contribution to sustainable development. Furthermore, to the best of our knowledge this work is the first so far to directly compare both the CSR and Sustainable Management concepts, clearly exposing their correspondent and opposing points based on a literature review, providing a useful input to bring forth more rigor to fill in the gap of the confusing, overlapping and blurred discussion around this topic so far.

9.2. Ecological Economics

Ecology and Economics have so far been separate research fields throughout their recent histories in the 20th Century, addressing distinct topics, applying different assumptions and supporting diverse interests in the policy process. The advent of Ecological Economics has reconciled both approaches: for a review on the topic, the works of Nørgård [NOR 13], Costanza [COS 96], Norgaard [NOR 89], Alier [ALI 87a], Alier and Schlüpmann [ALI 87b]; Vitousek *et al.* [VIT 86], Clark and Munro [CLA 75], Leontief [LEO 70], Ayres and Kneese [AYR 69], Mishan and Mishan [MIS 67], Cumberland [CUM 66], Galbraith [GAL 58] and Ciriacy-Wantrup [CIR 52] are relevant.

In fact, Ecological Economics aims at developing a more profound understanding of the complex connections between ecological and economic systems, using such knowledge to develop efficient and effective policies to construct a world which can be characterized by being ecologically sustainable, articulating a fair distribution and allocation of scarce resources to satisfy not only the present needs, but also safeguarding the satisfaction of future generations' demands. It is due to the fact that these approaches focus more incisively on the problems facing *Homo sapiens'* future existence and well-being, as well as the ecosystems on which civilization rests over the long term. As a result, it is clear that Ecological Economics is nowadays evidently present on an institutional level and global scale. Therefore, we can suggest that Ecological Economics consists of a transdisciplinary effort to bring a connection between the natural and social sciences broadly – especially environmentalism, ecology, management and economics – based on the premise that approaches which eliminate the associations within and between economic and natural systems fall into reductionist paradigms, and analysis taken under such roots are not rigorous as they can originate severe misperceptions and policy failures, given the fact that these days we increasingly observe a robust crystallization of the strength of real-world interdependencies [COS 87].

In light of the above, we can conceive Ecological Economics as an anthropocentric field of study, because it is, at its very core, concerned with the survival and well-being of *Homo sapiens* on this planet. Also relevant to highlight is the fact that it is simultaneously biocentric as it provides insights on the survival and well-being of all other life forms as well [RAP 93]. Hence, this concept requires "new approaches that are comprehensive, adaptive, integrative, multi-scale, and pluralistic, and that acknowledge the huge uncertainties involved" [COS 96, p. 978], as it is an attempt to design and objectivize a more effective interdisciplinary relationship which can work as a link towards "a truly comprehensive science of humans as a component of nature that will fulfil the early goals of ecology", attempting to provide a positive contribution which helps in rectifying "the tendency to ignore humans in ecology, while at the same time rectifying the parallel tendency to ignore the natural world in the social sciences" [COS 96, p. 979]. Consequently, Ecological Economics integrates elements of myriad disciplines to offer a cohesive, combined and integrated perspective on the several interdependencies happening on the dyad environment-economy, contributing to structural solutions towards environmental issues [BER 00a].

As the intellectual founders and antecedents of Ecological Economics we can highlight, in the field of Economics, Boulding, Daly, and Georgescu-Roegen; as well as Holling and Odum in the field of Ecology. At the end of the 1960s, Daly boosted a chief input to the long-lasting economic growth debate, as the author advanced the idea of a "steady state economy", linked at the aim of minimizing the use of materials and energy ("throughput") in the economy [DAL 96, DAL 92, DAL 91, DAL 68], having also produced a substantial work around international trade, sustainable welfare indicators and, a notable contribution, on the maximum physical scale of the economy. Boulding shared such academic interest in environmental issues. Among his contributions to this topic we can highlight the disparities between the "cowboy economy" and the "spaceship economy" [BOU 66]: while the first represented a metaphor for the local/national open economy, symbolized under the logics of a closed system – where people worry very little about the quality of the environment and nature, merely paying attention to local environmental problems, articulating a microsystem – Boulding sharply acknowledges that was not the correct path to take in the times ahead. To the author, the solution might reside in the migration towards new resources, hence suggesting the metaphor of the "spaceship economy", this symbolizing the world as a complex and interdependent whole, even if formed by fragmented pieces, consequently being limited on the very first instance on material and food supplies. The author, thus, somehow ended by suggesting Sustainable Management as a solution, advancing it as the most accurate survival strategy, which objectivated the economic use of materials, energy and environment, as well boosting the maximization of recycling substances, materials and products. This "spaceship metaphor" turned into a precursor for the modern interpretation of global environmental problems. Georgescu-Roegen is best known for his contributions to utility theory and activity analysis, enthusiastically criticizing standard neoclassical economics [GEO 76, GEO 71, GEO 66]. On the other hand, Holling's arguments on ecosystem stability and resilience [HOL 73] are the foremost denoted and discussed in theoretical ecology, and indeed the author's influence has surpassed this field of study to impregnate other disciplines, influencing approaches to integrated modeling and adaptive management [PER 98, GUN 95]. Specifically, it is noteworthy to highlight Holling's idea that (terrestrial) ecosystems do not inevitably track and follow a path of succession towards a climax: instead, they can develop in a recurrent cycle [HOL 85]. Odum has influenced Ecological Economics through the EMERGY analysis approach he coined [ODU 71], then applying this method to the combined study of economic-ecological exchanges from local to global scales [ODU 87].

Summarizing the above, we can see that, in their opposition from the prevailing mainstream view, ecological economists frequently cite Georgescu-Roegen's [GEO 71] theory. It refutes the standard model of economic growth firstly based on the second law of thermodynamics, which entails that there is always an energy deficit in a system, given the fact that, in entropy terms, the cost of any biological or economic action is always greater than the product. That standard model is also refuted on the argument that the free or operational energy (low entropy) used to replace such a deficit embodies a fixed and declining stock, thus "nature really does impose an inescapable general scarcity", so that it would be a "serious delusion to believe otherwise" [DAL 79, p. 69]. Ecological economists also refute the mainstream trend by arguing that "the basic relation of man-made and natural capital is one of complementarity, not substitutability" [DAL 94, p. 26]. This argument is, nevertheless, undermined due to the fact that it fails to reply to the basic dispute of the mainstream model, which assumes that growing resource scarcity would always generate price signals that would stimulate compensating economic and technological devices, such as resource substitution, recycling, exploration and increased efficiency in resource utilization [CLA 73].

Indeed, mainstream economists ground their models on the premise that the Earth's carrying capacity cannot be measurably accessed scientifically because it is merely the result of the state of knowledge and technology, therefore, it is biased. Consequently, they base their models trusting to human intelligence and ingenuity, advocating that nature imposes no limits to economic growth, postulating that, as people seek to satisfy their needs and preferences in order to achieve well-being, they choose from among an indefinitely large plethora of alternatives [BAR 13]. Basing themselves on such a premise, mainstream economists offer at least three arguments corroborating that knowledge and ingenuity are expected to always lessen resource shortages. First, they assume that reserves of natural resources are essentially functions of technology, in the sense that the more advanced the technology is, the more reserves become known and recoverable [LEE 93]. Second, they defend that advances in technology make it possible not only to grow available reserves but also to allocate and employ substitutes for resources that have the potential to turn scarce. Third, they claim that the power of knowledge incessantly diminishes the quantities of resources required to produce a continuous or cumulative torrent of consumer goods and services. Ecological economists, in an energetic contrast, reject such ideas based on a different conception of "the limiting factor": in this new era we live in, the limiting factor in development is not human-created capital, as in the past, but remaining natural capital [COS 91]. Knowledge would be as such a limiting factor in economic production for mainstream economists (considering it would even exist), even though, as long as knowledge progressed, the economy would also be able to expand and such problems would be surpassed. Drucker [DRU 93, p. 8] clearly defended this mainstream economics optimistic view on technological progress and economic growth: "The basic resource – 'the means of production', to use the economist's term, is no longer capital, nor natural resources (the economist's 'land'), nor 'labor" It is and will be knowledge." This evidently diverges from Daly's argument [DAL 85, pp. 274–275] that "technology and resource substitution" can unceasingly outpace resource scarcity, strongly advocating that economic growth faces (and indeed has to face) limits, because sources of raw materials (natural capital) are fixed and limited, restraining the global economy's potential growth. Daly [DAL 96] incisively pointed out that it would be an absolute illusion to consider that economic growth would still possible if only organizational, business, political and civil society's initiatives were labelled as "sustainable" or "green".

Ecological Economics, then, projects a perspective that, in its roots, opposes a strictly utilitarian conception of value, instead having developed contingent valuation methodologies to assign what through this approach is called shadow prices to intrinsic values [SAG 95]. This also comes from the fact that these approaches provide a central role to uncertainty, once they tightly argue that both ecological and social systems are complex (even chaotic). Therefore, events deriving from the interchange between the two systems are intrinsically unpredictable. As such, ecological economists argue that mainstream economics lacks representation of these systems' evolutionary nature and of its characteristic nonlinear causation [CHR 89], once those approaches are grounded on complete measurability, value neutrality, objectivity and unidimensional terms. Bearing in mind that particular processes in nature are essentially irreversible [COS 96, LUD 93, COS 92], CLA 75], these models suggest the need to conserve and advance natural capital [COS 92b] in order to retain the ecological life-support systems and the interconnected socioeconomic systems, providing inputs so that they remain resilient to change [PER 98, HOL 94, JAN 94, HAM 93]. The "precautionary principle" is, then, very present in Ecological Economics: such economists propose it as one way to manage the problem of true uncertainty, recommending that society should establish safe minimum standards to protect the planet's life-support systems [COS 96].

Such examples prove that Ecological Economics proposes viable alternatives to the theoretical foundations and policy recommendations of neoclassical welfare economics. In other words, Ecological Economics can be considered as a particular specialization of neoclassical economics as it concerns two fundamental questions: the issue of environmental externalities, and the optimal intergenerational allocation of non-renewable resources. Following this line, we can see that a revolution in neoclassical economics is taking place (since the 1970s), with which the central conventions of welfare economics are being revised and substituted with more realistic representations of consumer and firm behavior. In regards to this, Gowdy and Erickson [GOW 05, p. 207] sharply advocate that Ecological Economics be assumed today as "the only heterodox school of economics focusing on the human economy both as a social system and as one imbedded in the biophysical universe", accentuating its positive impact playing "a leading role in recasting the scope and method of economic science" as it comprises an holistic approach.

Ecological Economics acknowledges that ecological and economical rationality are not sufficient to, *per se*, obtain efficient and effective outcomes, hence, environmental decisions should be designed through a democratic scientific-political decision process [MUN 97]. Given the fact that Ecological Economics regards the socioeconomic system as a component of the overall ecosphere (on its analysis heightening its carrying capacity and scale issues in face of the growth of the human population and its activities, as well as the expansion of fair systems in wealth distribution), it becomes clear that the nucleus of Ecological Economics is associated with the goal of Sustainable Development, which is conceived as referring to both intra- and intergenerational equity, understanding economy as only a subsystem inserted as an active part of a larger local and global ecosystem that decisively imposes limits to the economy's physical growth [BER 00a].

To conclude this argumentation, we can state that co-evolution and diversity are the vital requests of both Ecological Economics, Sustainable Management and Sustainable Development. Following the line of Munda [MUN 97], the alarm about the carrying capacity of Earth symbolizes a withdrawal from traditional arguments in favor of environmental protection, once they no longer rest on prudential considerations, in the sense that 19th Century environmentalists, framed on a mindset which apprehended nature as full of divinity, looked upon its conservation less as an economic imperative than as a moral test. Hence, Ecological Economics projects an explicit apprehension for future generations and long-term sustainability, exploring questions around untraditional economic topics such as ethics, equity, regional development and multiculturalism [BER 00b, TUR 97], articulating its approaches through models with a wide range of values, providing a more ambitious and rigorous level of study as such models go beyond the partial insights of the current human generation (although these are not ignored).

9.3. Sustainable Management

In light of the above, having Ecological Economics as its theoretical foundation, we can find the roots of the concept of Sustainability back in the end of the 18th Century, where it became obvious that resources had a limited lifetime and were available in nature for human usage at a limited stock. Consequently, human beings could not use it to exhaustion to satisfy their current needs if they considered that such resources were required to remain obtainable in nature for the development of future generations – indeed, there was a mismatch in both ambitions, both needed to be calibrated [GLU 01, p. 9]. Anderson [AND 04] notes the Industrial Revolution era, which originated in England in the late 1700s, as the period since when the environmental awaking had its roots, as it was the period in history in which the most devastating environmental harm originated. It is also important to call attention to this era as the (even though silent) root for the emergence of the concept of Sustainability due to the fact that, according to Hobsbawm and Cumming [HOB 75], it marks the move towards the capitalistic economy, where wealth and profit became the valued goals of individuals and corporations.

Not disregarding these earlier acknowledgments, the true environmental movement instigated around the mid-1960s and speedily boosted over the following decades is currently cited as a cornerstone for an upsurge in Sustainability debates as during such time societal changes provoked weighty negative effects on the environment, which impacted society's awareness compelling it to start expecting businesses to take an active stand on assuming a great part of the accountability for the planet's environmental problems [BUC 93]. Hence, organizations found themselves compelled to accept the challenge of incorporating Sustainable Management initiatives in all of their business functions, facing a precipitous learning curve when adopting such management practices [NAT 99]. The second era of environmental awareness identified by Nattrass and Altomare [NAT 99] traversed the 1980s, when tragic environmental events and the growing environmental deterioration due to climate change harmed environmental and human welfare, as well as companies' financial records. Thus, organizations gathered efforts to implement management practices and policies towards sustainability as a means to proactively anticipate and best manage such scenarios. Consequently, those problems crystalized as vibrant alerts demanding that organizations should go beyond legal compliance to truly assume themselves as respectable corporate citizens [MCG 63].

With the advancement of time, strategic questions surrounding environmental issues gained notable urgency, turning Sustainable Management into an imperative by organizations. Thus, the 1990s coined the term "eco-efficiency" as this period establishes the third era of environmental consciousness, once organizations began to grasp that sustaining the *status quo* would not lead to a fruitful future [NAT 99]. In fact, this period was demarcated by a hands-on corporate response to environmental issues, as well (and possibly with sharper impacts) as by the awareness that companies could indeed profit from being environmentally mindful and underscoring unceasing enhancements towards environmental issues, given the fact that such an approach could help them in obtaining a competitive advantage over competitors [POR 95].

Nattrass and Altomare [NAT 99] suggest the new millennium as the final and current era of environmental awareness, in which organizations increasingly displayed high levels of integration of sustainability initiatives at both strategic and operational levels in their management policies and practices, this being so because they deconstructed the idea that environmental and organizational performances are two completely separate fields. Instead, organizations are increasingly acknowledging the positive outcomes, even if in regards to their financial performance, that can be originated if adopting Sustainable Management practices in daily life, thus alongside aligning company and environmental goals. In this era, by assuming environmental issues as a chief concern in all of their business functions, organizations remain competitive in their markets and clearly stand out as a message to be socially responsible and behave according to moral standards.

In light of the above, we can state that Sustainability has its roots on three pillars: economic growth, ecological balance and social responsibility. The advancement of time generalized this concept adding a plethora of ideas for its interpretation [ZIN 05]. However, its core remains unchangeable, and in current times it is absolutely highlighted as an urgent issue: it presents a dyadic dynamics, as it refers to both human beings' dependence on the environment, as well as to their reaction to global changes in such an environment through its present behavior in the economic, social and/or ecological domains. Malovics *et al.* [MAL 08] agree with such an argument, herewith, we can defend that Sustainable Management provides a refined management approach to conceive the relationship between business and society, not understanding corporate success, environmental conservation and social welfare as a zero-sum game, instead considering such a relationship as a win-win-win dynamics. Accordingly, we can also clearly see that this concept is grounded in the search for a long-term perspective in regards to human impact on the environment, which is compelled by the premise of attributing equal relevance to human resources, societal balance and the environment [LEP 10], in the first place by understanding the relevance of building sustainable business.

A more specific and widespread conceptualization for Sustainable Management is necessary, but the truth is it is complicated to crystalize a consistent and comprehensive definition on the first instance because it is a relatively new term. Both improved environmental and business performance are elementary goals of Sustainable Management, nevertheless the majority of research on this topic focuses on Environmental Management and Environmental Management Systems as paths to advance such outcomes [FLO 01].

Taylor [TAY 92] defines Sustainable Management as a management concept demanding the commitment of all the organization's stakeholders, as they recognize being an active part in the community, consequently assuming their responsibility quota on environmental conservation, sustainable development and societal welfare. Thus, in its core this concept involves conceiving the organization in its entirety instead of as a conjunction of fragmented smaller entities, being fully aware that the company is an active and integral part of the community [MAR 03], thus, managing the organization having the long-term as a motto and implementing a holistic approach. The truth is, environmentalism forces organizations to expand their corporate time-horizons because it compels them to be ahead of public opinion. Consequently, under a Sustainable Management paradigm, organizations are enhanced to commit to quality performance standards in the broad scope of the organization's activities; developing fruitful and close relationships with the customer as well as sustaining motivation and finding creative solutions through the constant engagement and commitment of/towards employees, by acknowledging employees are vital not only to the organization's profitable performance but also to successfully institute corporate change. Indeed, under this management paradigm, organizations seek to improve not only the quality of the environment but of all activities under the organization's (and its subsidiaries) scope. Consequently, organizations are increasingly recognizing environmentalism as a crucial factor in assuming themselves as leaders in the market, being the global scale of the competition standard.

Sharing the same logic but putting it in other words, Haden *et al.* [HAD 09] present the concept as respecting the organization-wide process of applying innovation via continuous learning and development to accomplish sustainability, waste reduction, social responsibility and a competitive advantage, in this sense fully integrating environmental goals and strategies into the organization's ones. So, in its very essence, Sustainable Management consists of an incessant process of assessment and improvement through the construction of environmental and management excellence, so it requires a deeper and ambitious approach to organizational actions as, at its very core, it makes us change attitudes, structures, policies and processes [TAY 92].

In building sustainable businesses, organizations are constantly under the influence of many forces impacting on the success of their Sustainable Management efforts. The *promoters* are forces that favor sustainable business, such as the corporate code of ethics and ethics committee, corporate social responsibility strategies, sector operators, government pressure, local communities and non-governmental organizations. The *inhibitors*, opposingly, embrace the dynamics that halt organizations from conducting business based on sustainability values, namely bad management, economic constraints, high costs of social responsibility programs and competitive environment. Nonetheless, Nelson [NEL 98] and Zairi [ZAI 00] proposed an approach based on three elements for building added societal value, arguing that organizations that have started to make a true headway into the adoption of a Sustainable Management paradigm tend to vividly demonstrate four characteristics: (1) they rely on value-based transformational leadership; (2) they objectivate a commitment to learning and innovation through global networks and partnerships; (3) they crystalize stakeholder linkages, hence taking advantage of mutual benefits via various modes of relationships; and (4) they make use of an extensive assortment of financial and non-financial performance measures reinforced by auditing, verification, reporting and recognition systems, to leverage their performance.

Thus, exploring Sustainable Management as a strategic organizational topic implies examining the means by which it affects the organization's competitiveness and profitability, and how it can be unified to the firm's strategic planning processes [BAN 02, JUD 98]: the natural-resource-based perspective of the firm [HAR 95], developed on the basis of the original resource-based view of the firm [WER 84, BAR 91], is indeed one of the predominant theories in regards to such an aspect, suggesting that a firm's unique resources and capabilities are its main sources of sustainable competitive advantage, basing such an advantage on the organization's relationship with the natural environment, condensing a conceptual framework which encompasses the interconnected strategies of pollution prevention, product stewardship and sustainable development. Very important to notice is the fact that firms are self-motivated to seek them, in the sense that we may argue that, because Sustainable Management provides outcomes which may be identifiable as public goods, organizations are, on their side, not able to entirely appropriate such value [TEE 07]. Consequently, we can contend that there are likely to be other reasons claiming organizations' attention to implement Sustainable Management structures, practices and policies [MAR 06a]. In regards to this, Banerjee [BAN 01] advises that the range of an organization's environmentally-based strategies oscillates from reactive to proactive: as to say, organizations can resist or merely conform and comply with environmental canons, or they can assess environmental issues as a chance to be innovative and obtain a competitive advantage. In fact, and as contended by Taylor [TAY 92, p. 674], Sustainable Management requires up-front investment and changes in the organizational mindset, but "the business advantages are real", once it "rewards its adherents with: cost reductions and improved efficiencies; new marketing outlets; enhanced corporate image; opportunities to sell new products and services; an improved competitive position; a more dedicated and motivated workforce; and the ability to set the agenda for the industry and public policy". Consequently, this concept emphasizes three dimensions of corporate performance: economic, social and environmental [STE 05].

9.4. Corporate Social Responsibility

Literature on Environmental Management points out that, organizations being the main cause of environmental problems, they should also play a vital role in addressing those issues and act in regards to them. Subsequently, organizations are, all over the world, progressively moving towards the adoption of advanced environmental practices that underpin their environmental performance as well as their organizational competitiveness. As per the above mentioned issues surrounding Ecological Economics and Sustainable Management, the current global organization is posing higher public expectations on organizations' social and ethical performance, as globalization has brought with it a broader set of challenges. Thus, new rules of corporate conduct have increasingly been considered: legitimacy, governance, equity, public/private-sector relationships, employment and environmental impact. This means, ethics are decisively present among the core criteria in assessing corporate performance [WIL 00]. Thus, a wide range of eco-initiatives has been launched by organizations as one organizational response to environmental degradation, supported by a developing Sustainable Management model. In regards to this, we can highlight CSR strategies, in the sense that these consist of opportunities provided by the development of business strategies allied with business objectives. CSR emerges, then, as a constituent of the new societal governance.

As in the case for Sustainable Management, Carroll [CAR 08], based on the contributions of Wren [WRE 05], stresses the Industrial Revolution "as a useful starting point". Hereby exposing a very synthetized summary, in the 1950s it is possible to, not disregarding the above, find the first solid inputs towards the evolution of the CSR concept, whose initial definitions were then expanded during the 1960s, proliferating throughout the 1970s. On the one hand, if fewer innovative classifications flourished throughout the 1980s, during that period there was, on the other hand, more empirical research on the topic, so that alternative topics – including corporate social performance, stakeholder theory and business ethics theory – started to mature and to garner attention both in academic work, as well as in the political agenda and in the civil society [CAR 99]. According to Muirhead [MUI 99], the period after that can be interestingly apprehended as the "prelegalization period" of corporate contributions and, until the present day, according to Eberstadt [EBE 73] corporations started to be conceptualized as institutions to which a plethora of social obligations are continually being addressed, consequently playing an increasingly active role in fulfilling them, alongside the government. This period indeed assumed itself as the "increasingly corporate period" [CAR 08, p. 4].

Several theoretical frameworks have been used to conceptualize CSR (for a review, see [ORL 11, MAT 08, AGU 07, MCW 06, MOI 01]). Defining CSR is a complex task mainly for two reasons, even though the literature presents a vast and increasing body of theoretical works and empirical research on the topic (as an example, see Crane *et al.* [CRA 08] as well as Lockett *et al.* [LOC 06]). On the one hand, it is an "essentially contested concept", presenting a great level of complexity and having fairly open rules of application [MOO 05, pp. 433–434]. In addition, CSR is categorized as a dynamic phenomenon [CAR 99], because it has been presented and used in empirical analysis as an "umbrella term" [CRA 05b] in the sense that it often intersects (considered as synonymous) with other conceptions of business-society relations [MAT 08]. Preston and Post [PRE 75, p. 9] presented such difficulties in defining CSR very well, pointing out the "large number of different, and not always consistent, usages" of such a concept, subsequently articulating "a vague and highly generalized sense of social concern that appears to underlie a wide variety of *ad hoc* managerial policies and practices", which "lack, however, any coherent relation to the managerial unit's internal activities or to its fundamental linkage with its host environment". Thus, CSR conceptualization has developed mirroring the influence of several theoretical approaches, namely agency theory, the resource-based view of the firm, institutional theory, stakeholder theory and stewardship theory (for a review, see Windsor [WIN 06], van Marrewijk [MAR 03], McWilliams, Van Fleet and Cory [MCW 02], Wartick and Cochran [WAR 85]; Carroll [CAR 79]).

Not neglecting the difficulties highlighted above, it is consensual in the literature around this topic the premise that CSR reflects social imperatives and the social consequences of business success resides at the nucleus of this concept, thus addressing the business' moral purpose. Steiner [STE 71, p. 164] clearly states this idea by arguing that, while business consists of and must remain essentially an economic institution, "it does have responsibilities to help society achieve its basic goals and does, therefore, have social responsibilities". In summary, we contend that an organization acting in a socially responsible way is one that performs and develops itself through the establishment and implementation of structures, policies and practices aimed at going beyond compliance and investing further not only into the numerous interdependencies between all stakeholders, but also (and tightly) into human capital and the environment. Such an argument is clearly presented by Davis [DAV 60, p. 73], whose ideas culminated on the premise that "the avoidance of social responsibility leads to gradual erosion of social power", as the author argued that organizational social responsibility consists of a nebulous idea, nevertheless should be integrated and objectively operationalized in a managerial context, because certain socially responsible organizations' decisions were able to be vindicated by the means of an extensive and intricate process of reasoning which, as outcomes, propitiated an honorable chance of carrying long-term economic gain to the organization, subsequently rewarding it for its socially responsible management performance. Frederick [FRE 60, p. 60] corroborated such an idea, stressing the relevance of CSR defending that "the economy's means of production should be employed in such a way that production and distribution should enhance total socio-economic welfare". Inspired by those authors, back in the 1970s Johnson [JOH 71, p. 69] provided further inputs to clearly understand the long-term orientation CSR seeks: based on the premise that utility maximization is the organization's prime motivation, organizations are then driven to achieve long-run profit maximization – thus, a socially responsible manager would be one interested not only in his/her own well-being but also in that of the others, imprinting a balance through which the fulfilment of all stakeholders' needs could be achieved, consequently objectivizing that business should serve a wider range of human values.

Two distinct cases can be analyzed as the basis for implementing CSR practices: the *normative* and the *business* case. These are not mutually exclusive, as an organization's motivation to engage in CSR activities might mirror a combination of the two [SMI 03]. The normative case locates the organizational motivation towards social responsibility on its desire to behave according to moral standards; the business case, on the other hand, focuses on the concept of rational self-interest, considering that paying attention to social responsibility may originate concrete outcomes providing the advantage of furthering the organization's economic success.

As such, CSR is distinguished both from the business responsibility of accomplishing vital profit-making and from the governmental social responsibilities [FRI 70], which lead Carroll [CAR 79, CAR 91] to systematize the concept by distinguishing its core economic, legal, ethical and philanthropic responsibilities. Benefiting from such inputs, Rochlin and Googins [ROC 05] defended the importance of CSR by maintaining that through the construction of a business strategy to align economic, social and environmental performance to long-term business values, CSR would turn part of the business and provide long-term value for both the company and society. Tuzzolino and Armandi [TUZ 81] developed a broader conceptualization of CSR by suggesting a need-hierarchy framework inspired on Carroll's [CAR 79] definition and subsequent proposals [CAR 91], an approach based on a reinterpretation of Maslow's [MAS 82] hierarchy of needs. Such contributions were also later reviewed [SCH 03, KAN 95, TUZ 81]. Tuzzolino and Armandi's [TUZ 81] suggestion does not redefine CSR, even though it adds an interesting point by contending that organizations, as well as individuals, display needs and goals that should be fulfilled, categorizing them into a broader scope than had previously been proposed by Carroll [CAR 91], who only mentioned economic, legal, ethical and philanthropic needs. Tuzzolino and Armandi [TUZ 81] indeed postulate physiological, safety, affiliative, esteem and self-actualization as organizational needs.

To achieve such goals, organizations acknowledge the need to involve all stakeholders in CSR policies and actions, which in a broader sense may be understood, following Zink's [ZIN 05, p. 1047] input, as "the ethical behavior of a company towards society". In this, we need to stress the fact that organizations adhere to CSR strategies on a voluntary basis [EUR 02, p. 7]. Manne and Wallich [MAN 72, p. 40] clarify the voluntary dimension surrounding CSR actions on the premise that an organization must be considered "at least in some measure a free agent", this meaning that "any of the foregoing social objectives are imposed on the corporation by law, the corporation exercises no responsibility when it implements them". Nonetheless, it is also clear that some CSR policies and practices are instigated in compliance to a legal foundation. Davis [DAV 73, p. 313] provides further insights on the relationship between law enforcement and voluntary action to understand its interconnection at the core of the CSR concept, advocating that social responsibility would have a proactive dynamics: "It is the firm's obligation to evaluate in its decision-making process the effects of its decisions on the external social system in a manner that will accomplish social benefits along with the traditional economic gains which the firm seeks."

The European Union provides additional insights to better understand the concept of CSR, defending that it comprises, in line with the issues mentioned above, two dimensions: *internal* and *external*. The *internal* dimension embraces human resources management, health and safety at work, adaptation to change, management of environmental impacts and natural resources; the *external* one includes local communities, human rights, global environmental concerns and the business partners/suppliers/consumers triangle. Undeniably, a socially responsible organization designs its structures, outlines its policies, articulates its practices and orients its actions through socially responsible integrated management, marked by socially responsible investment, reporting and auditing, quality in work, as well as by the implementation of social- and eco-labels [EUR 02].

Thus, and as supported by Matten and Moon [MAT 08], CSR (and the concepts covered by its "umbrella") consist of visibly articulated and communicated organizational policies and practices mirroring business accountability and proactive action towards the extensive societal good. Subsequently, concerns with corporate social performance, stakeholder relationships, connections and actions affecting financial performance, corporate citizenship and new applications of business ethics have stretched CSR theory and practice [GAR 04]. This idea can be strengthened discussing both internal as well as external benefits an organization can take advantage of by implementing CSR strategies [BRA 06, MCW 06]. Grounding such a discussion is the premise that organizations produce sustainable competitive advantages by effectively controlling their rare resources and capabilities, which are valuable because they are not possible to be perfectly imitated, thus no perfect substitutes are available. Hence, investment in socially responsible activities and disclosure may positively impact on the fundamental intangible resources, namely those associated with employees, as it can boost an organization's know-how and corporate culture – this would be the case for *internal benefits*. Likewise, it can also foster fundamental intangible resources by affecting corporate image – this would be the case for *external benefits*.

It is noteworthy that, taking a macro level on the analysis, the assumption of CSR varies between countries, as it is contextualized by national institutional frameworks [CHA 05, VIS 05]. On a micro level, it differs among organizations: as Matten and Moon [MAT 08, p. 405] sharply point out, "the precise manifestation and direction" of CSR lands "at the discretion of the corporation", an idea also shared by van Marrewijk [MAR 10]. Accordingly, organizations have a discretionary power on the decision and execution of which CSR approach to implement, then facing a different scope of impacts, varying as a function of the chosen strategy's depth. Actually, choosing the accurate CSR strategy positively effects business by reducing costs and risks, maximizing profits, fostering competitive advantage, increasing market share, enhancing employee motivation as well as customers' confidence and loyalty, consequently improving corporate reputation and legitimacy, aspects which end up "creating synergistic value" [KUR 08, p. 86]. Dey and Sircar [DEY 12] culminate this argumentation by considering that, in order to achieve such outcomes, CSR efforts must be positioned at the organization's very center, thus internalized on its structures, policies and practices through an allied incorporation dynamics, a goal that must be prompted not only by the organization's desire to foster its operational efficiency, to enhance its competitive advantage and, hence, to build a positive global corporate image, but indeed as a condition of developing it as a sustainable business.

In light of the above, reviewing the literature we can retrieve a collection of CSR strategies. *Implicit* CSR strategies are not considered as a voluntary and deliberate corporate decision, they are rather perceived as a response to, or replication of, the organization's institutional environment; on the other hand, *explicit* CSR practices objectify the outcome of an organization's deliberate, voluntary and often strategic decisions [POR 06]. Also important to keep in mind is the fact that organizations implementing implicit CSR strategies might behave in the same way as those organizations implementing explicit CSR strategies.

The literature also proposes the factors affecting the choice of the most appropriate strategy and specifies the challenges within the organization and the level of development it aims to achieve [BOM 11, MAR 10]. In fact, organizations can choose different strategies for different aspects of sustainability – namely *resign*, *defensive* and *offensive* strategies [BOM 11]. A resign strategy can be observed in organizations in which it is decided not to initiate the implementation of sustainability, a case commonly observed in organizations with a fragile innovation capacity and situated in contexts marked by a lack of pressures and incentives towards such an aim. Organizations with a fragile innovation capacity may also opt for a defensive strategy, while organizations with a high level of innovation are, opposingly, more likely to implement offensive strategies. Nonetheless, organizations can accumulate both a defensive and an offensive strategy, deciding it through a casuistic basis (meaning, according to specific products or services). The literature presents additional contributions in regards to other classifications of CSR strategies: "obstructionist, defensive, accommodative and proactive" [SAU 05, FIS 04, CAR 00, WAR 85, CAR 79]. Rejecting any form of ethics or social responsibility which mismatches the organization's economic interest, organizations are acting within an *obstructionist* strategy; but when they discard only ethical responsibilities and shelter their own interests inside the legal framework, they are adopting a *defensive* strategy. By its end, *accommodative* strategy is observed when organizations support only specific ethical responsibilities, particularly those of special stakeholders through a decision on a casuistic basis, not initiating proactive actions towards the common good. Opposingly, *proactive* companies differentiate themselves as they fully recognize social responsibilities, actively compromising to both minimize their negative environmental impact and satisfy all stakeholders' needs.

Looking at the analysis on a broader spectrum, we can argue that CSR can be coupled with the ideas of Sustainability. This was once the establishment of a corporate social contract based on CSR strategies and practices [BOW 91, DAV 83], which has been under sharp scrutiny since the advent of globalization, as the implementation of the complex interdependencies brought about by that new global order required a constant connection of the following fields within Sustainability: economic, financial, environmental, workforce and social criteria. The discussion around CSR has thus been facing a reorientation, as it has been gradually compelled to dissect how such a commitment should be made, instead of inquiring why to substantially compromise to CSR [SMI 03].

9.5. Where do the concepts match and mismatch?

The vitality and the frequency of the debate around Ecological Economics, Sustainable Management and CSR is evident. However, the proliferation of CSR definitions, theoretical approaches, assessment processes and tools, as well as the growing themes covered under the Sustainable Management "umbrella" and its diffusion at a global scale – which have proliferated in a more intense rhythm during the past decade – have added uncertainty and confusion to both academic discussions as well as to managerial policies and strategies' definition and implementation [BAN 05, CAR 99]. Indeed, there has been definitional unclarities on the first instance because both are relatively recent concepts, so rigor implies they still need to mature over time (we need to be aware that their boost was only observed mainly around the 1990s). Hence, the prominent themes which continued to grow and take center stage in the 1990s included corporate social performance, stakeholder theory, business ethics, sustainability and corporate citizenship, in a way that, though initially defined in terms of the natural environment, then evolved into a more encompassing concept that embraced the larger social stakeholder environment, CSR. Especially in the 2000s, the CSR movement has crystalized to be a global phenomenon [CAR 08].

As such, we can propose that, although Sustainable Management and CSR have evolved from slightly different historical pathways, they are pushing towards a common future. They both share the same vision, which intends to balance economic responsibilities with social and environmental ones. In fact, in current theoretical debates and empirical research both CSR and Sustainable Management aim to balance economic prosperity, social integrity, and environmental responsibility into a complex and interdependent relationship, regardless of whether they conceptualize environmental subjects as a subset of social issues or as the third element of sustainability, through the triple bottom line [MON 08]. Therefore, a conceptualization of CSR that assimilates both economic, social and environmental dimensions in a complex and intricated interdependence dynamics; and the triple bottom line conceptualization of Sustainable Management, which equally embraces economic, social and environmental dimensions in a fusion logics, are very similar. This is so because that way both approaches would signal that organizations must balance the three foundations of the triple bottom line to achieve long-term sustainability and social responsibility. Based on these assumptions, we see a notorious trend in current research which seems to propose that, due to their communal environmental and social concerns, CSR and Sustainable Management are increasingly converging, despite their paradigmatic differences.

As such, ambiguous definitions and constructs may prevent managers from identifying CSR and Sustainable Management goals for their organizations, and may also prevent academics from performing empirical research on coherent standards, as both concepts are currently neither well-defined nor clearly bounded, on the first instance because commonly agreed constructs exist. Based on the above discussion, we hereby present the foremost mismatches that can be perceived from a rigorous analysis of the conceptual constructs so far available around Sustainable Management and CSR, interconnecting and systematizing all the information discussed in the three previous sections of this work.

In the first instance, we suggest that a clear initial mismatch can be observed on the historical tradition that was the basis of both terms and their related concepts. Indeed, the topics covered by each concept, respective theoretical approach and conceptual umbrella are different in the scope that has been traditionally addressed to each of them. Sustainable Management links environmental and social management with business strategy, and it also integrates environmental and social information into sustainability reporting [SCH 06]. The truth is that, by historical tradition we can see that research on social concerns has been grounded prevalently in CSR strategies and actions; on the other hand, research on environmental issues has been the case usually for environmental management strategies and practices. In fact, CSR strategies, practices and policies have mainly been concerned with the social impact of organizational performance, marginalizing for a great period of time the environmental dimension of organizational actions: indeed, reviewing literature we can see that special attention has been given to the connection between social responsibility strategy and the business model [TEE 10], to the relationship between corporate social responsibility strategy and social capital [SPE 03] and to the link between social responsibility strategies and branding [POP 11]. Hence, historical tradition reports that under the CSR concept environmental issues consist only of a subdivision of broader social performance dimensions; but in what refers to the Sustainable Management approach, both the environmental and the social dimensions are deeply involved, assuming, with no doubt, vivid organizational concerns, thus transformed progressively into an important part of the organization's sustainability paradigm.

Indeed, until relatively recently (in the second half of the 20th Century) the business of social responsibility has been mainly based on the entrepreneurs' goodwill and personal altruism. However, it is now an integral part and a strategic issue towards the sustainable development of organizational structures [BAL 15]. One explanation for the fact that in CSR policies and practices the environmental dimension has by tradition received significantly less attention could be, as evidenced in Carroll's [CAR 99] literature review, that the environmental breadth was not encompassed in the early definitions for this term. Thus, it can be argued that it might have influenced future and current definitions to not include it either. In fact, either the environmental dimension has not been included in the CSR definition, or such an inclusion has not been explicitly bounded, clearly dissecting which approaches to be taken in order to objectively operationalize such a relationship. In order to understand this argument, attention can be driven at the World Business Council for Sustainable Development's conceptual proposal, once it differentiates between *corporate social responsibility* and *corporate environmental responsibility* – subsequently, issuing two separate and distinct definitions of CSR. Even though, once more it is noteworthy to mention that neither of those proposed definitions include the environmental dimension [WOR 00]. However, when CSR is explained in more depth, the environmental dimension and the social dimension are equally emphasized, and when that link is observed it is due to blurred references to Sustainable Management and Sustainable Development standards and core terms.

Sustainable Management consists of an approach beyond social obligation, as often some CSR strategies in organizations are only oriented towards this. Consequently, we suggest that this argument, through which we propose that there is an historical mismatch on the topics addressed to both CSR and Sustainable Management, develops into the assumption that CSR may focus more often on the tension and not so much on the cooperation between the triple bottom line of economic, social and environmental performance. We base this on the premise that contemporary businesses must address economic prosperity, social equity and environmental integrity before they can claim to have socially responsible behavior or sustainable practices.

As a second mismatch between both concepts, we suggest attention be brought towards the reasons behind the adoption of each of them. As discussed in the third section of this chapter, the adoption of CSR policies and practices can oscillate throughout a spectrum in which we can observe both normative or business reasons. So, we suggest that, through this mismatch, organizations have a more discretionary decision-making power in what refers to the adoption of CSR policies and practices, or at least to say, they commonly decide on a casuistic basis which CSR policies and practices they wish to implement, within which time frames and with which operative methods to achieve the desired results. In fact, we advocate that the most common corporate response to today's global challenges has been neither strategic nor operational, but purely cosmetic public relations and superficical media campaigns, which hardly provides a coherent framework for CSR activities – such initiatives indeed mainly only aggregate clumsy and uncoordinated actions aimed at publicly revealing an organization's social sensititity. Consequently, the moral appeal (or the voluntary reason to adopt CSR strategies, if we want to put it in other words), seems to be at stake, underestimated by more self-interested goals.

This idea is based on Carroll's [CAR 79] proposed popular four-part definition of CSR, suggesting that organizations assume four responsibilities towards societal welfare: economic, legal, ethical and philanthropic (we can here clearly see the environmental dimension being neglected, as per the explanation already provided when presenting the first mismatch). Nevertheless, it is true that Sustainable Management involves all of those four dimensions, but historical tradition and empirical evidence indeed shows that some organizations may only choose to be socially responsible and active in special fields. They may still present active strategies and practices of CSR even though neglecting some of the proposed four dimensions of impact, subsequently not being fully committed to a Sustainable Management paradigm. If truly embedded towards a Sustainable Management paradigm, organizations actively and deeply acknowledge that all organizational strategies, policies and practices actively reflect in societal well-being. They cannot just opt to fulfil responsible goals in some areas, as conservation of the planet and societal welfare are comprehended as a whole, they are imperative aims, requiring a broader commitment from the organization, fully entrenching its basilar structures. To reinforce this mismatch, we base it on the ideas of van Marrewijk [MAR 03], as the author supports that the principle of self-determination (more the case for CSR) is balanced by the principle of communion (the case by excellence for Sustainable Management). Hence, the capacity to create added value depends on the organization's willingness, commitment and duty to be responsible for its impact in the community and to adjust itself to environmental changes.

So, we suggest that the adoption of CSR strategies is mainly grounded on the organizations' (in the figure of its management team) self-interest, leading it to either comply with legislation and action standards in vigor (normative case), and/or to pursue the achievement of a competitive advantage, as organizations often understand that the adoption of CSR actions may provide them with resources they value, an additional source of value in their value chain (business case). It is, nevertheless, also true that CSR strategies can be adopted in an organization in light of a voluntary willingness, moved towards a broader consciousness that organizational performance impacts the community as a whole. However, this is not the most frequent case, if we analyze once more through an historical perspective – this idea is supported by Hartman *et al.* [HAR 07], who manifestly report the contrast between CSR as a business case and as an ethical reaction, plainly stating that both approaches were not only different, but indeed evidently separate and disconnected.

Sustainable Management may, therefore, be characterized as more anticipatory and preventive; and CSR, opposingly, as more reactive. In light of the above, we hereby suggest another mismatch between both concepts, which relates to the issues discussed previously, as these concepts imply a different commitment towards society, requiring a different engagement level from organizations, management teams and each person. Thus, the complexity and the scope of each concept is markedly distinct. Following that logic, we also suggest that CSR may focus more on the tension – and not so much on the cooperation – between the triple bottom line of economic, social and environmental performance, contrasting to what can be observed if discussing the Sustainable Management concept. Each level of analysis includes and transcends the previous ones, as each orientation represents a higher level of complexity. Hence, we suggest that a micro analysis is more the case for CSR; Sustainable Management, on the other hand, consists of a holistic approach, directed towards a broader scope, requiring a macro analysis [MAR 03]. We argue that CSR represents the microeconomic dimension of the macroeconomic concept of Sustainable Management, being also noticeably related to the concept of Sustainable Development.

We advocate, thus, that CSR acts only as a precondition for Sustainable Management: business sustainability is a consequence of the application of CSR strategies. In other words, we suggest that to fulfil their purpose, CSR strategies must be integrated into the overall business strategy [DEY 12], so should be embedded across the organization horizontally and vertically [FRA 01]. Inspired by Jones [JON 80], who postulated that CSR initiatives should be conceived as a process, we then argue that CSR strategies may be conceptualized as an integral part of the Sustainable Management concept and managerial approach, a remarkable contribution into the business environment to the achievement of the Sustainable Development objectives, yet depending on the compromise the organization wishes to make (as already explained in the discussion around the reasons to engage in CSR actions, namely the differences between the normative, the business and the voluntary cases). We defend that CSR is located in wider responsibility systems in which business, governmental, legal and social actors operate according to standards of mutual responsiveness, interdependency, choice and capacity, according to Matten and Moon [MAT 08]. So, it is located in broader systems managed according to the sustainability imperative, articulated within a sustainable management paradigm. As such, we can postulate that CSR is an operative tool of Sustainable Management.

This assumption shares the line of Lyon [LYO 04], who emphasizes that to incorporate CSR into long-term strategies and decision-making criteria, organizations must transition from a target-driven to a value-driven culture. Indeed, and as pointed out by Heslin and Ochoa [HES 08], a sophisticated ambition level on CSR interventions implies a supporting institutional framework and the respective value system, which may be achieved if in the organization we truly assist in the engagement towards the implementation of a Sustainable Management paradigm, decisively affecting the organizations' values, mission, vision, structure and objectives. Consequently, we advocate that organizations must build on their corporate values to create an organizational culture that is receptive to change and can sustain a CSR strategy over the long-term, towards a real Sustainable Management paradigm. This argument is supported by Maon *et al.* [MAO 09], who state that, in order to achieve a Sustainable Management paradigm and effectively have CSR simultaneously as their objectivation and as an objective pre-condition towards it, the first step would involve translating values, visions or policy statements into commitments, expectations and guiding principles, directing efforts towards goal setting and the development of targets and performance measures, based on the premise that, to be a sustainable organization, actions must be institutionalized into the organization and considered an integral part of its culture. This argument is also supported by the idea Cramer [CRA 05a: 588] had already intensely pointed out: "In any company, drawing up short- and longer-term strategies is a familiar procedure. What is often still missing up till now is the integration of the three P's (planet, people and profit) into the strategy and the action plans which derive from it."

9.6. Conclusion

This work aimed at, through a literature review, exposing the concepts of Ecological Economics, Sustainable Management and CSR, in order to verify the conceptual confusion and overlap between the latter two concepts. We conclude that the debate has been marked by definitional unclarity surrounding both terms and their conceptual umbrella frequently used as if they were synonymous, primarily due to their relatively recency. In fact, only since the 1990s have we witnessed a more intense discussion on the topic. Nevertheless, clear distinctions between both concepts can be highlighted, which we presented as mismatches if comparatively analyzing both conceptual structures and their preconized approaches. We have distinguished three such mismatches, all of which are related even though different from one another.

The first is based on the historical tradition surrounding both concepts. CSR strategies, practices and policies have mainly been concerned with the social impact of organizational performance; opposingly, Sustainable Management vividly acknowledges the environmental domain as an active and integral part of the triple bottom line, as it consists of an approach that goes beyond social obligation. The second mismatch refers to the reasons that from the basis of the organizations' decision towards the adoption of CSR strategies or of a Sustainable Management paradigm. CSR policies and practices can oscillate throughout a spectrum in which we observe normative, business and/or voluntary reasons, which we argue to mean that organizations have a more discretionary decision-making power with regards to the adoption of CSR policies and practices, as they can opt on a casuistic basis which CSR policies and practices they wish to implement, within which time frames and with which operative methods. Historical tradition and empirical evidence show that some organizations may only choose to be socially responsible and active in special fields, not being fully committed into a Sustainable Management paradigm. So, by this mismatch we suggest that the adoption of CSR strategies is mainly grounded on the organizations' self-interest, either to comply with the law (normative case) and/or to achieve competitive advantage, as organizations often understand that the adoption of CSR may provide them with valuable resources, an additional input to incorporate in their value chain. Sustainable Management may, therefore, be characterized as more anticipatory and preventive, CSR more reactive. Hence, the third mismatch arises as these concepts imply a different commitment level towards society, requiring a different engagement from organizations, management teams and each individual. Thus, the complexity and the scope of each concept is markedly distinct. Subsequently, we suggest that a micro analysis is more the case for CSR, but Sustainable Management consists of a holistic approach, requiring a macro analysis [MAR 03]. We argue that CSR represents the microeconomic dimension of the macroeconomic concept of Sustainable Management, thus, CSR acts only as a precondition for Sustainable Management: business sustainability is a consequence of the application of CSR strategies; hence, we can postulate that CSR is an operative tool of Sustainable Management.

Consequently, we advocate that such concepts should be used in their original semantic sense in order to prevent them becoming more diffuse, as the overlap creates blurred contributions and harms empirical research on rigorous standards. Confusing conceptualizations may also hinder organizations from assertively designing and implementing strategies that actively direct organizational performance towards sustainability. In addition, civil society debates become distorted and unclear, political agendas find obstacles to clearly define strategies, policies and practices to achieve sustainable development goals.

This chapter provides a useful input as it stresses that these two concepts may be considered "intrinsically linked" and CSR can be seen as the business contribution to sustainable development, so that organizations are seen as contributing to sustainable development "by managing their operations in such a way as to enhance economic growth and increase competitiveness whilst ensuring environmental protection and promoting social responsibility" [EUR 02, p. 7]. Thus, and based on where the organization's CSR strategies are located in the spectrum, progress towards sustainability in organizations is an ongoing dynamic which can waver throughout a series of phases, namely rejection, ignorance, compliance, efficiency, proactive strategy and corporate sustainability [HOL 10].

To the best of our knowledge, this work is the first to directly compare both the concepts of CSR and Sustainable Management, clearly exposing their corresponding and opposing points based on a literature review, in order to provide a useful input to bring forth more rigor to fill in the gap of the confusing, overlapping and blurred discussion around the topic. Nevertheless, it also aims to foster research to provide more contributions in this regard, as important research questions remain. A primary challenge focuses on the fact that, in line with Dahlsrud [DAH 08], CSR definitions are commonly a describing phenomenon, failing to provide a clear direction on the management of challenges within such a phenomenon. Consequently, we still need to truly understand how CSR originates, configures and develops as a socially constructed case within a specific context; as well as the way through which such a phenomenon is then transversally assimilated into the design and implementation of organizational strategies, policies and practices. Furthering this suggestion, in line with McWilliams *et al.* [MCW 06], we also advocate that there is a need to improve the measurement precision of the private and social returns of CSR initiatives, to better evaluate its contributions towards Sustainable Development. As Post [POS 78] argued, any conceptual and theoretical approach dealing with the intricated connection between business and society should, at its core, trial the wide-ranging and enduring organization-society interaction. Thus, future research around CSR should also shed more light on the complex network between organizations and their direct/indirect stakeholders. In addition, we recommend that it would be important to expand the focus of research by including CSR and Sustainable Management imperatives in the context of globalization. We also suggest the relevance of further research around the vigorous debate regarding managerial motives – instrumental [SIE 09] versus non-instrumental [MAR 09] – that drive environmental sustainability in organizations.

9.7. References

[AGU 07] AGUILERA R.V., RUPP D.E., WILLIAMS C.A. *et al.*, "Putting the S back in corporate social responsibility: A multilevel theory of social change in organizations", *Academy of Management Review*, vol. 32, no. 3, pp. 836–863, 2007.

[ALI 87a] ALIER J.M., "Economía y ecología: Cuestiones fundamentales", *Pensamiento Iberoamericano*, vol. 12, pp. 41–60, 1987.

[ALI 87b] ALIER J.M., SCHLÜPMANN K., *Ecological Economics: Energy, Environment, and Society*, Wiley-Blackwell, Oxford, 1987.

[AND 04] ANDERSON R., "Climbing mount sustainability", *Quality Progress*, vol. 37, no. 2, pp. 32–37, 2004.

[AYR 69] AYRES R.U., KNEESE A.V., "Production, consumption, and externalities", *The American Economic Review*, vol. 59, no. 3, pp. 282–297, 1969.

[BAL 15] BALABANOV V., BALABANOVA A., DUDIN M., "Social responsibility for sustainable development of enterprise structures", *Asian Social Science*, vol. 11, no. 8, pp. 111–118, 2015.

[BAN 01] BANERJEE S.B., "Managerial perceptions of corporate environmentalism: Interpretations from industry and strategic implications for organizations", *Journal of Management Studies*, vol. 38, no. 4, pp. 489–513, 2001.

[BAN 02] BANERJEE S.B., "Corporate environmentalism: The construct and its measurement", *Journal of Business Research*, vol. 55, no. 3, pp. 177–191, 2002.

[BAN 05] BANSAL P., "Evolving sustainably: A longitudinal study of corporate sustainable development", *Strategic Management Journal*, vol. 26, no. 3, pp. 197–218, 2005.

[BAR 91] BARNEY J., "Firm resources and sustained competitive advantage", *Journal of Management*, vol. 17, no. 1, pp. 99–120, 1991.

[BAR 13] BARNETT H.J., MORSE C., *Scarcity and Growth: The Economics of Natural Resource Availability*, Routledge, New York, 2013.

[BER 00a] VAN DEN BERGH J.C., Ecological economics: Themes, approaches, and differences with environmental economics, Tinbergen Institute Discussion Paper, No. 00-080/3, Tinbergen Institute, Amsterdam, 2000.

[BER 00b] BERKES F., COLDING J., FOLKE C., "Rediscovery of traditional ecological knowledge as adaptive management", *Ecological Applications*, vol. 10, no. 5, pp. 1251–1262, 2000.

[BOM 11] VAN BOMMEL H.W., "A conceptual framework for analyzing sustainability strategies in industrial supply networks from an innovation perspective", *Journal of Cleaner Production*, vol. 19, no. 8, pp. 895–904, 2011.

[BOU 66] BOULDING K.E., "The economics of the coming spaceship earth", in JARRET H. (ed.), *Environmental Quality in a Growing Economy*, Johns Hopkins University Press, Baltimore, 1966.

[BOW 91] BOWIE N.E., "New directions in corporate social responsibility", *Business Horizons*, vol. 34, no. 4, pp. 56–66, 1991.

[BRA 06] BRANCO M.C., RODRIGUES L.L., "Corporate social responsibility and resource-based perspectives", *Journal of Business Ethics*, vol. 69, no. 2, pp. 111–132, 2006.

[BUC 93] BUCHHOLZ R.A., *Principles of Environmental Management: The Greening of Business*, Prentice Hall, New York, 1993.

[CAR 79] CARROLL A., "A three dimensional model of corporate performance", *Academy of Management Review*, vol. 4, no. 4, pp. 497–505, 1979.

[CAR 91] CARROLL A., "The pyramid of corporate social responsibility: Toward the moral management of organizational stakeholders", *Business Horizons*, vol. 34, no. 4, pp. 39–48, 1991.

[CAR 99] CARROLL A., "Corporate social responsibility – Evolution of a definitional construction", *Business and Society*, vol. 38, no. 3, pp. 268–295, 1999.

[CAR 00] CARROLL A., BUCHHOLTZ A.K., *Business and Society: Ethics and Stakeholder Management*, South-Western College Publishing, Cincinnati, 2000.

[CAR 08] CARROLL A., "A history of corporate social responsibility: Concepts and practices", in CRANE A., MCWILLIAMS A., MATTEN D. *et al.* (eds), *The Oxford Handbook on Corporate Social Responsibility*, Oxford University Press, Oxford, pp. 19–46, 2008.

[CHA 05] CHAPPIE W., MOON J., "Corporate Social Responsibility in Asia: A seven country study of CSR website reporting", *Business and Society*, vol. 44, pp. 415–441, 2005.

[CHR 89] CHRISTENSEN P.P., "Historical roots for ecological economics: Biophysical versus allocative approaches", *Ecological Economics*, vol. 1, no. 1, pp. 17–36, 1989.

[CIR 52] CIRIACY-WANTRUP S.V., *Resource Conservation*, University of California, Berkeley, 1952.

[CLA 73] CLARK C.W., "The economics of overexploitation", *Science*, vol. 181, no. 4100, pp. 630–634, 1973.

[CLA 75] CLARK C.W., MUNRO G.R., "The economics of fishing and modern capital theory: A simplified approach", *Journal of Environmental Economics and Management*, vol. 2, pp. 92–106, 1975.

[COM 92] COMMON M., PERRINGS C., "Towards an ecological economics of sustainability", *Ecological Economics*, vol. 6, no. 1, pp. 7–34, 1992.

[COS 87] COSTANZA R., "Social traps and environmental policy", *BioScience*, vol. 37, no. 6, pp. 407–412, 1987.

[COS 91] COSTANZA R., "Ecological economics: A research agenda", *Structural Change and Economic Dynamics*, vol. 2, no. 2, pp. 335–357, 1991.

[COS 92a] COSTANZA R., CORNWELL L., "The 4P approach to dealing with scientific uncertainty", *Environment: Science and Policy for Sustainable Development*, vol. 34, no. 9, pp. 12–42, 1992.

[COS 92b] COSTANZA R., DALY H.E., "Natural capital and sustainable development", *Conservation Biology*, vol. 6, no. 1, pp. 37–46, 1992.

[COS 96] COSTANZA R., "Ecological economics: Reintegrating the study of humans and nature", *Ecological Applications*, vol. 6, no. 4, pp. 978–990, 1996.

[CRA 05a] CRAMER J.M., "Experiences with structuring corporate social responsibility in Dutch industry", *Journal of Cleaner Production*, vol. 13, no. 6, pp. 583–592, 2005.

[CRA 05b] CRANE A., MATTEN D., "Corporate citizenship: Missing the point or missing the boat? A reply to van Oosterhout", *Academy of Management Review*, vol. 30, no. 4, pp. 681–684, 2005.

[CRA 08] CRANE A., MCWILLIAMS A., MATTEN D. *et al.* (eds), *The Oxford Handbook on Corporate Social Responsibility*, Oxford University Press, Oxford, 2008.

[CUM 66] CUMBERLAND J.H., "A regional interindustry model for analysis of development objectives", *Papers of the Regional Science Association*, vol. 17, no. 1, pp. 65–94, 1966.

[DAH 08] DAHLSRUD A., "How corporate social responsibility is defined: An analysis of 37 definitions", *Corporate Social Responsibility and Environmental Management*, vol. 15, no. 1, pp. 1–13, 2008.

[DAL 68] DALY H.E., "On economics as a life science", *Journal of Political Economy*, vol. 76, no. 3, , pp. 392–406, 1968.

[DAL 79] DALY H.E., "Entropy, growth, and the political economy of scarcity", in SMITH, V.K. (ed.), *Scarcity and Growth Reconsidered*, The Johns Hopkins University Press, Baltimore, pp. 67–94, 1979.

[DAL 85] DALY H.E., "Moving to a steady-state economy", in EHRLICH P.R., HOLDREN J.P. (eds), *The Cassandra Conference: Resources and the Human Predicament*, Texas A&M Press, Texas, pp. 271–287, 1985.

[DAL 91] DALY H.E., *Steady-State Economics*, 2nd edition, Island Press, Washington D.C., 1991.

[DAL 92] DALY H.E., "Allocation, distribution, and scale: Towards an economics that is efficient, just and sustainable", *Ecological Economics*, vol. 6, no. 3, pp. 185–193, 1992.

[DAL 94] DALY H.E., "Operationalizing sustainable development by investing in natural capital", in JANSSON A., HAMMER M., FOLKE C. *et al.* (eds), *Investing in Natural Capital: The Ecological Economics Approach to Sustainability*, Island Press, Washington, D.C., pp. 22–37, 1994.

[DAL 96] DALY H.E., *Beyond Growth: The Economics of Sustainable Development*, Beacon Press, Boston, 1996.

[DAV 60] DAVIS K., "Can business afford to ignore social responsibilities?", *California Management Review*, spring, vol. 2, pp. 70–76, 1960.

[DAV 73] DAVIS K., "The case for and against business assumption of social responsibilities", *Academy of Management Journal*, vol. 16, no. 2, pp. 312–322, 1973.

[DAV 83] DAVIS K., "An expanded view of the social responsibility of business", in BEACHAMP T.L., BOWIE N.E. (eds), *Ethical Theory and Business*, 2nd edition, Prentice-Hall Inc., New Jersey, 1983.

[DEY 12] DEY M., SIRCAR S., "Integrating corporate social responsibility initiatives with business strategies: A study of some Indian companies", *The IUP Journal of Corporate Governance*, vol. XI, no. 1, pp. 36–51, 2012.

[DRU 93] DRUCKER P.F., *Managing for the Future*, Routledge, New York, 1993.

[EBE 73] EBERSTADT N.N., "What history tells us about corporate responsibilities", *Business and Society Review/Innovation*, autumn, pp. 76–81, 1973.

[ELK 94] ELKINGTON J., "Towards the sustainable corporation", *California Management Review*, vol. 36, no. 2, pp. 90–100, 1994.

[EUR 02] EUROPEAN COMMISSION, *Corporate Social Responsibility – A Business Contribution to Sustainable Development*, Office for Official Publications of the European Communities, Luxembourg, 2002.

[FLO 01] FLORIDA R., DAVISON D., "Gaining from green management: Environmental management systems inside and outside the factory", *California Management Review*, vol. 43, no. 3, pp. 64–84, 2001.

[FRA 01] FRANKENTAL P., "Corporate social responsibility – A PR invention?", *Corporate Communications: An International Journal*, vol. 6, no. 1, pp. 18–23, 2001.

[FRE 60] FREDERICK W.C., "The growing concern over business responsibility", *California Management Review*, vol. 2, no. 4, pp. 54–61, 1960.

[FRI 70] FRIEDMAN M., "The social responsibility of business is to increase its profits", *New York Times*, no. 13, pp. 122–126, 1970.

[GAL 58] GALBRAITH J.K., "How much should a country consume?", in JARRET H. (ed.), *Perspectives on Conservation*, The John Hopkins Press, Baltimore, pp. 89–99, 1958.

[GAR 04] GARRIGA E., MELÉ D., "Corporate social responsibility theories: Mapping the territory", *Journal of Business Ethics*, vol. 53, no. 1–2, pp. 51–71, 2004.

[GEO 66] GEORGESCU-ROEGEN N., *Analytical Economics: Issues and Problems*, Harvard University Press, Cambridge, 1966.

[GEO 71] GEORGESCU-ROEGEN N., *The Entropy Law and the Economic Process*, Harvard University Press, Cambridge, 1971.

[GEO 76] GEORGESCU-ROEGEN N., *Energy and Economic Myths*, Pergamon, New York, 1976.

[GLÜ 01] GLÜCK A., "Das Prinzip Nachhaltigkeit–Zukunftsorientiertes Denken und Handeln in ausgewählten Lebensbereichen", *Politische Studien, Sonderheft. Das Prinzip Nachhaltigkeit Zukunftsorientiertes Handeln in ausgewählten Lebensbereichen*, vol. 52, no. 1, pp. 1–77, 2001.

[GOL 94] GOLLEY F.B., "Development of landscape ecology and its relation to environmental management", *Ecosystem Management: Principles and Applications*, vol. 2, pp. 34–41, 1994.

[GOW 05] GOWDY J., ERICKSON J.D., "The approach of ecological economics", *Cambridge Journal of Economics*, vol. 29, no. 2, pp. 207–222, 2005.

[GRO 92] DE GROOT R.S., *Functions of Nature: Evaluation of Nature in Environmental Planning, Management and Decision Making,* Wolters-Noordhoff B.V., Groningen, 1992.

[GUN 95] GUNDERSON L.H., HOLLING C.S., LIGHT S.S. (eds), *Barriers and Bridges to the Renewal of Ecosystems and Institutions*, Columbia University Press, New York, 1995.

[HAD 09] HADEN S.S., OYLER J.D., HUMPHREYS J.H., "Historical, practical, and theoretical perspectives on green management: An exploratory analysis", *Management Decision,* vol. 47, no. 7, pp. 1041–1055, 2009.

[HAM 93] HAMMER M., JANSSON A.M., JANSSON B-O., "Diversity change and sustainability: Implications for fisheries", *Ambio*, vol. 22, pp. 97–105, 1993.

[HAR 95] HART S.L., "A natural-resource-based view of the firm", *Academy of Management Review*, vol. 20, no. 4, pp. 986–1014, 1995.

[HAR 07] HARTMAN L.P., RUBIN R.S., DHANDA K.K., "The communication of corporate social responsibility: United States and European Union multinational corporations", *Journal of Business Ethics*, vol. 74, no. 4, pp. 373–389, 2007.

[HES 08] HESLIN P.A., OCHOA J.D., "Understanding and developing strategic corporate social responsibility", *Organizational Dynamics*, vol. 37, pp. 125–144, 2008.

[HOB 75] HOBSBAWM E.J., CUMMING M., *Age of Extremes: The Short Twentieth Century, 1914–1991*, Abacus, London, 1975.

[HOL 73] HOLLING C.S., "Resilience and stability of ecological systems", *Annual Review of Ecological* Systems, vol. 4, no. 1, pp. 1–24, 1973.

[HOL 85] HOLLING C.S., *Resilience of Ecosystems: Local Surprise and Global Change*, Cambridge University Press, Cambridge, 1985.

[HOL 94] HOLLING C.S., "An ecologist view of the Malthusian conflict", in LINDAHL K.K., LANDBERG H. (eds), *Population, Economic Development, and the Environment,* Oxford University Press, New York, pp. 79–103, 1994.

[HOL 10] HOLTON I., GLASS J., PRICE A.D., "Managing for sustainability: Findings from four company case studies in the UK precast concrete industry", *Journal of Cleaner Production*, vol. 18, no. 2, pp. 152–160, 2010.

[JAN 94] JANSSON A., *Investing in Natural Capital: The Ecological Economics Approach to Sustainability,* Island Press, Washington, D.C., 1994.

[JOH 71] JOHNSON H.L., *Business in Contemporary Society: Framework and Issues,* Wadsworth, Belmont, 1971.

[JON 80] JONES T.M., "Corporate social responsibility revisited, redefined", *California Management Review*, vol. 22, no. 3, pp. 59–67, 1980.

[JUD 98] JUDGE W.Q., DOUGLAS T.J., "Performance implications of incorporating natural environmental issues into the strategic planning process: An empirical assessment", *Journal of Management Studies*, vol. 35, no. 2, pp. 241–262, 1998.

[KAN 95] KANG Y.C., WOOD D.J., "Before-profit social responsibility: Turning the economic paradigm upside down", *Proceedings of the International Association for Business and Society*, vol. 6, pp. 809–829, 1995.

[KNE 15] KNEESE A.V., AYRES R.U., D'ARGE R.C., *Economics and the Environment: A Materials Balance Approach*, Routledge, New York, 2015.

[KUR 08] KURUCZ E.C., COLBERT B.A., WHEELER D., "The business case for corporate social responsibility", in CRANE A., MCWILLIAMS A., MATTEN D. *et al.* (eds), *The Oxford Handbook* on *Corporate Social Responsibility*, Oxford University Press, Oxford, pp. 83–112, 2008.

[LEE 93] LEE K.N., *Compass and Gyroscope: Integrating Science and Politics for the Environment*, Island Press, Washington, D.C., 1993.

[LEE 08] LEE M., "A review of the theories of corporate social responsibility: Its evolutionary path and the road ahead", *International Journal of Management Reviews*, vol. 10, no. 1, pp. 53–73, 2008.

[LEO 70] LEONTIEF W., "Environmental repercussions and the economic structure: An input-output approach", *The Review of Economics and Statistics*, vol. 52, no. 3, pp. 262–271, 1970.

[LEP 10] LEPINEUX F., ROSE J.J., BONANNI C. *et al.*, *La RSE. La responsabilité sociale de l'entreprises : théories et pratiques*, Dunod, Paris, 2010.

[LOC 06] LOCKETT A., MOON J., VISSER W., "Corporate social responsibility in management research: Focus, nature, salience and sources of influence", *Journal of Management Studies*, vol. 43, no. 1, pp. 115–136, 2006.

[LUD 93] LUDWIG D., HILBORN R., WALTERS C., "Uncertainty, resource exploitation, and conservation: Lessons from history", *Science*, vol. 260, pp. 17–36, 1993.

[LYO 04] LYON D., "How can you help organizations change to meet the corporate responsibility agenda?", *Corporate Social Responsibility and Environmental Management*, vol. 11, no. 3, pp. 133–139, 2004.

[MAL 98] MALTHUS T.R., *An Essay on the Principle of Population*, Reeves & Turner, London, 1798.

[MAL 08] MALOVICS G., NAGYPAL N.C., KRAUS S., "The role of corporate social responsibility in strong sustainability", *Journal of Socio-Economics*, vol. 37, no. 3, pp. 907–918, 2008.

[MAN 72] MANNE H.G., WALLICH H.C., *The Modern Corporation and Social Responsibility*, American Enterprise Institute for Public Policy Research, Washington, D.C., 1972.

[MAO 09] MAON F., LINDGREEN A., SWAEN V., "Designing and implementing corporate social responsibility: An integrative framework grounded in theory and practice", *Journal of Business Ethics*, vol. 87, no. 1, pp. 71–89, 2009.

[MAR 67] MARX K., *Capital*, Vintage, New York, 1867.

[MAR 03] VAN MARREWIJK M., "Concepts and definitions of CSR and corporate sustainability: Between agency and communion", *Journal of Business Ethics*, vol. 44, no. 2, pp. 95–105, 2003.

[MAR 06a] MARCUS A., ANDERSON M., "A general dynamic capability: Does it propagate business and social competencies in the retail food industry?", *Journal of Management Studies*, vol. 43, no. 1, pp. 19–46, 2006.

[MAR 06b] MARCUS A., KAISER S., *Managing Beyond Compliance: The Ethical and Legal Dimensions of Corporate Responsibility*, North Coast Publishers, Ohio, 2006.

[MAR 09] MARCUS A., FREMETH A.R., "Green management matters regardless", *Academy of Management Perspectives*, vol. 23, no. 3, pp. 17–26, 2009.

[MAR 10] VAN MARREWIJK M., "Strategic orientations: Multiple ways for implementing sustainable performance", *Technology and Investment*, vol. 1, pp. 85–96, 2010.

[MAS 82] MASLOW A., *Toward a Psychology of Being*, Van Nostrand Reinhold, New York, 1982.

[MAT 08] MATTEN D., MOON J., "'Implicit' and 'explicit' CSR: A conceptual framework for a comparative understanding of corporate social responsibility", *Academy of Management Review*, vol. 33, no. 2, pp. 404–424, 2008.

[MCG 63] MCGUIRE J.W., *Business and Society*, McGraw-Hill, New York, 1963.

[MCW 02] MCWILLIAMS A., VAN FLEET D.D., CORY K., "Raising rivals' costs through political strategy: An extension of the resource-based theory", *Journal of Management Studies*, vol. 39, no. 5, pp. 707–723, 2002.

[MCW 06] MCWILLIAMS A., SIEGEL D.S., WRIGHT P.M., "Corporate social responsibility: Strategic implications", *Journal of Management Studies*, vol. 43, no. 1, pp. 1–18, 2006.

[MIL 57] MILL J.S., *Principles of Economics*, Parker, London, 1857.

[MIS 67] MISHAN E.J., MISHAN E.J., *The Costs of Economic Growth*, Staples Press, London, 1967.

[MOI 01] MOIR L., "What do we mean by corporate social responsibility?", *Corporate Governance*, vol. 1, no. 2, pp. 16–22, 2001.

[MON 08] MONTIEL I., "Corporate social responsibility and corporate sustainability: Separate pasts, common futures", *Organization & Environment*, vol. 21, no. 3, pp. 245–269, 2008.

[MOO 05] MOON J., CRANE A., MATTEN D., "Can corporations be citizens? Corporate citizenship as a metaphor for business participation in society", *Business Ethics Quarterly*, vol. 15, no. 3, pp. 429–453, 2005.

[MUI 99] MUIRHEAD S.A., *Corporate Contributions: The View from 50 Years*, The Conference Board, New York, 1999.

[MUN 97] MUNDA G., "Environmental economics, ecological economics, and the concept of sustainable development", *Environmental Values*, vol. 6, no. 2, pp. 213–233, 1997.

[NAT 99] NATTRASS B., ALTOMARE M., *The Natural Step for Business*, New Society Publishers, Canada, 1999.

[NEL 98] NELSON J., "Leadership companies in the twenty-first century: Creating shareholder value and societal value", *Visions of Ethical Business, Financial Times Management*, vol. 1, pp. 21–26, 1998.

[NOR 89] NORGAARD R.B., "Three dilemmas of environmental accounting", *Ecological Economics*, vol. 1, no. 4, pp. 303–314, 1989.

[NØR 13] NØRGÅRD J.S., "Happy degrowth through more amateur economy", *Journal of Cleaner Production*, vol. 38, pp. 61–70, 2013.

[ODU 71] ODUM H.T., *Environment, Power, and Society*, Wiley, New York, 1971.

[ODU 87] ODUM H.T., "Models for national, international and global systems policy", in BRAAT L.C., VAN LIEROP W.F. (eds), *Economic-Ecological Modelling*, Elsevier Science Publishing, New York, 1987.

[ORL 03] ORLITZKY M., SCHMIDT F.L., RYNES S.L., "Corporate social and financial performance: A meta-analysis", *Organization Studies*, vol. 24, no. 3, pp. 403–441, 2003.

[ORL 11] ORLITZKY M., SIEGEL D.S., WALDMAN D.A., "Strategic corporate social responsibility and environmental sustainability", *Business & Society*, vol. 50, no. 1, pp. 6–27, 2011.

[PER 98] PERRINGS C., "Resilience in the dynamics of economy-environment systems", *Environmental and Resource Economics*, vol. 11, nos 3–4, pp. 503–520, 1998.

[POP 11] POPOLI P., "Linking CSR strategy and brand image: Different approaches in local and global markets", *Marketing Theory*, vol. 11, no. 4, pp. 419–433, 2011.

[POR 95] PORTER M.E., VAN DER LINDE C., "Toward a new conception of the environment-competitiveness relationship", *Journal of Economic Perspectives*, vol. 9, no. 4, pp. 97–118, 1995.

[POR 06] PORTER M.E., KRAMER M.R., "The link between competitive advantage and corporate social responsibility", *Harvard Business Review*, vol. 84, no. 12, pp. 78–92, 2006.

[POS 78] POST J.E., *Corporate Behaviour and Social Change*, Reston Publishing, Reston, 1978.

[PRE 75] PRESTON L., POST J.E., *Private Management and Public Policy: The Principle of Public Responsibility*, Prentice-Hall, New Jersey, 1975.

[RAP 93] RAPPORT D.J., "Book review of Man, Nature, and Technology", *Ecological Economics*, vol. 7, pp. 79–83, 1993.

[RIC 17] RICARDO D., *On the Principles of Political Economy and Taxation*, Penguin Books, Harmondsworth, 1817.

[ROC 05] ROCHLIN S.A., GOOGINS B.K., *The Value Proposition for Corporate Citizenship*, The Center for Corporate Citizenship at Boston College, Chestnut Hill, 2005.

[SAG 95] SAGOFF M., "Carrying capacity and ecological economics", *BioScience*, vol. 45, no. 9, pp. 610–620, 1995.

[SAU 05] SAUSER W.I., "Ethics in business: Answering the call", *Journal of Business Ethics*, vol. 58, no. 4, pp. 345–357, 2005.

[SCH 03] SCHWARTZ M.S., CARROLL A., "Corporate social responsibility: A three-domain approach", *Business Ethics Quarterly*, vol. 13, no. 4, pp. 503–530, 2003.

[SCH 06] SCHALTEGGER S., WAGNER M., "Integrative management of sustainability performance, measurement and reporting", *International Journal of Accounting, Auditing and Performance Evaluation*, vol. 3, no. 1, pp. 1–19, 2006.

[SIE 09] SIEGEL D.S., "Green management matters only if it yields more green: An economic/strategic perspective", *Academy of Management Perspectives*, vol. 23, no. 3, pp. 5–16, 2009.

[SMI 03] SMITH N.C., "Corporate Social Responsibility: Whether or how?", *California Management Review*, vol. 45, no. 4, pp. 52–76, 2003.

[SPE 03] SPENCE L.J., SCHMIDPETER R., HABISCH A., "Assessing social capital: Small and medium sized enterprises in Germany and the U.K.", *Journal of Business Ethics*, vol. 47, no. 1, pp. 17–29, 2003.

[STE 71] STEINER G.A., *Business and Society*, Random House, New York, 1971.

[STE 05] STEURER R., LANGER M.E., KONRAD A. *et al.*, "Corporations, stakeholders and sustainable development: A theoretical exploration of business–society relations", *Journal of Business Ethics*, vol. 61, no. 3, pp. 263–281, 2005.

[TAY 92] TAYLOR S.R., "Green management: The next competitive weapon", *Futures*, vol. 24, no. 7, pp. 669–680, 1992.

[TEE 07] TEECE D.J., "Explicating dynamic capabilities: The nature and microfoundations of (sustainable) enterprise performance", *Strategic Management Journal*, vol. 28, no. 13, pp. 1319–1350, 2007.

[TEE 10] TEECE D.J., "Business models, business strategy and innovation", *Long Range Planning*, vol. 43, nos 2–3, pp. 172–194, 2010.

[TUR 97] TURNER R.K., PERRINGS C., FOLKE C., "Ecological economics: Paradigm or perspective", in VAN DEN BERGH J.C., VAN DER STRAATEN J. (eds), *Economy and Ecosystems in Change: Analytical and Historical Approaches*, Edward Elgar, Cheltenham, 1997.

[TUZ 81] TUZZOLINO F., ARMANDI B.R., "A need-hierarchy framework for assessing corporate social responsibility", *Academy of Management Review*, vol. 6, no. 1, pp. 21–28, 1981.

[VIE 94] VIEDERMAN S., *The Economics of Sustainability: Challenges*, Jessie Smith Noyes Foundation, New York, 1994.

[VIS 05] VISSER W., MIDDLETON C., MCINTOSH M., "Corporate citizenship in Africa", *Journal of Corporate Citizenship*, vol. 18, pp. 17–124, 2005.

[VIT 86] VITOUSEK P.M., EHRLICH P.R., EHRLICH A.H. *et al.*, "Human appropriation of the products of photosynthesis", *BioScience*, vol. 36, no. 6, pp. 368–373, 1986.

[WAL 03] WALSH J.P., WEBER K., MARGOLIS J.D., "Social issues and management: Our lost cause found", *Journal of Management*, vol. 29, no. 6, pp. 859–881, 2003.

[WAR 85] WARTICK S.L., COCHRAN P.L., "The evolution of the corporate social performance model", *Academy of Management Review*, vol. 10, no. 4, pp. 758–769, 1985.

[WER 84] WERNERFELT B., "A resource-based view of the firm", *Strategic Management Journal*, vol. 5, no. 2, pp. 171–180, 1984.

[WIL 00] WILSON I., *The New Rules of Corporate Conduct: Rewriting the Social Charter,* Quorum Books, Westport, 2000.

[WIN 06] WINDSOR D., "Corporate social responsibility: Three key approaches", *Journal of Management Studies*, vol. 43, no. 1, pp. 93–114, 2006.

[WOR 00] WORLD BUSINESS COUNCIL FOR SUSTAINABLE DEVELOPMENT, *Corporate Social Responsibility: Making Good Business Sense*, World Business Council for Sustainable Development, Geneva, 2000.

[WRE 05] WREN D.A., *The History of Management Thought*, John Wiley & Sons Inc, New Jersey, 2005.

[ZAI 00] ZAIRI M., "Social responsibility and impact on society", *The TQM Magazine*, vol. 12, no. 3, pp. 172–178, 2000.

[ZIN 05] ZINK K.J., "Stakeholder orientation and corporate social responsibility as a precondition for sustainability", *Total Quality Management and Business Excellence*, vol. 16, nos 8–9, pp. 1041–1052, 2005.

List of Authors

J. Paulo DAVIM
Department of Mechanical Engineering
University of Aveiro
Portugal

Dimas de Oliveira ESTEVAM
UNESC – Universidade do Extremo Sul Catarinense
Santa Catarina
Brazil

Diana FERNANDES
Department of Management
School of Economics and Management
University of Minho
Braga
Portugal

Hailong FU
Northeast Petroleum University
Daqing
China

Delfina GOMES
Department of Management
School of Economics and Management
University of Minho
Braga
Portugal

Cristiana Cerqueira LEAL
Department of Management
School of Economics and Management
University of Minho
Braga
Portugal

Carolina Feliciana MACHADO
Department of Management
School of Economics and Management
University of Minho
Braga
Portugal

Benilde OLIVEIRA
Department of Management
School of Economics and Management
University of Minho
Braga
Portugal

Mirela PANAIT
Petroleum-Gas University of Ploieşti
Romania

Adriana Toledo PEREIRA
ISEG/UL Lisbon School of Economics and Management
University of Lisbon
Portugal

Marius Gabriel PETRESCU
Petroleum-Gas University of Ploieşti
Romania

João Leite RIBEIRO
Department of Management
School of Economics and Management
University of Minho
Braga
Portugal

Bruna ROCHA
Department of Management
School of Economics and Management
University of Minho
Braga
Portugal

Maria João SANTOS
ISEG/UL Lisbon School of Economics and Management
University of Lisbon
Portugal

Yasemin SEN
Management and Organization Department
School of Business
Istanbul University
Turkey

Adrian STANCU
Department of Business Administration
Faculty of Economics Sciences
Petroleum-Gas University of Ploieşti
Romania

David STARR-GLASS
Empire State College
State University of New York
USA

Marian Cătălin VOICA
Department of Business Administration
Faculty of Economics Sciences
Petroleum-Gas University of Ploieşti
Romania

Yue WANG
Northeast Petroleum University
Daqing
China

Index

D, E

F, G

H, I

L

M

N, O

P

Q, R

S

T, V, W

Other titles from

ISTE

in

Innovation, Entrepreneurship and Management

2020

ANDREOSSO-O'CALLAGHAN Bernadette, DZEVER Sam, JAUSSAUD Jacques, TAYLOR Robert
Sustainable Development and Energy Transition in Europe and Asia (Innovation and Technology Set – Volume 9)

BEN SLIMANE Sonia, M'HENNI Hatem
Entrepreneurship and Development: Realities and Future Prospects (Smart Innovation Set – Volume 30)

CHOUTEAU Marianne, FOREST Joëlle, NGUYEN Céline
Innovation for Society: The P.S.I. Approach (Smart Innovation Set – Volume 28)

CORON Clotilde
Quantifying Human Resources: Uses and Analysis (Technological Changes and Human Resources Set – Volume 2)

CORON Clotilde, GILBERT Patrick
Technological Change (Technological Changes and Human Resources Set – Volume 1)

CERDIN Jean-Luc, PERETTI Jean-Marie
The Success of Apprenticeships: Views of Stakeholders on Training and Learning
(Human Resources Management Set – Volume 3)

DELCHET-COCHET Karen
Circular Economy: From Waste Reduction to Value Creation
(Economic Growth Set – Volume 2)

DIDAY Edwin, GUAN Rong, SAPORTA Gilbert, WANG Huiwen
Advances in Data Science
(Big Data, Artificial Intelligence and Data Analysis Set – Volume 4)

DOS SANTOS PAULINO Victor
Innovation Trends in the Space Industry
(Smart Innovation Set – Volume 25)

GOGLIN Christian
Emotions and Values in Equity Crowdfunding Investment Choices 1: Transdisciplinary Theoretical Approach

GUILHON Bernard
Venture Capital and the Financing of Innovation
(Innovation Between Risk and Reward Set – Volume 6)

LATOUCHE Pascal
Open Innovation: Human Set-up
(Innovation and Technology Set – Volume 10)

MAKRIDES Andreas, KARAGRIGORIOU Alex, SKIADAS Christos H.
Data Analysis and Applications 3: Computational, Classification, Financial, Statistical and Stochastic Methods
(Big Data, Artificial Intelligence and Data Analysis Set – Volume 5)
Data Analysis and Applications 4: Financial Data Analysis and Methods
(Big Data, Artificial Intelligence and Data Analysis Set – Volume 6)

MASSOTTE Pierre, CORSI Patrick
Complex Decision-Making in Economy and Finance

MEUNIER François-Xavier
Dual Innovation Systems : Concepts, Tools and Methods
(Smart Innovation Set – Volume 31)

MICHAUD Thomas
Science Fiction and Innovation Design (Innovation in Engineering and Technology Set – Volume 6)

MONINO Jean-Louis
Data Control: Major Challenge for the Digital Society
(Smart Innovation Set – Volume 29)

MORLAT Clément
Sustainable Productive System: Eco-development versus Sustainable Development
(Smart Innovation Set – Volume 26)

SAULAIS Pierre, ERMINE Jean-Louis
Knowledge Management in Innovative Companies 2: Understanding and Deploying a KM Plan within a Learning Organization
(Smart Innovation Set – Volume 27)

2019

AMENDOLA Mario, GAFFARD Jean-Luc
Disorder and Public Concern Around Globalization

BARBAROUX Pierre
Disruptive Technology and Defence Innovation Ecosystems
(Innovation in Engineering and Technology Set – Volume 5)

DOU Henri, JUILLET Alain, CLERC Philippe
Strategic Intelligence for the Future 1: A New Strategic and Operational Approach
Strategic Intelligence for the Future 2: A New Information Function Approach

FRIKHA Azza
Measurement in Marketing: Operationalization of Latent Constructs

FRIMOUSSE Soufyane
Innovation and Agility in the Digital Age
(Human Resources Management Set – Volume 2)

GAY Claudine, SZOSTAK Bérangère L.
Innovation and Creativity in SMEs: Challenges, Evolutions and Prospects
(Smart Innovation Set – Volume 21)

GORIA Stéphane, HUMBERT Pierre, ROUSSEL Benoît
Information, Knowledge and Agile Creativity
(Smart Innovation Set – Volume 22)

HELLER David
Investment Decision-making Using Optional Models
(Economic Growth Set – Volume 2)

HELLER David, DE CHADIRAC Sylvain, HALAOUI Lana, JOUVET Camille
The Emergence of Start-ups
(Economic Growth Set – Volume 1)

HÉRAUD Jean-Alain, KERR Fiona, BURGER-HELMCHEN Thierry
Creative Management of Complex Systems
(Smart Innovation Set – Volume 19)

LATOUCHE Pascal
Open Innovation: Corporate Incubator
(Innovation and Technology Set – Volume 7)

LEHMANN Paul-Jacques
The Future of the Euro Currency

LEIGNEL Jean-Louis, MÉNAGER Emmanuel, YABLONSKY Serge
Sustainable Enterprise Performance: A Comprehensive Evaluation Method

LIÈVRE Pascal, AUBRY Monique, GAREL Gilles
Management of Extreme Situations: From Polar Expeditions to Exploration-Oriented Organizations

MILLOT Michel
Embarrassment of Product Choices 2: Towards a Society of Well-being

N'GOALA Gilles, PEZ-PÉRARD Virginie, PRIM-ALLAZ Isabelle
Augmented Customer Strategy: CRM in the Digital Age

NIKOLOVA Blagovesta
The RRI Challenge: Responsibilization in a State of Tension with Market Regulation
(Innovation and Responsibility Set – Volume 3)

PELLEGRIN-BOUCHER Estelle, ROY Pierre
Innovation in the Cultural and Creative Industries
(Innovation and Technology Set – Volume 8)

PRIOLON Joël
Financial Markets for Commodities

QUINIOU Matthieu
Blockchain: The Advent of Disintermediation

RAVIX Joël-Thomas, DESCHAMPS Marc
Innovation and Industrial Policies
(Innovation between Risk and Reward Set – Volume 5)

ROGER Alain, VINOT Didier
Skills Management: New Applications, New Questions
(Human Resources Management Set – Volume 1)

SAULAIS Pierre, ERMINE Jean-Louis
Knowledge Management in Innovative Companies 1: Understanding and Deploying a KM Plan within a Learning Organization
(Smart Innovation Set – Volume 23)

SERVAJEAN-HILST Romaric
Co-innovation Dynamics: The Management of Client-Supplier Interactions for Open Innovation
(Smart Innovation Set – Volume 20)

SKIADAS Christos H., BOZEMAN James R.
Data Analysis and Applications 1: Clustering and Regression, Modeling-estimating, Forecasting and Data Mining
(Big Data, Artificial Intelligence and Data Analysis Set – Volume 2)
Data Analysis and Applications 2: Utilization of Results in Europe and Other Topics
(Big Data, Artificial Intelligence and Data Analysis Set – Volume 3)

UZUNIDIS Dimitri
Systemic Innovation: Entrepreneurial Strategies and Market Dynamics

VIGEZZI Michel
World Industrialization: Shared Inventions, Competitive Innovations and Social Dynamics
(Smart Innovation Set – Volume 24)

2018

BURKHARDT Kirsten
Private Equity Firms: Their Role in the Formation of Strategic Alliances

CALLENS Stéphane
Creative Globalization
(Smart Innovation Set – Volume 16)

CASADELLA Vanessa
Innovation Systems in Emerging Economies: MINT – Mexico, Indonesia, Nigeria, Turkey
(Smart Innovation Set – Volume 18)

CHOUTEAU Marianne, FOREST Joëlle, NGUYEN Céline
Science, Technology and Innovation Culture
(Innovation in Engineering and Technology Set – Volume 3)

CORLOSQUET-HABART Marine, JANSSEN Jacques
Big Data for Insurance Companies
(Big Data, Artificial Intelligence and Data Analysis Set – Volume 1)

CROS Françoise
Innovation and Society
(Smart Innovation Set – Volume 15)

DEBREF Romain
Environmental Innovation and Ecodesign: Certainties and Controversies
(Smart Innovation Set – Volume 17)

DOMINGUEZ Noémie
SME Internationalization Strategies: Innovation to Conquer New Markets

ERMINE Jean-Louis
Knowledge Management: The Creative Loop
(Innovation and Technology Set – Volume 5)

GILBERT Patrick, BOBADILLA Natalia, GASTALDI Lise,
LE BOULAIRE Martine, LELEBINA Olga
Innovation, Research and Development Management

IBRAHIMI Mohammed
Mergers & Acquisitions: Theory, Strategy, Finance

LEMAÎTRE Denis
Training Engineers for Innovation

LÉVY Aldo, BEN BOUHENI Faten, AMMI Chantal
Financial Management: USGAAP and IFRS Standards
(Innovation and Technology Set – Volume 6)

MILLOT Michel
Embarrassment of Product Choices 1: How to Consume Differently

PANSERA Mario, OWEN Richard
Innovation and Development: The Politics at the Bottom of the Pyramid
(Innovation and Responsibility Set – Volume 2)

RICHEZ Yves
Corporate Talent Detection and Development

SACHETTI Philippe, ZUPPINGER Thibaud
New Technologies and Branding
(Innovation and Technology Set – Volume 4)

SAMIER Henri
Intuition, Creativity, Innovation

TEMPLE Ludovic, COMPAORÉ SAWADOGO Eveline M.F.W.
Innovation Processes in Agro-Ecological Transitions in Developing Countries
(Innovation in Engineering and Technology Set – Volume 2)

UZUNIDIS Dimitri
Collective Innovation Processes: Principles and Practices
(Innovation in Engineering and Technology Set – Volume 4)

VAN HOOREBEKE Delphine
The Management of Living Beings or Emo-management

2017

AÏT-EL-HADJ Smaïl
The Ongoing Technological System
(Smart Innovation Set – Volume 11)

BAUDRY Marc, DUMONT Béatrice
Patents: Prompting or Restricting Innovation?
(Smart Innovation Set – Volume 12)

BÉRARD Céline, TEYSSIER Christine
Risk Management: Lever for SME Development and Stakeholder Value Creation

CHALENÇON Ludivine
Location Strategies and Value Creation of International Mergers and Acquisitions

CHAUVEL Danièle, BORZILLO Stefano
The Innovative Company: An Ill-defined Object
(Innovation between Risk and Reward Set – Volume 1)

CORSI Patrick
Going Past Limits To Growth

D'ANDRIA Aude, GABARRET Inés
Building 21st Century Entrepreneurship
(Innovation and Technology Set – Volume 2)

DAIDJ Nabyla
Cooperation, Coopetition and Innovation
(Innovation and Technology Set – Volume 3)

FERNEZ-WALCH Sandrine
The Multiple Facets of Innovation Project Management
(Innovation between Risk and Reward Set – Volume 4)

FOREST Joëlle
Creative Rationality and Innovation
(Smart Innovation Set – Volume 14)

GUILHON Bernard
Innovation and Production Ecosystems
(Innovation between Risk and Reward Set – Volume 2)

HAMMOUDI Abdelhakim, DAIDJ Nabyla
Game Theory Approach to Managerial Strategies and Value Creation
(Diverse and Global Perspectives on Value Creation Set – Volume 3)

LALLEMENT Rémi
Intellectual Property and Innovation Protection: New Practices and New Policy Issues
(Innovation between Risk and Reward Set – Volume 3)

LAPERCHE Blandine
Enterprise Knowledge Capital
(Smart Innovation Set – Volume 13)

LEBERT Didier, EL YOUNSI Hafida
International Specialization Dynamics
(Smart Innovation Set – Volume 9)

MAESSCHALCK Marc
Reflexive Governance for Research and Innovative Knowledge
(Responsible Research and Innovation Set – Volume 6)

MASSOTTE Pierre
Ethics in Social Networking and Business 1: Theory, Practice and Current Recommendations
Ethics in Social Networking and Business 2: The Future and Changing Paradigms

MASSOTTE Pierre, CORSI Patrick
Smart Decisions in Complex Systems

MEDINA Mercedes, HERRERO Mónica, URGELLÉS Alicia
Current and Emerging Issues in the Audiovisual Industry
(Diverse and Global Perspectives on Value Creation Set – Volume 1)

MICHAUD Thomas
Innovation, Between Science and Science Fiction
(Smart Innovation Set – Volume 10)

PELLÉ Sophie
Business, Innovation and Responsibility
(Responsible Research and Innovation Set – Volume 7)

SAVIGNAC Emmanuelle
The Gamification of Work: The Use of Games in the Workplace

SUGAHARA Satoshi, DAIDJ Nabyla, USHIO Sumitaka
Value Creation in Management Accounting and Strategic Management: An Integrated Approach
(Diverse and Global Perspectives on Value Creation Set –Volume 2)

UZUNIDIS Dimitri, SAULAIS Pierre
Innovation Engines: Entrepreneurs and Enterprises in a Turbulent World
(Innovation in Engineering and Technology Set – Volume 1)

2016

BARBAROUX Pierre, ATTOUR Amel, SCHENK Eric
Knowledge Management and Innovation
(Smart Innovation Set – Volume 6)

BEN BOUHENI Faten, AMMI Chantal, LEVY Aldo
Banking Governance, Performance And Risk-Taking: Conventional Banks Vs Islamic Banks

BOUTILLIER Sophie, CARRÉ Denis, LEVRATTO Nadine
Entrepreneurial Ecosystems (Smart Innovation Set – Volume 2)

BOUTILLIER Sophie, UZUNIDIS Dimitri
The Entrepreneur (Smart Innovation Set – Volume 8)

BOUVARD Patricia, SUZANNE Hervé
Collective Intelligence Development in Business

GALLAUD Delphine, LAPERCHE Blandine
Circular Economy, Industrial Ecology and Short Supply Chains (Smart Innovation Set – Volume 4)

GUERRIER Claudine
Security and Privacy in the Digital Era (Innovation and Technology Set – Volume 1)

MEGHOUAR Hicham
Corporate Takeover Targets

MONINO Jean-Louis, SEDKAOUI Soraya
Big Data, Open Data and Data Development (Smart Innovation Set – Volume 3)

MOREL Laure, LE ROUX Serge
Fab Labs: Innovative User (Smart Innovation Set – Volume 5)

PICARD Fabienne, TANGUY Corinne
Innovations and Techno-ecological Transition (Smart Innovation Set – Volume 7)

2015

CASADELLA Vanessa, LIU Zeting, DIMITRI Uzunidis
Innovation Capabilities and Economic Development in Open Economies (Smart Innovation Set – Volume 1)

CORSI Patrick, MORIN Dominique
Sequencing Apple's DNA

CORSI Patrick, NEAU Erwan
Innovation Capability Maturity Model

FAIVRE-TAVIGNOT Bénédicte
Social Business and Base of the Pyramid

GODÉ Cécile
Team Coordination in Extreme Environments

MAILLARD Pierre
Competitive Quality and Innovation

MASSOTTE Pierre, CORSI Patrick
Operationalizing Sustainability

MASSOTTE Pierre, CORSI Patrick
Sustainability Calling

2014

DUBÉ Jean, LEGROS Diègo
Spatial Econometrics Using Microdata

LESCA Humbert, LESCA Nicolas
Strategic Decisions and Weak Signals

2013

HABART-CORLOSQUET Marine, JANSSEN Jacques, MANCA Raimondo
VaR Methodology for Non-Gaussian Finance

2012

DAL PONT Jean-Pierre
Process Engineering and Industrial Management

MAILLARD Pierre
Competitive Quality Strategies

POMEROL Jean-Charles
Decision-Making and Action

SZYLAR Christian
UCITS Handbook

2011

LESCA Nicolas
Environmental Scanning and Sustainable Development

LESCA Nicolas, LESCA Humbert
Weak Signals for Strategic Intelligence: Anticipation Tool for Managers

MERCIER-LAURENT Eunika
Innovation Ecosystems

2010

SZYLAR Christian
Risk Management under UCITS III/IV

2009

COHEN Corine
Business Intelligence

ZANINETTI Jean-Marc
Sustainable Development in the USA

2008

CORSI Patrick, DULIEU Mike
The Marketing of Technology Intensive Products and Services

DZEVER Sam, JAUSSAUD Jacques, ANDREOSSO Bernadette
Evolving Corporate Structures and Cultures in Asia: Impact of Globalization

2007

AMMI Chantal
Global Consumer Behavior

2006

BOUGHZALA Imed, ERMINE Jean-Louis
Trends in Enterprise Knowledge Management

CORSI Patrick *et al.*
Innovation Engineering: the Power of Intangible Networks

Printed in the USA/Agawam, MA
September 16, 2026

910661.026